LITERATURE AND HISTORY
OF
AVIATION

LITERATURE AND HISTORY
OF
AVIATION

Advisory Editor: JAMES GILBERT

SKY STORMING YANKEE

THE LIFE *of* GLENN CURTISS

by Clara Studer

ARNO PRESS

A NEW YORK TIMES COMPANY

Reprint Edition 1972 by Arno Press Inc.

Reprinted from a copy in The Newark Public Library

LC# 76-169438
ISBN 0-405-03780-5

Literature and History of Aviation
ISBN for complete set: 0-405-03789-9
See last pages of this volume for titles.

Manufactured in the United States of America

SKY STORMING YANKEE

The Life of Glenn Curtiss

GLENN CURTISS IN HIS FAMOUS JUNE BUG, THE
EXPERIMENTAL PLANE WHICH CONTRIBUTED LAND-
MARK CHAPTERS TO THE HISTORY OF AMERICAN
FLYING. THE PHOTOGRAPH WAS TAKEN ON JULY
4, 1908.

SKY STORMING YANKEE

THE LIFE *of* GLENN CURTISS

by Clara Studer

1937

STACKPOLE SONS   NEW YORK CITY

1

F O R E W O R D

I WAS detached from my ship in order to report for flying instruction to Glenn Curtiss at Hammondsport, New York, in June, 1911. He had only recently returned from San Diego, where he had been conducting many interesting experiments, the most important of which was the development of what was called, at that time, the hydro-aeroplane.

At the time I arrived at Hammondsport, my only knowledge of aviation and aviators was what little I had seen during a brief visit to Issy-les-Moulineaux, just outside Paris during the previous winter. Many of you are aware of the characteristics of the French people and some of you are familiar with the scenes at the French aerodromes in those early days: the excitement, the extraordinary costumes, and the still more extraordinary characteristics of the aviators.

I was young and impressionable and, quite naturally, expected to witness somewhat the same scene at Hammondsport, and I had a very clear picture in my mind as to the manner of man Glenn Curtiss would be. His name had appeared in big headlines in papers throughout the world; he had won the *Scientific American* Trophy two years in succession. He had, in 1909, at Rheims, France, won the speed classic of the world, the Gordon Bennett Cup; he had won the *New York World* prize of $10,000 for the flight from Albany to New York, and many other notable events. I was therefore greatly surprised when I got off the train to see him, quiet, simply dressed in ordinary business clothes, diffident and modest to a degree which was really embarrassing. I was rather reserved and a bit diffident myself. That, coupled with my completely upset mental picture of him, did not put me at ease. He did his best to make me feel at home, taking me around through the shops and explaining what was going on, particularly in the way of improvements in design.

As I hardly knew one end of an aeroplane from the other, this did not help matters much. He then took me to his house, which was just across the road, and offered me a glass of buttermilk. I hate buttermilk, but I was too embarrassed to say so, so I tried to drink it. It made me suddenly and violently ill. Looking back upon it, I regard my long and very close friendship with Glenn Curtiss as dating from exactly that time—a very human event.

There was only one complete aeroplane at Hammondsport, the one in which I later learned to fly. Work was being pushed forward on the Navy aeroplanes when I arrived. So far as I know, there were never any actual plans for these. In some respects they were to be similar to planes already built, also with no plans. In other respects they were to be different. The workmen were supposed to remember how the earlier planes were built, but the differences were in the heads of Glenn Curtiss and Henry Kleckler.

The white walls of the shop were covered with sketches made by Curtiss and Kleckler for the benefit of the workmen. This seemed to answer the purpose remarkably well until a new hand, having been told to clean up the shop, whitewashed right over all the sketches. This little episode delayed completion of the first plane about two weeks, for nobody, not even Curtiss, could reproduce the sketches. All the changes had to be worked out over again.

In the winter of 1911-1912 Curtiss again went to San Diego and we moved our small outfit out there to continue our experimental work and also to keep in touch with his. During that winter and spring I acted as his test pilot and tried out his new ideas. He was always changing, always improving. And while there is no way of knowing how many ideas he may have had and never spoken of, I can say definitely that I can not remember a single idea that he ever spoke of in those early days that did not prove, when developed, to have definite merit.

He had already conceived the idea of a flying boat and during this winter he developed one. This I regard as one of the greatest accomplishments of Curtiss, and the flying boat today, regardless of its size or its nationality, is essentially simply an expansion of the very early Curtiss design. You can trace the ancestry of the present big boats of the British and United States services, and also of the commercial lines, right through the Curtiss H-16's built for the British during the war, the famous *America*—built in 1914 for a projected flight across the Atlantic—the so-called "H" boats, with 200 horsepower engines, and the earlier United States Navy flying boats directly back to his original conception.

Glenn Curtiss gave up really active participation in the aviation business years ago, but I can assure you that he never lost interest. I shot with him in Scotland, played about with him in Paris, visited him in Florida and saw him many times in Washington and in other places. He not only was posted on the latest developments in aviation, but he always seemed to have new and interesting ideas.

I do not believe that many people shared with me the knowledge that even just before the illness which resulted in his death, he was very actively engaged in the development of a very new and radical design of an aircraft combined with an entirely new method of arresting it aboard ships. It may well be that we lost something of immense value, for death ruthlessly terminated his work. I am positive that no one was sufficiently in his confidence in regard to this flying boat to carry on the work.

Glenn Curtiss was a remarkable American. He had no engineer's degree, but he was an engineer of the highest order. Mathematical formulae rather confounded him and he did not seem to need them. He did not carry slide rules and comptometers in his pockets; he must have had them in his head. He never claimed greatness as an engineer, and therefore he was all the greater.

CAPTAIN JOHN H. TOWERS,
United States Navy

THE CONTENTS

PART I.   MYSTERY OF MOTIVE POWER

    Mechanical Turn
    Bicycle Doctor
    "She Works Like a Charm"
    Light, Strong Motors for Gas Bags
    The Fastest Mile

PART II.   COOPERATIVE SCIENCE

    With No Man Aboard
    And Carrying a Man
    Red Wing and White Wing
    Curtiss' June Bug
    Experiments Ended

PART III.   AVIATION LOSES ITS AMATEUR STANDING

    Customer for an Aeroplane
    The Fastest Man
    Showing America
    The Aeroplane Goes to Court
    Down the Hudson

THE CONTENTS (*Concluded*)

PART IV.   ALL THAT GOES UP

Bolts from the Blue
Pontoons and Hulls
North Island
Aviators' Home
Summer of 1914

PART V.   GLORY BE TO WINGS

A Keel a Day
Just Before Sundown

A NOTE ON ILLUSTRATIONS

An album of rare photographs which dramatize the career of Glenn Hammond Curtiss and his associates in the development of automotivation appears at the back of this volume. A descriptive caption is printed opposite each illustration.

ACKNOWLEDGMENT

This history of Glenn Curtiss and his associates could not have been written without the generous help of Lyman J. Seely and J. Lansing Callan. Many others lent a hand in clarifying the story and the author is especially grateful to Gilbert Grosvenor, William Chauncy Langdon, Wm. C. Chadeayne, G. Leonard Waters, Frank H. Russell, Don C. Seitz, Harry C. Genung, James Bauder, Henry Kleckler, James W. Smellie, R. G. Betts, Augustus Post, Ernest Jones, Beckwith Havens, Paul J. Zimmerman, Dr. Alfred F. Zahm, George Keeler, Jane Moore, Ervin Jaycox, Henry J. Wehman, Mrs. Love, Mrs. Will Damoth, Mrs. Lulu Mott, Lyman T. Seely, and the publishers of the Hammondsport Herald. Since Harry M. Benner was official photographer during most of the flying period, he is responsible for many of the photographs taken at Hammondsport.

SKY STORMING YANKEE
The Life of Glenn Curtiss

I.

MYSTERY OF MOTIVE POWER

Mechanical Turn

CLAUDIUS CURTISS, who came to Hammondsport, New York, in 1864, to preach the gospel at the Methodist Church, was a "pleasant, nice-appearing" man of medium height. A genial minister with an ample waistline, his sermons never overtaxed the minds of his congregation and nudged their consciences only gently.

The Reverend Claudius Curtiss liked the grape-growing community so well that he decided, after a few years, to retire from preaching and invest a portion of his savings in a house on the side of a hill and a little vineyard of his own. His tall, tight-lipped, black-haired wife was actually responsible for the decision, as she was responsible for the fact that there were savings to be invested and for nearly everything else in his life.

Years of living in parsonages had reinforced rather than destroyed Mrs. Ruth W. Curtiss's spirit and her financial equanimity.

They had one child, Frank R., who ran true to minister's-son traditions and was something of a trial to his parents. But when he was twenty-one he married Lua Andrews, of local pioneer stock, and they set up housekeeping in a rented cottage in the part of town known as the Lake Front. Claudius Curtiss was elated and Ruth Curtiss was hopeful that the marriage would have a wholesome influence on their son, would keep him out of village barrooms.

Of all the Finger Lakes—Cayuga, Onondaga, Owasco, Skaneateles and the others—Keuka has the most irregular shore line and therefore is the most beautiful. The spring-fed waters of Lake Keuka temper the Valley and make the climate some ten degrees warmer than that of the neighboring country. The growing season for grapes begins sooner and lasts longer; the fruit ripens two weeks earlier than in the Chautauqua Belt. This makes for less acid fruit and makes it possible for grapes of several different kinds to thrive. And sweetness and variety of the fruit are essential in the production of sparkling wines.

The steeply sloping hillsides afford what wine growers know as perfect air drainage and the general character of Pleasant Valley bears such a marked resemblance to the champagne districts of France, that they deliberately named the post office in the Pleasant Valley Wine Cellars, Rheims, New York. Though they pronounced it mostly "Reems."

The rugged contours responsible for its champagne industry also make the region good scenic playground material. It occurred to J. P. Barnes, a natural promoter, that the ravine to the north of town might well be turned into as profitable a source of revenue as Watkins Glen, near Ithaca, New York.

For the first half mile the bed of the stream lies between cleancut stone walls; then comes a series of waterfalls. Beyond this are other cataracts, rimmed by a border of sturdy pine trees. Barnes built in stairsteps, railings, bridged over the falls; officially re-christened it the "Glen" and charged admission. Various concessions were installed along the slope. For several years it proved a successful enterprise, then its popularity declined. Fellow townsmen liked to tease Barnes by asking him what ever happened to his Glen. With some bitterness he would mutter that he didn't know "what ever became of the damned old gully."

But a few sentimental souls still remembered it. Lua Curtiss was one of those who went there now and then. The Glen was the prettiest place she knew, so pretty she thought she ought to name her first baby after it. With another "n" added "to make it look more like a name," she called him Glenn Hammond Curtiss. The middle name was taken from the town itself, or its first settler, Lazarus Hammond.

This whimsy of naming her son after a local landmark was typical of Lua Curtiss. Then too a name like Glenn Hammond Curtiss had sweep and resonance, was much less commonplace than Harry or Jim or Charlie; or Frank, like his father. She hardly imagined that some day she would petition the court for the right to sign herself, Mrs. Glenn H. Curtiss, Senior, so distinguished had the name become. Still to Lua Curtiss anything may have seemed possible. Life had been mostly dull and troublesome for her, and she had acquired the habit of fabricating a glorious other life in her dreams.

Even then, as a young village matron, she "sang her troubles away right lustily" as she dabbled in china and landscapes, just as she still did when she was an old woman. When she was eighty, undisturbed by the fact that she was stone blind, she went blithely on applying colors to canvass with comparatively intelligible results.

The home of Frank and Lua Curtiss was not far from the little harness shop where Frank sold new and mended old harness as well as other leather horse fittings. Their two children were born in the house near the Lake; Glenn Hammond on May 21, 1878, and a year later, his sister Rutha.

Part of the legal tender a hardware dealer had to accept fifty years ago was the scrap metal, the broken parts of old machines and implements turned in by farmers. In the back of George Keeler's store was a pile of scrap iron. Because he thought he had better find out what was rattling around in his old iron pile, Keeler went outside one day and found a little shaver joyously burrowing in the collection of junk. He was Frank Curtiss's boy, then not quite three years old.

The incident—as George Keeler, for many years Mayor of Hammondsport, proudly pointed out—would tend to indicate that even at that green age Glenn Curtiss felt the urge to assemble parts into a whole which might work.

When Glenn and Rutha were five and four their jolly grandfather died and Frank Curtiss moved his family up on the hill to live with his mother. The following year he too died, at the early age of twenty-seven.

For a while Lua Curtiss stayed on in the old Curtiss house, then she remarried and moved away to Rock Spring, New York, taking Rutha with her. Glenn was left behind to keep his grandmother company, to help tend the cows and work in the tiny vineyard in the nearly perpendicular backyard. There was plenty of work for a boy to do there, from January when the new shoots had to be willow-tied, until about October the twentieth when the last grapes were picked. All those Grandma Curtiss did not require for cordial or jelly-making were loaded onto a slender-bodied grape-wagon to be carried off to a wine cellar.

The heavy-set gray frame house, with its two stories and square cupola on top was much too large for one elderly woman and her grandson. It crouched on a bluff above a lower tier of houses and directly over an old cellarway that made a gorgeous play cave for Glenn and his friends. Since it was surrounded by plenty of rock ammunition, this was a logical stronghold in their never-ending feud with the Low Town boys. When he was eleven or twelve years old Glenn became leader of the Hill Gang, not because he lived nearest to the cave but because even then his lead seemed good to follow.

From September to June, Glenn attended Hammondsport Union Free School. According to "Ervie" Jaycox, a classmate, he was no better or worse than the other boys in school room deportment. Jaycox remembers well the day Glenn and he were caught whispering about some plans to go red raspberry picking on Harry Champlin's side hill. "Prof" Cates, their angular Quaker principal, picked them both up by their collars and shifted them, with his extension ladder arms, from desks to platform where he administered a good "lamming."

In arithmetic Glenn usually scored 98 or better, but grammar and spelling left him floundering. He managed to keep up with his class, but his teachers often wished audibly that he would keep his mind on his studies. He had already begun to develop that gift for absorption in a mechanical problem which was to be the bone and sinew of his life. New wrinkles in bicycle making were his special delight. He had always had a bike of his own since the first little secondhand high wheel his Grandpa Curtiss had bought for him long before he was old enough to start to school.

Within easy reach of his bed he kept a pile of the current technical magazines, while under his bed was a whole library of back files of *The Bearings—Cycling Authority of America*, *The Wheel and Cycle Trade Review* and the *Bicycling World*. Piled up in a corner of the room were hundreds of trade catalogs and pamphlets. The odd sums his grandmother gave him, when she sensed his pressing need for money, and the occasional quarters and dimes earned here and there by delivering papers or bundles on his bike, were spent mostly on subscriptions to magazines. With the rest he sent for advertised gadgets. Those he could not afford to buy he made himself from looking at the pictures. The words "clip this coupon and receive our handsome catalog" were irresistible bait to him.

Grandma Curtiss was wise enough to know when to let a boy alone. So long as Glenn looked after his chores and was regular in his school attendance, she permitted him considerable liberty. She never scolded when she noticed that the lamp in his room was burning late nights.

For all her forbidding exterior, she was an understanding soul in her way.

Yet the extreme reserve which clamped down on him during adolescence was an inevitable by-product of her sternly erect manner toward him. Grandma Curtiss had a mind as forceful, as masculine as her tiny black mustache and little black chin whiskers which inspired such awe in Glenn's playmates. They never quite knew what to make of the old lady.

When Glenn had a birthday party, for example, she served the starched and ruffled guests a mess of corned beef and cabbage. The children ate their way through it with dazed gusto, for it was really a delectable dish of corned beef and cabbage. But they had expected party cake and lemonade—which did not disturb Grandmother Curtiss at all. It was Glenn's birthday and corned beef and cabbage was his favorite dish.

If Glenn's grandmother had been more talkative, she might have told him the secret of her sublime disregard for other people's opinion. Some convictions she managed to transmit undiluted to her grandson, but on that point she failed him.

When Glenn was fifteen he left school, in response to his mother's urging, and went to live with his family. They had moved to Rochester so that his sister Rutha, who had lost her hearing, might attend the school for the deaf there.

Since funds were far from plentiful in his mother's household, he decided without regret, to consider his education finished and look for a steady job. He found employment easily with the Western Union Telegraph Company and his bicycle joined the fleet of wheels in a rack against the sidewalk at the Four Corners, where the messenger boys sat on a bench against the wall waiting their turns. At the rate of ten cents per telegram, a boy could easily triple his earnings with a bicycle to speed him around town. Because Glenn had the knack of making friends without ever having much say, the other messengers liked the serious-faced smalltown boy, who went about his duties in such a methodical manner. They knew he had plenty of grit in spite of his shy way and were not surprised when he saved the life of another boy who fell through the thin ice that winter.

They understood too how foolish he felt when spectators tried to tell him what a brave lad he was, and liked him the better for his embarrassment.

The Curtiss boy had devious ways of improving on their sports, such as a skate-sail or a more efficient paddle. Lake Erie was their favorite playground, summer and winter, and Glenn helped them make the most of their hours on it or in it.

Business limped so badly during 1894 that the volume

THE LIFE OF GLENN CURTISS

of telegrams dwindled. There was work for only a few of the messenger boys; the others were laid off, Glenn Curtiss among them. His home was near Kodak Park, but there were no vacancies there either. By haunting the premises day after day he gained the attention of some of the salesmen and learned a lot about photography. One of them sent him to talk to a customer of his who needed a man to travel around the state snapping pictures at retail.

Glenn got the job and spent the spring of 1895 trying to pursuade mothers they wanted to have pictures taken of their babies or their rose bushes or their aged parents. With his tripod, camera, black cloth and film strapped to the back of his bicycle he covered a good portion of western New York with fairly profitable results.

This roving existence did not appeal to him, though, and he was glad to find work in Rochester that summer with the Eastman Company. They paid him $3.50 a week for the not very exciting job of stenciling the numbers "1" to "6" on the short lengths of film and "1" to "12" on the long ones. These numbers were stamped by hand on the strips of black paper used to back the film. The strips in turn had to be pasted to one end of the strips of film. Impatient of the slow process, Glenn worked out a device, later perfected, which increased one man's output of pasted end strips from four hundred to nearly four thousand a day.

When October and slacktime found him laid off again, Glenn decided to climb onto his bicycle and pedal himself home to Hammondsport. And Mrs. Ruth Curtiss, who had been sore-lonely in the big house on the hill and had written many times urging him to come, let him know without saying so in words how glad she was to have him back under her grandmotherly wing.

Possibly her shrewd mind dared to acknowledge that

in Glenn there was something of his rather unaccountable mother who wrote poetry and painted pictures instead of keeping her house and her husband in order. In Grandma Curtiss' heart there was great pity for her son's wife. People were different, drifters or practical people, that was all. She was confident Glenn would turn out to be one of the practical ones, thought maybe she could help him to travel that road. There is no question but that her grandson was her favorite human being.

It was not in her nature to nag at a boy, but she rooted in his young mind the sensible thought that "if you're smart enough you can amount to something some day—not be a little two-by-four fellow, but an important business man who makes a lot of money."

The old lady sensed the cut steel quality in his hazel-gray eyes, with its promise of mental stamina; she could not know of course that she was planting the seed of a mortal conflict. Certainly Ruth Curtiss knew her way about in the world of practicality. She sensed the damaging influence of idealism, of too much imagination, and the need for resolute action based on sharp thinking. Most of Glenn Curtiss's life, from the day he earned his first nickel, was a battle between the practical, stern strain—partly inherited, partly acquired from his grandmother—and the gentler strain that made it impossible deliberately to hurt another man's feelings; to say anything that, as he expressed it, "might not sound so nice."

Grandma Curtiss had high aspirations for this grandchild she loved so fiercely, in which there was no room for compromise. Big things were going on in the world, fabulous fortunes in the making. The word "millionaire" was coming into use and events were swollen with change. Her Glenn could be a big factor in his time, maybe a big rich man some day.

Most of the troubles in his life were due to the fact that Grandma Curtiss tried to make him, because of her devotion, the kind of man he wasn't and couldn't be. Or because he tried so doggedly to make good her ideal. In his early ventures he had her counsel to guide him. And he did possess one essential qualification of the business executive: the gift of leadership. He never asked any man to do him a favor, yet all his life the things he wanted done were done and by men best suited to do them. Still he lacked a main ingredient of the business magnate: the ability to rebuff a persistent salesman. At various times in his life a decisive No would have saved him years of torment. This inability to steer clear of an unsound proposition, was a serious handicap. He also had a disconcertingly unbusinesslike way, because of his ingenuous yearning to please, of promising the same plum to several different people.

The only really important success he had in a business way was due to a world war and a real estate boom. His claim to greatness is owed largely to his sense of vision, the fanaticism of the highly geared experimental mind. And Lua Andrews Curtiss, Ruth Curtiss's daughter-in-law, with an undeniable creative urge in her, was the instrument through which he inherited the surging curiosity and imagination of his great, great-uncles, the Morse brothers, inventors of the electric telegraph. Without those same traits he could never have become, rather than the big man of business, the "Fastest Man of the Earth and the Skies" in 1909, nor one of the greatest mechanical geniuses of all time.

Bicycle Doctor

A S HE was leaving Smellie's Drug Store, late one afternoon in 1895, G. Leonard Waters pulled up short and stared. Somebody was riding a bicycle around the Square at what his practiced eye told him was a decidedly rapid clip. "Who in the world is this," the best bicycle rider in Hammondsport wondered, "coming into my territory? I'd better get acquainted."

He hailed the stranger and they proceeded to introduce themselves in the manner of a couple of lanky seventeen-year-olds with a common interest.

If "Tank" Waters had not been something of a new-comer at the time he would have recognized the other boy. Most of the older residents of Hammondsport remembered him as an awkward gandershank who was always tinkering with something. Reticent, rather than bashful, full of ideas often impractical on the face of them, but somehow convincing; deliberate, sometimes to the point of laziness, he had emerged as a personality even earlier than most boys in small towns.

The boy Tank Waters saw riding around the Square that evening had learned a good deal about bicycle riding and racing during his years in Rochester. Bill Appel,

Frank Kammer, Al Zimbrick, the local speedsters, had kept the papers filled with their exploits at the Rochester Athletic Club cinder track and at Driving Park on Lake Avenue. Sprinting practice went on wherever there was asphalt, and Glenn and the other Western Union boys spent most of their free time in pedalling practice on one fine stretch where there were no cross streets.

Back in Hammondsport, Glenn teamed up with Tank to build up more experience. There was a cycle path made of cinders running alongside the highway between Bath, the county seat, and Hammondsport. Bicycle riders did not ride roads: the brass tag on their handle bars signified that they had paid the dollar-a-year tax which went for upkeep of the cinder paths. Boys and men, women and girls, all over the world fell in line with one of the great advances in locomotion—the first practical form of individual transportation.

Instead of travelling four miles an hour on foot or eight an hour behind a horse, an active person on a bicycle went scorching up the road at ten to twenty miles.

When the high wheel was replaced by the safety bicycle, and particularly when the pneumatic tire came into use, they rode and bought bicycles as fast as they were built, bringing on the bicycle boom of 1890 to 1897. There were a hundred plants in this country turning out more than a million bicycles a year. The bicycle trust of the day, the American Bicycle Company, formed, strangely enough, when signs of a decline were discernable, was a sixty million dollar corporation.

Women with bustles, puffed sleeves and enormous hats cruised around the country. Men who were getting a trifle old and stiff in the joints for sprint racing showed their stamina by making century runs and having their chests decorated with strings of bars. Promoters staged track races for red-headed girls, for boys under sixteen, and for mothers of twins.

On the race tracks Skeeter Zimmerman finally abandoned the high wheel and increased his speed on the safety. Eddie Ball of Buffalo, Fred Titus, the Big Four of the New York Athletic Club and a hundred others were drawing crowds to the race tracks that sprang up all over New York state. The Hammondsport boys did most of their practicing up the Valley at Stony Brook Farm where Harry Champlin had a half mile track for his race horses. They usually met there after supper to race until, exhausted, they went to sleep in the haymow.

At dawn they shook themselves awake and got in a little practice before going home for breakfast. Sometimes on frosty mornings they had to run around the course on foot in order to get the chill out of their limbs. One morning Tank Waters conceived the warm-up scheme of having each boy drop his cap, to be picked up by the boy on the bicycle behind and dropped again for the next boy to pick up, in a sort of relay.

A farmer who was passing with a load of produce on the road above halted his team and watched them quietly, then he sang out, as he flicked his whip, "I seen you, boys, I seen you doing that hand-ee-cap race."

His spontaneous pun seemed very funny to the bicycle riders, especially to Glenn who adored puns and jokes and used to warm up occasionally and "spring some good ones." Outside of technical material, the only reading matter he honestly enjoyed was a good joke book. It was a little-boy side of him which he never outgrew. Joke books answered the same sort of need in him as the newspaper comic strips are consistently answering in grown men and boys today. Next to jokes Glenn liked bets and during their practice periods at Stony Brook he was forever trying to "make a little bet" with one of the other boys. Another pet pastime of his was thinking up freak tests of riding skill. "I'll ride across it if you will," he would propose, indicating an eight inch board across a ditch. The other boy would accept the challenge and frequently go down sprawling. Glenn always took the hurdle, whatever it was, with neatness and dispatch. His judgment of distance and his sense of balance were both nearly infallible.

When the village merchants heard that the boys were getting good enough to put on an exhibition, they offered a prize for a big championship race around the Valley. Two miles and a half from the Square to the turning point beyond the P. V. Wine Cellars and then on to the ancient Drover's Inn, and back towards Lake Keuka and the starting point; altogether it was between five and six miles. Quite a distance in dirt road days.

The contestants left the monument on Pulteney Street at the crack of a pistol and pedalled as fast as they could all the way. Glenn, making the round in that strangely effortless fashion of his, reached the finish line with his nearest competitor still puffing away a half mile behind. It was his first racing victory.

After that he and Tank Waters, Albert Cook and Bill Damoth, raced regularly at the county fairs in their end of the state and other small town meets. It was strenuous doing, for train connections with Hammondsport were so poor that even if the boys had had the money for tickets, it would have been impossible to go by train on the day of the races. So they turned out early in the morning and rode to the meets over terrible roads—long stretches of deep sand or rough clay with an occasional stretch of shale or gravel road. They would ride twenty-five to fifty miles over bad roads in the morning and then face the starting pistol at two o'clock in the afternoon.

But the Hammondsport teams turned the trick time and again, and almost invariably Glenn won the principal event of the day. Most of the races were held on ordinary half-mile dirt tracks, well chopped up by trotting horses; consequently the low-geared machines the boys from Hammondsport had to use on the steep hills and bad roads about their town gave them an advantage. They began to think they were ready to outride comers from anywhere.

Once Glenn and Tank ventured as far as the Waterville Fair, expecting to walk off with the honors as a matter of habit. They discovered that, though they could race roads, they couldn't race track—not good hard track. Instead of taking first and second prizes they took fourth and fifth places. To even matters up they invited De Tample, the winner, to a road race at Hammondsport. There they took him down the Lake road and left him to come straggling in over the hills alone.

At propelling a bicycle, Glen was the local pride, but at another favorite sport he was notoriously bad. Although he liked being out-of-doors, his nature was too restless for fishing. Almost before they were started he would say, "What do you say we go home?" As the others had no intention of turning back Glenn spent the rest of the time making a paddle or an oar, or mending a loose oar-lock.

"Your doorbell don't ring, I notice."

Leo Masson, answering a vigorous knock at the door of his house, admitted that the bell had not been functioning for some time.

"I'll fix it for you if you want me to," said the boy taking a screw-driver out of his pocket.

In short order the bell was in pieces and back together again, ready to respond to a pushing finger's command.

Mr. Masson was pleased, and as he paid the boy a quarter, he asked with a smile, "Who are you?"

"Glenn Curtiss. I guess your bell will be all right now."

Leo Masson had failed to recognize the boy because he had grown considerably during his years in Rochester; because his heavy black eyebrows and intent expression that was almost a frown made him look nearer twenty-five than seventeen.

Glenn's first salaried job in the town was with Saylor, a local photographer, who had a little shop near the Lake front; but he soon found outside occupations. When Seymour Hubbs' acetylene plant went out of order, Glenn repaired it. In studying its eccentricities he figured out that a double drip system would give greater efficiency than the single tank arrangement then in general use. So he made an acetylene outfit with two tanks instead of one and started his first independent business venture in a little el-room off the Ward house near the Lake. With his acetylene outfit he lighted his own place and some of the adjoining stores, at so much a month.

In his spare time he also repaired bicycles for the other boys. Grandmother Curtiss was convinced it was time to give up his job. "Hmmm I shouldn't think you'd want to work all your life for somebody else," was her way of putting it.

In Canal Time, when Hammondsport was still an important shipping center, most of the business had been conducted on the shore of Lake Keuka. When, with the growth of railroads, the towpath of the Erie Canal fell into disuse along with the channels that fed it, Hammondsport's business center gradually moved away from the water. Plenty of old structures were left standing empty there for callow young businesses.

In his bicycle repair shop and acetylene lighting plant

near the Lake Front, Glenn also offered for sale what stock was left over from his father's harness shop. Mostly he fixed punctures, stretched bicycle chains, straightened handlebars sold spring saddles and other gadgets. His own bike had always had a way of blossoming out with little contrivances to increase comfort and speed, and the boys came to him as a matter of course for expert attention.

There were two bicycle dealers in the town: James H. Smellie, druggist; and George A. Lyon, jeweler. Bicycles as a sideline did not seem out of place in either of their stores. Tank Waters clerked in the drugstore, and he and Glenn Curtiss had come to be known as "Smellie's pet cycle boys." They rode his machines at races. Theirs were the glory and the medals, his the advertising advantages. Smellie was an enterprising man, a Canadian, the first man in that part of the country to turn his pharmacy into a general store for everything except groceries. He was ready to try anything once, and when Glenn set his heart on a shop on the Square, Smellie agreed to finance him. Putting a patch on a tire cost fifteen cents; seven and a half of which Glenn kept and seven and a half went to Smellie.

The shop prospered after a fashion and very soon Smellie allowed Glenn to take over his bicycle selling for him. He paid for the machines, Glenn got rid of them. The profits, if any, were divided between them.

In 1898, Glenn Curtiss, then twenty years old, and already a fairly prosperous citizen, married the only woman he seems ever to have cared for. Lena Neff, a descendant of a substantial pioneer family in the Finger Lakes region, was as marked in her reticence as Glenn himself. After their marriage they lived with Grandmother Curtiss in the stodgy old gray frame house on the hill.

Glenn's official re-christening, his coming of age as a business man, was proclaimed in the sign he had put up over the last shop on the north side of the Square. It read:

G. H. CURTISS, DEALER IN HARNESS AND HORSE
FURNISHINGS, ALSO BICYCLES AND SUNDRIES

Backed up by the painted letters, it was much easier
to pluck up the courage to correct an occasional customer
with, "How about calling me G.H.?"

Gradually they did remember to. Since he liked it and
looked much older than he was, why not? So they reasoned
and the boyish "Glenn" fell into disuse.

There was a pleased glint in his grandmother's eyes
when she first heard him addressed "G.H." Her boy
would get there. Not seventy-five yet, she wasn't so old but
what she might live to see the day. She was convinced now
that it was in mechanics that he would make his mark.
Glenn was clever at making things that worked, he would
find ways to speed up living, ways that people would spend
good money for. His eagerness to justify her fond hopes
quickly was partly responsible for a sudden burst of business expansion.

He was doing well in Hammondsport, so well that he
hired his former classmate, Will Damoth, as his assistant.
They handled only the wellknown makes of bicycles like
Eddie Ball's favorite, the National, but sometimes they
got a stray order for a fancy Eagle racer or a Sterns racer
with orange rims. The sale of bicycles was reasonably brisk,
much more so than that of Horse Furnishings. But Glenn
somehow liked the idea of carrying on his father's line
of business. And they did have occasional calls for harness
strap or a new side saddle.

The time had come, he announced to his staff of one,
to do a little branching out. He rented a store in Bath and
hired Barney Feagle to run it. But he wanted first hand

supervision of practically everything he did, so Will Damoth and he took turns staying alternate days and nights in Bath, eight miles away. Then he opened still another link in his chain of cycling headquarters in Corning.

Since Curtiss was often away at the tracks winning races to sell more bicycles, additional assistance was needed in the Hammondsport shop. Young Carlton Wheeler was therefore employed as a part-time helper. Carlton learned to repaint bicycles, repair punctures and to straighten wobbly wheels. He thought he was lucky to be drawing ten cents an hour for these duties, for money was one of the scarcest things about the shop, which a customer once threw into state of embarrassment by presenting a dollar bill in payment for a twenty-five cent item. The total amount of change in the cash drawer, and in the pants pockets of G.H. Curtiss and his entire staff was exactly thirty cents.

It was characteristic of Hammondsport and the way it felt about Glenn Curtiss that it not only laughed off the financial deficiency of the moment but actually relished its dramatic portent. Somebody grabbed a camera, chirped, "stand still," and snapped a picture of Curtiss, staff and two cyclist customers. Curtiss, holding the dollar bill was supposed to look chagrined.

The picture still exists in vivid evidence of the local conviction that G.H. was bound to make his mark some day. Any boy who was as absorbed in his work, who could ride a bike as superbly, and furthermore was as disinterested in social distractions—who never looked twice at the girls or drank a drop—well, he'd win out. He had to.

The sale of standard makes of bicycles showed a very small margin of profit, perhaps twenty percent, which was little more than enough to pay the overhead. Customers for the expensive "racing" bicycles were few, and Curtiss soon discovered that the only mystery connected with this $125 "racing" model was why anyone should pay so much for it. The net factory cost of making and assembling the parts he found to be less than twenty dollars. Somewhere between the factory and the ultimate customer five times that amount disappeared.

He decided to take a larger split in the profits. In Addison, N. Y., ten miles from Corning, he found a shop quite as capable of sticking two wheels in a tubular frame as any of the manufacturers of the highly advertised goods, and willing to take a fraction of their wholesale price. Curtiss contracted for thirty or forty machines to be made under a trademark of his own. He called these first bicycles HERCULES, the name which he later used on his early motors.

These bicycles earned at least twice the profit he could have made by selling any of the standard makes. And that was the end of it. Bicycles had become a stock commodity to be turned out with no special effort, in quantity, and marketed. Curtiss's enthusiasm for them was gone as it always was for anything finished, working. But he had discovered another form of experiment which provided reason for contentment.

"She Works Like a Charm."

GENERATING power off the hoof, in small doses, was a painfully slow process. It took nearly a hundred years for the big steam boilers to hatch chicks. Patience, indestructible drive and a quality right next door to genius were essential to the job of instilling commercial dependability into fuel explosions.

In 1897 a few motor tricycles and quadracycles groped their way along the roads. About the same time Kenneth Skinner of Boston began importing, from France, the first satisfactory small motor in use in this country, the De Dion.

Ritchie G. Betts, editor of the *Bicycling World*, and some of his associates decided that since the public seemed to be losing sight of the value of the exercise of pedal-pushing, there might be an upturn in the bicycle business if they could do away with the footwork, especially up hills and against headwinds. The two wheels in line, would give a single track vehicle which could travel over many roadways not possible to three and four wheels.

With such reasoning they persuaded Charles H. Metz of the Waltham Manufacturing Company, who had built a number of De Dion-driven tri and quadracycles to build

37

a motored bicycle. In 1900 Metz turned out the first commercially built motorcycle.

Amateur designers of course had been wrestling with homemade devices for generating more power mechanically. Glenn Curtiss, like the rest of them, could not resist trying to hitch a motor up to something. Answering an advertisement by E. R. Thomas of Buffalo, he sent for a set of castings for a tiny air-cooled motor. When the package arrived at his little lean-to shop near the Lake Front, Glenn brought them to Frank Neff next door to be machined.

Neff, thirty years grayer, less erect, standing by his lathe in the same machine shop, is still sure that "clamped to a bicycle, it worked real good." But, he adds, with a shake of his head, "twarn't enough power in it; twarn't fast enough for Glenn."

The fragile construction of racing bicycles of 1896 was not adapted to the strains necessarily inherent in a power-driven vehicle. The motors had to be of such low horsepower they were of little value making hills in the Finger Lakes region. Glenn Curtiss junked his first motor and went about the business of expanding his bicycle shop for the time being.

A year later he bought another set of rough castings for a somewhat larger engine. The castings and shaft were comparatively inexpensive. The trick lay in turning them into a finished engine.

Three miles up the Valley the Kirkham boys, Charles and Clarence, had rented an old mill with its own water power and turned it into a machine shop which was building up a reputation for skilled workmanship. Curtiss took his second set of castings there to be machined. Rings were fitted to the pistons, the shaft was painstakingly lapped to meet the bearings of the crank case and connecting rod. In the back room of Smellie's Drug Store, Curtiss, Tank Waters, the Kirkhams and Will Damoth assembled the engine.

But to make an engine propel a motorcycle certain other items were necessary. There must be a coil and spark distributor. They had to have a carburetor and they must devise a driving mechanism.

Dr. Philias Alden in his office on the Square had a machine for giving patients electric treatments for various ailments. A jump spark-coil out of this, the boys argued, should serve as a valuable addition to the vitals of their motor. They talked Dr. Alden into lending them this part out of his machine, and Curtiss devised a make-and-break distributor.

He made a carburetor from a half-pint sized tomato can, in the top of which he fitted a gauze screen. Through this the gasoline vaporized and passed through a pipe to the cylinder.

The finished product was hardly an ambitious creation. It had a single cylinder, a 2-inch bore and a 2½-inch stroke. And like all by-guess-and-by-God machinery it was a joint product of mechanical intuition, machinist's skill and trade journal dogma.

At first the motorcycle into which it was intended to transform a bicycle worked on a friction roller pulley. Sometimes Curtiss set this to drive the front wheel, sometimes he shifted it to drive against the real wheel. He fussed with it a long time. This problem of motive power was something noisy and messy and baffling into which to sink his teeth.

Sometimes after hours of work it could be made to run for a few minutes, then it would choke up and stop. The carburetor gave trouble and had to be modified considerably. The electrical equipment was far from adequate.

Eventually Curtiss mounted his motor in a bicycle frame and announced he was ready to give a demonstration.

One Hammondsporter guessed he could get as far as the Post Office, two blocks away upgrade, if he pedalled hard enough, and guessed correctly. Curtiss pedalled hard, opened and closed the throttle and jumped the spark, but no explosion came from the motor.

At the Post Office he paused for breath and headed the machine down hill. The motor suddenly touched off a package of fire crackers under a tin can: Curtiss sailed the three blocks down to the Lake Front at the foot of the street in a cloud of smoke. Further experiment satisfied him that the motor still had insufficient power for that country. He ordered another set of castings, had them machined by the Kirkhams and again started to build a cycle around it.

This new engine was a large one with a cylinder bore of 3½ inches and a piston stroke of 5 inches. The outfit, without the bicycle and connections, weighed 190 pounds. If it kept running the weight would not matter so much, but if it stalled on a steep hillside, then came the sore problem of wherewith to push it to the top.

This machine had so much power it started off with a series of explosions that nearly tore it from the framework. But when it settled down to work Curtiss found himself roaring through the village at a speed of thirty miles an hour. It carried him up the milelong North Urbana Hill and tore right on until the empty gasoline tank brought him to a stop in Wayne, eight miles to the north.

Luckily one progressive Wayne-ite had a gasoline stove and excitedly drained its tank to supply Curtiss with fuel for his motored ride to Hammondsport. Having worked on the upgrade, he was confident his creature could carry him back down again without a hitch. He was sure he had begun to see daylight in the matter of a formula for working power.

That night his grandmother mentioned casually that she'd heard he had gone to Wayne in a hurry that day.

He admitted as much and added: "Say, Grammer, she worked like a charm. And next time I can build a better one."

"I have a notion you can too, son," the old woman said quietly. And he knew that in her heart she was very proud of what he had done and of what he might do about automotivation.

Whatever time and money he could snatch from his bicycle business Curtiss now spent on the design and construction of his fourth and fifth motorcycles. Since these machines showed astonishing speed and he rode them easily, he began entering them at racing meets.

Orders for machines like those he rode began to drift in and the question of financing came up. Banker A. B. Pratt advanced a few hundred dollars, but that was hardly enough capital to start a manufacturing business on. J. Seymour Hubbs, local financier, whose high opinion of Curtiss's ability dated back to the time he had put the Hubbs acetylene lighting plant back into condition, agreed to put up the first thousand dollars. His business acumen told him though that this borrower who was racing around the country at near mile-a-minute speed might not be a good physical, even though a nearly perfect moral risk.

"First," said Mr. Hubbs, "you get me an insurance policy on your life for one thousand dollars."

The policy was obtained and Hubbs posted the money. Victor Masson, Lynn D. Masson, Henry Miller and Professor M. C. Plough, principal of the high school, each put up five hundred dollars. The total amount was less than five thousand, but with it Curtiss in 1901 started his motorcycle factory in a one-story wooden shed in his grandmother's back yard.

Financially it was a tight squeeze and often C. O. D. express shipments of parts needed to complete machines on order lay for days and weeks in the local express office before Curtiss could raise the cash to get them out. De Witt Clinton Bauder, lordly and hard headed old Dutchman, then president of the Bank of Hammondsport as well as head of the P. V. Wine Cellars, gave him some help by indirection in these emergencies. He did not feel justified in loaning the bank's funds to the infant manufacturing venture, but he did cultivate the habit of dropping around to see the express agent and growling, " 'Spose you hold that stuff till Glenn can pay for it." He knew well enough that the expressman would take this to mean that sooner or later the bank would, if necessary, see that the payments were met.

The Curtiss motorcycles were very fast but they were also tricky, and in order to be sure of making a good showing at the races Curtiss had to be his own demonstrator, as well as chief engineer and factory manager. He had to go out and prove his machines were the fastest in order to get volume business. But aside from the practical angle and the rewards Curtiss liked to win. If he knew beforehand that he could not possibly come out in front he did not start. Often he took desperate chances, or chances that looked that way to everybody but himself. But if from his own elastic point of view it was a question of staying out or breaking his neck, he stayed out.

Once he built a speed machine for a race at Coney Island. When he designed it he did not know what the track was like. He took it around once, dismounted, wheeled his motorcycle to one side, and erased his name from the entry list.

Another track racer was amazed at this move. "Looks funny to me," he blurted, "you've got the fastest machine here and you are scared to ride it."

"All right, fellow, go in and win it yourself, if that's the way it looks to you." Curtiss handed over the motorcycle.

The other man gladly mounted and made one lap of the track at a moderate speed and a second one wide open. He shut off the motor, just in time to avoid being swept over the top of the track. His face was white as he returned the machine, which he now realized was built too long to take the banks, to its owner.

Glenn Curtiss's first important motorcycle race was won in New York City on Memorial Day in 1902 during one of the early events sponsored by the New York Motorcycle Club. The streets of the route were blocked off and the combined roar of the machines left wrecked nerves behind all along the side streets.

It was Curtiss's first experience with professionalism, but many of the other riders had already established reputations, made names. Other manufacturers were backing their products with high pressure advertising and hiring professional riders. To them and to the public the man from Hammondsport was a nobody.

When Curtiss made a trial run over the course the other contestants realized that this lanky stranger might bear watching.

The man from Hammondsport rode a machine unique in several ways. It had a double frame with a loop at the bottom wide enough to permit his single cylinder motor to rest in a vertical position. Instead of bicycle chains he used a flat belt with a lever and pulley for increasing its tension. The motor had a 3-inch bore, 3-inch stroke and ball bearings for the crank shaft. Because of these inno-

THE LIFE OF GLENN CURTISS

vations Curtiss was handicapped so heavily that one of his opponents shot across the finish line ahead of him. He won the time prize, though, since he covered the course faster than anyone else, and finished in second place. The performance at the meet of this one, his first really successful motorcycle, brought an order for two machines like it from New York City and another from nearer home; practically a business boom.

Curtiss went straight to work on a better model. The ball-bearings were abandoned because they wore ruts in the ball-races. Sometimes the steel balls would split and chew a bearing completely. Roller bearings were substituted. He worked out several other schemes for increasing the efficiency of his new machines, one of the most vital in motorcycle evolution being the twist grip control.

Although the motor he used in the New York meet was superior to any of its predecessors, Curtiss decided it was still a weak sister. Multi-cylinder motors were few and far between in 1902, but Curtiss decided to double his cylinder strength in the next model. He spent most of his free time during the fall and winter of 1902 reading up on and analyzing the problems of high speed combustion engines.

No time was wasted before the drafting board. His designs matured in his own head and he was able to develop them vividly enough in his mind to transfer his ideas to others. Again the Kirkhams and Jerry Dalton, in charge of the electric light plant at Bath, were called into consultation. The Curtiss plant now had a regular working force of three men: Will Damoth, Claude Miller and John Osborn.

The castings finally arrived and were, by slow degrees, machined and assembled. The crank shaft and connecting rod bearings were carefully lapped to make a perfect fit.

Meantime a more substantial cycle frame was put together after Curtiss' design to withstand the tortional strains of this larger power plant. Several types of manifolds were cast and welded, but they could never get an equal mixture of gasoline in both cylinders. The big National Cycling Association's meet, was booked for Memorial Day. On the twenty-eighth of May the motor was just barely able to chug. They worked most of that night and it showed no improvement. The eccentricities of gas distribution had them stumped.

It was a case of give up or go on blindly.

"Pack it up and take it to Bath right away or we'll be too late for the train to New York." Those were the boss's orders.

Oh well, maybe G. H.'d get a good idea in time.

The machine was delivered to Curtiss at the shed near the starting line late on the afternoon of the 29th. There hadn't been enough car fare to bring along a helper, so he unpacked his tool kit and went to work on the motor. He worked alone all that evening and most of the night muddling over the fact that one cylinder was starved with a thin mixture, whereas the other was choked by a rich mixture to the point of backfiring.

At about three in the morning he had a brainstorm; took a sixteenth inch drill and began making little holes in the induction pipe leading to the overfed cylinder. Each time he drilled a hole he tested the engine. When he had just enough holes to balance the mixture perfectly the motor ran like a sewing machine. Then with motor oil soaked into his hands, smeared on his face up into his light brown hair he lay down beside his machine and slept for a few hours.

Two important events were scheduled for the next day, a hill climbing contest at Riverdale, on the Hudson, in the morning and the national championship track race at Empire State track in the afternoon.

A still grimy but very determined Curtiss showed up at the starting line for the hill climb at ten in a leather jacket, leather hip boots, leather cap and goggles. The fact that his costume was in strange contrast to the more sporty cycling togs of his professional competitors did not disturb Curtiss at all. Let the others play to the grandstand. Besides, this machine of his, with supplementary exhaust holes drilled in the exhaust pipe, forced him at top speed to ride in a halo of burned motor oil. Against this the leather costume was his only protection.

At Riverdale he won, with his two-cylinder motor, hands down and head up, as always. It was his habit still to sit calmly erect in the saddle of his machine. He had not yet learned the distinct advantage of the hairpin position adopted by the grandstand performers.

That afternoon Curtiss entered at Empire State track the most important race of his career up to that time. It was his first national championship event with a gold medal offered by the New York Motorcycle Club. Because he knew just what he had to do and had designed and built a machine to accomplish it—even made it work at long last—he won the ten-mile national championship and the gold medal in his usual workmanlike manner.

The cup which he won that day, when it was delivered, had been engraved

GEORGE H. CURTISS

because when he was asked to repeat his initials over long distance telephone he had said "G.H.—G. like in George." And George was the name he was known by in print for several months. On another trophy the G.H. appeared correctly, but his last name emerged as CURTICE.

It did not take very long for committee officials to

master the correct spelling of the name of the man from Hammondsport, N. Y. And his prestige as a manufacturer grew in direct ratio to his fame on the tracks. With very slight financial underpinning, no manufacturing background, he drove his wedge into the field. Few of his competitors suspected that he was just past twenty-five. They would have thrown up their hands in horror had they dreamed how crude his plant equipment was, that most of his helpers were green country boys.

Yet they could not afford to ignore him as a designer. On his machines he constantly added this or lopped off that feature. More often than not they followed his lead. Sometimes they thought his departures too radical or just superfluous gimcracks.

Sometimes his maturer, much more financially stable competitors had to pinch themselves to realize that the G.H. Curtiss who occasionally drifted into their councils, turned up at automotive shows with his displays—though he never at any time had much to say—was the same as the man who was forever showing what those machines of his had, at race tracks.

Dressed in a black sweater and woolen racing tights, as he usually was in later events, his body adjusted to the exact angle best designed to cut down wind resistance, he came to signify the utmost precision in racing form, as well as super speed and daring. Yet he was also the same vague, casually put together individual whose coat always seemed too ample for his wiry frame.

As pallid rain water or quick silver on a rampage they learned to accept him for what he was, both in street clothes or on a motorcycle. Though some of them had to school themselves not to gape in astonishment at the sharp discrepancy between the two incarnations of G. H. Curtiss.

Light, Strong Motors for Gas Bags

THOMAS SCOTT BALDWIN was known as "Captain" Baldwin. The balloonists who floated about the landscape in the early 1900's were known as "Captain." Captain J. Leo Stevens of New York, Captain H. E. Honeywell of St. Louis and Captain C. L. Bumbaugh of Indianapolis, were other popular aerial skippers. But Baldwin, at fifty was probably the best known and certainly the most aggressive.

To his intimates this jovial gentleman was plain "Uncle Tom." He had dipped into many professions and his initiative was inexhaustable. Born in Marion County, Missouri, he put in time as a newsboy, lamplighter, messenger boy, printer's devil, typesetter and train butcher. Then he joined the circus as an acrobat and earned the distinction of being the only man to walk blindfolded from Seal Rock to Cliff House over San Francisco Bay on a slack wire.

In 1880 he perfected the modern type parachute and, at a flat rate of a dollar a foot of drop, he picked up many a thousand dollars in demonstrations both in this country and abroad. His courage and daring were as dependable as his sense of humor. By the time he got around to ballooning his tightrope figure was a robust memory, but his smile was as ready and beaming as ever and his complexion as rosy.

Tom Baldwin built his own balloons. They were bulbous cloth creatures, coated with several layers of varnish and covered with netting to hold the basket. In shape they were virtually identical to the first balloons sent aloft by the Montgolfier brothers. Building them was simple enough. Keeping them afloat was no great trick either. Baldwin had made some five thousand flights; free ballooning was old stuff to him. He was anxious now to give his gas bags a sense of direction, make them less dependent on fickle air currents. Santos Dumont had followed up his circumnavigation of the Eiffel Tower in October, 1901, with flights in his dirigible around the fields near Paris. And the acclaim accorded Dumont's feats helped to convince the showman Baldwin that here was a bet not to be overlooked.

He experimented with several alleged internal combustion engines, always to be disappointed when they failed to live up to all the essential requirements. Dependable motive power in 1903 was still an unborn quantity. The motors available were too wheezy, not strong enough and far too heavy for the things called air ships. Captain Tom thought he would have to toss the whole tantalizing scheme overboard in disgust when his solution came bounding up a Los Angeles side street one day on a motorcycle.

This his ear long trained in disillusion told him was not a simple pfutt—pfutt—pfutt single-cylinder engine, but a twin-cylinder affair which purred like a happy kitten. He trailed the machine to its first stopping place.

"Well, Sonny, how is everything?" he began, eager to make conversation.

The boy guessed everything was all right.

"What I want to know," bluntly, "is where did you get that whiz-wagon?"

The trade name HERCULES painted on the gas tank

signified nothing to him and the owner was not sure just where his second-handed machine had originated. But Captain Tom kept at the boy until he finally dug out of a remote pocket the directions sheet that went with his two wheels in line. From the tattered circular Baldwin copied off the name: G. H. Curtiss Manufacturing Company, Hammondsport, N. Y.

He hurried home and wrote a letter to that address, asking for a price quotation on a high-powered engine proportioned to weight for use in a dirigible balloon. After a few weeks he received an answer from the Curtiss plant, naming a reasonable enough figure, and he fired back an order for a rush delivery.

Months went by and he did not have his engine, although he had written several reminders and received as many politely apologetic answers. But no engine. He did not dream, of course, that he might have had his motor almost immediately if some member of the Curtiss staff had known how to suggest in a discreet way that he put up full cash in advance. Production of motors at a plant with shop equipment consisting of only a drill press and a lathe was necessarily slow; merchandising cautious.

But Captain Tom was not the sort of fellow to start something he couldn't finish. He wanted a motor built by the same plant that was responsible for the HERCULES he had seen operating that motorcycle in Los Angeles. The Captain was a direct actionist at heart; he bought himself a ticket to Hammondsport and boarded an Eastbound train, leaving his balloon plant in charge of his two youthful assistants, Lincoln Beachey, a red-headed seventeen-year-old, and Roy Knabenshue, only a year or so older.

Captain Tom promptly took in the unprofessional flavor of the plant and sensed that G. H. Curtiss was just a youngster despite his shaggy frown.

"Hello sonny," was his bluff greeting. "My name's Baldwin. Where's that engine I ordered?"

And the head of the G. H. Curtiss Manufacturing Co. dropped his businesslike gravity, grinned sheepishly and tried to explain about the delayed shipment. They sat down to talk it over and Curtiss came out of the conference with the conviction that this customer was a thoroughly likable and trustworthy fellow. From that day on he was "Uncle Tom" while Baldwin continued to call him "Sonny" as he did all the "boys."

Production was shoved ahead on the engine that was to power a dirigible, and Baldwin stayed in Hammondsport to sit in on its progress and make sure there were no more delays. When it was finished he personally took it back to California, where his arrival was eagerly awaited by his two young helpers.

Together they tackled the complicated task of installing the engine, whose air-cooled cylinders were designed for use in motorcycles running thirty to sixty miles an hour. At that speed plenty of cooling air surged through the fins. Dirigible balloons at the time had a maximum speed of from ten to fifteen miles, but Baldwin's ingenuity was equal to this basic speed discrepancy. In a few months he had his apparatus adjusted so that the engine got enough air from the propeller draft to keep it going at least long enough to make a short exhibition flight.

The consuming ambition of balloonists of the day was to fly a complete circle, returning to the starting point. With his power plant designed by Glenn Curtiss, Captain Baldwin performed this feat in his first dirigible, the *California Arrow,* at Oakland in August 1904. Nobody in this country had ever before accomplished it successfully.

"To say that I was pleased with the working of the engine is to put it mildly," was his warm endorsement to the reporters who scampered up to interview him when he landed. He promptly placed an order for a bigger engine with the Curtiss plant.

The *California Arrow*, only dirigible flown successfully at the Louisiana-Purchase Exposition at St. Louis in 1904, was equipped with a two-cylinder five horsepower motor. Baldwin's second Curtiss engine was installed in his new *City of Portland*. It was a big, powerful brute of seven straining horsepower.

Lincoln Beachey flew this ship and threw some plain and fancy jitters into the crowds at the Lewis and Clark Exposition, the same year. They watched him land the balloon on top of Portland, Oregon's Chamber of Commerce building; take off again after a twenty minute respite and fly straight back home to his starting-point. The applause was tumultuous; this time the little Beachey chap and his chief had really outdone themselves.

On Baldwin's next engine order Glenn Curtiss let himself go completely berserk. By doubling the number of cylinders in "V" shape construction he produced an eighteen-horsepower plant that was still not heavy enough to anchor the *City of Los Angeles* to the ground, but strong enough to send her barging all over the sky.

Baldwin's enthusiasm was so strong that it brought quick response from others in the form of orders to Curtiss, orders for light and strong motors. All of them wanted increased power, better cooling qualities, better lubrication, lighter weight, than anything the Curtiss plant had ever done before. One after another these requirements were met. At the same time Curtiss was still building, selling and racing motorcycles.

Then a fire in Baldwin's factory early in 1906 destroyed the original *California Arrow*, the *City of Portland* and his entire plant equipment. Only the new *California Arrow* was safe and sound in Hammondsport where he had shipped her for motor installation.

"Might as well shut up shop out here and move to Hammondsport altogether," was Captain Tom's decision. And thereafter the sight of bulging bags cruising around Pleasant Valley and over Lake Keuka became a commonplace one. Other aerial navigators followed Baldwin's lead. Balloons were built and inflated in the Glen, whose sharp-cut canyon formed a natural hangar, and were floated out over the town, barely missing the steep cliffs on the way.

In Steuben County the aeronauts were generally known as "balloonatics." But they meant no disrespect and were careful about accenting the third syllable rather than the second and fourth. The balloonatics were popular in Hammondsport because they were bringing cash business to the town. The little Curtiss shop on the hill, which started with three men in 1901, had, thanks partly to them, ten men in 1905 and a hundred in 1908. Meanwhile a group of mechanics was learning about aircraft engines, a force of skilled aircraft mechanics was in training.

Curtiss, as head of the plant, was surrounded by eccentric individuals from all over the country who had heard of his knack for creating power. They came worrying him with schemes for rotary valves, sleeved valves, radial engines, for the most fantastic balloons. And Curtiss welcomed particularly the airmen among them. "Why wouldn't I?" he excused his tolerance to Ritchie Betts, editor of the *Bicycling World and Motorcycle Review*. "I get twice as much money for my motors from those aviation cranks."

Still in his twenties, he had his chain of bicycle stores, his bicycle contracts and his motorcycle business, as well as more and more orders for dirigible motors to work at. Usually his plant was running twenty-four hours a day, with Curtiss himself on an eighteen-hour shift. By 1907 they were building and selling between five and six hundred motorcycles a year. With agencies all over the country, most orders, incidentally, came in from the California agency.

The success of the Curtiss output inspired a Rochester merchant to offer Curtiss a large factory and ample capital if he would move to that town. But when the moneyed men of Hammondsport heard of the offer their local pride was stirred. They made Curtiss a counter proposition which he accepted. In October 1905 the G. H. Curtiss Manufacturing Company was incorporated with a capital stock of forty thousand dollars. A. B. Pratt, R. G. Hall and Curtiss were the directors.

The earlier motors and motorcycles had been trade-named HERCULES. Curtiss fancied the clank of tradition inherent in the name. And only when it developed that a California manufacturer had applied the name to a motorcycle at an earlier date did he consent to change it. It did not occur to him to use his own name as a trademark until Will Demoth of the factory staff proposed it. Originally it appeared in old English letters after a stencil designed by Claude Jenkins, then in the familiar conventionalized fac-simile of Curtiss's own signature.

In 1903 Curtiss lost his grandmother, less than a year after the death of his little son, Carlton N., only eleven months old. And he was more grieved by the two deaths than it was in his nature to show. Ruth Curtiss's rigorous soul had grown a little brittle with the years, and she could not overcome the shock of losing her great-grandson who was very dear to her because he was so like his father. She did not quite manage to finish out her eightieth year. She had retired within herself more than ever during the months she lingered on after the baby's funeral, and had taken less dish in Glenn's affairs. But she held on to her belief that the man she had helped to mould would make the world sit up and take notice some day.

In his motor experiments Curtiss found the way to sheathe his grief. He worked strenuously, gave scant attention to anything except engines and motorcycles, orders, bills and payrolls. His natural diffidence now made him seem almost dour. The wistfulness of the boy was gone for those years from 1903 to 1907.

Not satisfied with the strain that racing, manufacturing and inventing put on his mind and body, he took on, as a side line, automobiles. In Waltham, Massachusetts, during a motorcycle meet, he saw the first Orient Buckboard, bought one and took on the Hammondsport agency. Any motor-driven vehicle fascinated him and he could not resist the lure of the little slot-sprung Orient.

When the first one was delivered to him he invited young Nancy Van Gelder, who happened to be passing his shop on the Square, to come for a ride in it. One of his helpers gave a mighty pull to the ten-foot strap and they bounded all the way to the bottom of Sweet Wine Hill. But the Buckboard refused to climb back up.

He found customers for two of the Orients in Hammondsport. Arthur Bauder and J. S. Hubbs both let him sell them Orients, though their power was only theoretically sufficient to make them useful on the rutty sandy hill roads. Later Curtiss helped to undermine his own motorcycle business by taking the agency for the five hundred dollar four-cylinder Ford, and for a while he was agent for the Frayer-Miller automobile.

Another experimental diversion of his was a simple three-wheeled wind wagon, built to test the efficiency of dirigible propellers. The front wheel was used for steering, the rear ones carried the load of the motor and the aerial propeller. With this creation he made so many horses climb fences on a trip up Pleasant Valley that he never dared to give it another workout. The one trip brought him some profitable notoriety, though.

Dr. J. P. Thomas of New York City, who was producing a special dietetic bread, bought a twin-cylinder Curtiss motor for his own wind wagon and drove it around the square at Broadway and 72d Street. His ride was a sweeping mechanical triumph, though he was arrested for blocking traffic. The Doctor thought the venture well worth whatever fine and trouble it cost him. He called up Henry Wehman, Curtiss's New York City agent, and asked if his plant could supply a more powerful four-cylinder, air-cooled engine. Since Wehman was sure Curtiss was working on just such a motor for Captain Baldwin, the Doctor proposed they go to Hammondsport and take a look at it.

At the plant the motor was put on a test stand and the prospective customer was invited to watch its performance. Both Wehman and the mechanic operating it knew that the bearings in the brand new engine were very stiff and knew there were no facilities in the shop for cooling it. It was impossible to run it for more than three minutes on the stand without burning it up.

The motor was started. It ran beautifully with a grateful roar for two minutes. Then Wehman signalled the mechanic to shut it off so he could invite him into the house for a talk with Curtiss and to sample some of the local champagnes. Meanwhile the motor cooled off. It was not the only time that Hammondsport's major industry, grape-growing abetted the town's minor industry, motors.

Computing probable horsepower and drinking vintage champagne kept Dr. Thomas involved for the better part of an hour: long enough for the motor to reach a temperature at which it could safely be tried out again. Then Wehman proposed casually, "Well, Doctor, if you still have any doubts about the motor, let's go out and see it run. I think you will satisfy yourself it has the power claimed for it."

The motor started promptly, ran until Wehman waved to the mechanic to shut her down and so pleased the customer that he insisted on writing a check for it on the spot. He persuaded the wily salesman to accept another check for fifty dollars to reimburse him for time lost on the trip to Hammondsport.

Motorcycles of various types and capacities were built by the Curtiss Manufacturing Company, including the Rear Seat motorcycle-built-for-two and also the Flexible Side Car to be attached to a standard motorcycle. But Curtiss's chief interest, because there was more suspense to it, was designing light motors for lighter-than-air craft for men like Tom Baldwin, who had pitched their hangar-tents in Hammondsport to be near his engine shop.

Among them were Charles O. Jones, who built a dirigible which he flew with some success at Hammondsport, but in which he later crashed fatally during an exhibition flight in Maine, and Dr. George N. Tomlinson, of Syracuse, another Curtiss motor customer, who was much more successful. During the Hudson-Fulton Celebration in 1909 he shared with Baldwin the distinction of being one of the first two men to fly around the Statue of Liberty.

Stores in town were closed whenever one of the new air-ships was reported ready for trial. None of the clerks, nor any of the customers, wanted to miss a launching, nor even the storekeepers themselves. An impromptu field day was declared for June 27, 1907, when word got around that Captain Baldwin's newest ship was ready for testing.

It had the specially designed air-cooled motor in it and an arrangement of shaft-driven twin propellers. The object of the propellers, rotating in opposite directions, was to offset the gyroscopic, twisting effect of a single propeller.

Rain put off the flight for twenty-four hours, but that only gave the outing more publicity, more people a chance to get there on time. At Kingsley Pasture at the head of Lake Keuka, Curtiss and his assistants inspected the motor installation; then they tested the gearing of the new-type propellers. And the big bag slowly sucked in gas.

When she was ready Captain Baldwin took off. He circled Pleasant Valley, returned to Kingsley Pasture and reported that she handled pretty well but that the new gearing made her a trifle nose-heavy. The longitudinal balance of those early dirigibles was maintained mostly by the pilot, who shifted his own weight to make the proper adjustment.

Curtiss, who had never betrayed any interest in flying before, said coolly, after the pilot had finished his report:

"Uncle Tom, would you trust me with that gadget for a few minutes? I think maybe I can get the idea better if I try it out myself."

Baldwin's tone was just as contained as he answered him: "Sure, take her up if you want to, Sonny."

He wasn't worried, but the other men standing around were, though they knew well enough what Curtiss could do on the ground with a familiar machine. They knew also that these tiny dirigibles often drifted faster than they rose, that there were fairly high trees, electric poles and houses on three sides. If the ship collided with any of them before the balloon gained enough altitude the chances were right for a smashup and a fire.

Henry Kleckler, foreman at the factory, started trotting down the field under the balloon as if to catch the boss should he fall out. He was frightened. Another of the factory hands called the boss in plain upstate Anglo-Saxon, "a gol-darned fool."

But the balloon cleared the trees. At an altitude of approximately a hundred feet Curtiss sailed over the trees fringing the road, steered the ship across the valley, made a wide turn and sailed back to the starting point. He nosed her down, cut the motor and settled the ship on the ground directly in front of the tent that housed her.

"Not bad sport," he told his men down on the ground, "but there is no place to go."

And having tried flying, he was through with it. Because they paid top prices he went on selling the balloon builders all the light, strong engines they wanted to order. But he couldn't see any sense to what they were doing and had little or no respect for the aviation fiends as such. Which was all part and parcel of Grandmother Curtiss's own four-square philosophy.

He determined to concentrate on putting more power into motorcycles, to ride them for records and boost business at the plant.

The Fastest Mile

I T WAS not for his engine building that newspaper stories tagged him, as early as 1905, "that amazing Mr. Curtiss." It was for his ability as a speed merchant at the tracks. It did not matter much to his public that he himself had designed the machines he rode. It was the stretch he covered on them in so few minutes and seconds that made him that amazing Mr. Curtiss.

It was a curiously appropriate label. His abilities as a "hellrider" were undeniably amazing, and the "Mister Curtiss" was quite in character with the detached gravity of the Scotch-Yankee motorcyclist from Up-state.

The Federation of American Motorcyclists, formed in September 1903, at a meet at the Manhattan Beach cement bicycle track in Brooklyn, sought to control motorcycle racing and to limit the sizes of motors and weights of machines. A maximum weight limit of 110 pounds was imposed and rigidly enforced by the F. A. M. rules. If the scales at the track showed him half a pound overweight an entrant sometimes had to strip off his belt guides, pedal clips and even his stock saddle in order to qualify. Eventually the weight limit was discarded. Power and speed were essential and frantic trimming of weights resulted in weakened machines. It forced, in some cases, the use of wooden rims and racing bicycle tires instead of the heavier steel rims and regular motorcycle tires.

At Ormond Beach, Florida, in January 1904, Glenn Curtiss had established his first important world's record on a motorcycle when he covered a distance of ten miles in 8 minutes, 54 2/5 seconds. It stood as a record for motorcycles of 61 cubic inches displacement for more than seven years.

During the next two years his collection of trophies grew steadily. And his fellow racers liked him even when he outrode them.

At the national F. A. M. meet in 1904 he met William C. Chadeayne, another manufacturer who rode his own machines. He had bought the Thomas Auto-Bi interests in Buffalo, N. Y., when E. R. Thomas became absorbed in the four-wheeled Thomas Flyer. Billy or "Old Never-quit" Chadeayne crossed the continent by motorcycle in fast 47½ day record-time in 1905 when only two other machines had motored all the way across the United States. He raced against Glenn Curtiss many times but was never able to beat him. And whenever he wasn't racing against Curtiss he was trying to help him win.

What most impressed the other contestants about Curtiss was the fact that he was never cocksure about a victory. Usually he scratched his head, wrinkled up his heavy eyebrows while the timekeepers were making up their reports and said, "Gee, I guess I didn't do much."

More than once Curtiss proved that when his machine was slower than the ones it had to compete with it was possible to out-smart his opposition.

For the hill climb at the F. A. M. meet in Waltham, Massachusetts, in August 1905, he knew another entrant had a speedier machine and that in order to win the climb he would have to take the curves faster. Prospect Hill at Waltham had so sharp a turn, he found on going over the course, that in order to stay on the road the entrants would have to slow down so much they could hardly hope to regain full speed before the finish.

At the point where this turn occurred the road had been cut down several feet below its original level, leaving an almost perpendicular dirt wall around the bend. That night they borrowed a pair of shovels from the road crew and Curtiss and Tank Waters got up before daylight and shoveled enough dirt to fill in two short stretches of ditch beside the course, one of them at the approach, the other at the upper end of the turn. The first stretch he hoped would permit him to shoot across and strike the dirt wall, the second should give him a chance to get back on the roadway. There was considerable hazard of course in the possibility of a spill in the soft dirt of the improvised bank.

When time was called for the hill climb, Curtiss sailed up the steep bank around the curve and back onto the road without a hitch, winning the race by a comfortable margin. "He made the hair stand on the heads of even those who fancied themselves hardened, with his reckless daring when he tore up the hill like a human whirlwind," according to a startled newspaper account.

His own comment to Tank Waters was a casual, "Well, anyway I made it."

In August 1907 the annual F. A. M. meet was held at Providence, Rhode Island. Curtiss studied the road leading up Francis Hill, the course for the hill climb, carefully. It was an unusually tricky course. The finish line was at the head of the street just beyond a right-angled turn across the car tracks where the road came to a dead end. Common sense demanded that the riders throttle down before they reached the turn.

Stanley Kellogg had an Indian entered which had made that same hill climb in faster time than Curtiss possibly could on the fastest machine he had with him. And Kellogg was the sort of a rider who could be counted on to repeat if not better a fine performance. Curtiss decided that he would take the turn at full (sixty mile) speed and head for the eight-inch curb on the far side of the street. He would try to slide around the curbing sideways on the iron bands of his wheels and so check his speed to a stop in front of the judges' position. It was the only conceivable way to beat Kellogg, so he decided to risk his neck.

The start was made over Belgian blocks, although the surface of the hill proper was macadam. Curtiss streaked up the incline, made the right-angle turn wide open and struck the curbstone with his wheel. But the forward momentum was too great. He rolled and bounded over the sidewalk, took the backs off both his hands and scraped his right leg badly. He had come in several seconds ahead of all the other contestants, but in the excitement of his spill the timers forgot to stop their watches. Although he had won, the prize according to racing practice went to Kellogg.

They were a hard-riding lot who demonstrated the early motorcycles. The Indian team was the strongest combination in the field. It included Oscar Hedstrom, Jacques De Rosier, Fred Hoyt, Bert Barrows of Springfield, and later Stanley Kellogg of Bridgeport and B. A. Swenson of Providence. William Ray, Jr., of Brooklyn, imported a record-holding 14-horsepower Reugeot from France and expected to clean up on the field. Glenn Curtiss however was able to win from him.

He did not personally win all the trophies taken by the machines and motors built at his plant. But nobody other than Curtiss could get the terrific speed out of his machines that he could, except on occasion Tank Waters, his trusty second in the bicycle racing days. There were others who rode competently for him, Al Cook, Will Damoth, both Hammondsport boys, and Hank (Henry J.) Wehman.

Frequently when there were two Curtiss machines entered, they managed to nose out first and second place even though, for no reason in particular so far as any competitor could figure out, Curtiss stuck obstinately to the belt drive rather than the chain drive which was inherently faster.

In the winter of 1906-1907 Curtiss concentrated on preparing two machines for a big, officially timed meet, the Florida Speed Carnival. He wanted the one mile record for the small single-cylinder motorcycle rated at $2\frac{1}{2}$ horsepower and he wanted the world's one-mile record for the larger twin-cylinder machine. He knew the competition would be stiff. There were several manufacturers of motorcycles now in the field with much stronger backing than he had and facilities for turning out very fast machines.

Whether or not he won these two routine events, Curtiss decided suddenly on a fantastic experiment a few weeks before the meet. He was working on an eight-cylinder air-cooled engine of "V" type, destined for use in one of Baldwin's dirigibles. It occurred to him that he might test this motor and show the world some real speed by installing it in an elongated motorcycle frame.

The strain, he knew, would be terriffc. His stock motorcycle fittings were designed for machines with a maximum of less than ten horsepower. He knew that the ordinary motorcycle wheel and tire would not stand the strain of forty horses.

He had to devise a means of transmitting the tremendous power of that big motor to the drive wheel. This detail and others were worked out quietly in the dead of a Hammondsport winter. No use talking about it ahead of time until he had some notion whether the dizzy scheme would work. There was some sharp intake of breath by the men at the factory when they learned what was afoot. This did seem like stretching things too far. Still G. H. ought to know what he was doing.

An automobile wheel, with beveled gears and a substantial tire was used at the rear. The stoutest of motorcycle wheels was in front for the steering. The width of the tires was about 2½ inches as compared to the usual 1¾ inch width of the motorcycle tire of 1907 or the 4 inch width of motorcycle tires today. The usual Curtiss belt transmission was abandoned in favor of beveled gears and a shaft running through the lower frame. The machine was geared almost 1¼ to 1 on the rear wheel, or nearly five times as high as the average motorcycle of the day.

The motor was tested on the block in the factory in December. To make certain that everything was up to snuff it was taken back into the shop and completely dismantled for examination.

Time was very short. Curtiss wanted the big motor set into the cycle frame as soon as possible so the men worked with feverish intensity. Young Carlton Wheeler, working too fast and with too much energy, as he tightened a stud-bolt that helped to hold one of the cylinder heads in place, snapped off one of the cooling flanges.

A blaze of blue invective from the boss startled Wheeler almost as much as the damage he had done. He could not have been more startled if a cold potato had suddenly started shooting sparks. And country boys do not like being bawled out. A city shop worker would have shrugged off the unpleasant incident, but Carlton threw his tools into his bag and marched out of the place. He was *through*.

Few people ever saw Glenn Curtiss that angry. Those who did never forgot it. A man who could cuss like that and almost never did! It seemed like rank waste of a great gift to those who knew of his accomplishment.

The accident was annoying but not disastrous, as it turned out. An extra cylinder-head casting was found in the Kirkham shop and this was quickly machined, fitted into place and the motor was as good as ever. It was installed in the big frame and Curtiss prepared to test it out before shipping it South.

But the test was prevented by a heavy fall of snow. In an effort to determine whether he could balance the thing or not a path was shoveled through the snow behind the factory. The monster machine was dragged up the hill. Curtiss got on it and they pushed him downhill.

"Well I guess it will stay up alone when I get more room." He decided to chance it without a road test. With his two standard racing machines and his two-wheeled monstrosity, he was forced to start for Ormond Beach without the slightest certainty that the big fellow would run under power.

Tank Waters came along as his starter. Tank knew just how much you could beat the gun. Tom Baldwin grabbed his derby and came along too because he was too excited about the project to stay away. On the train to Florida they debated what might happen when the big motor let go. The ordinary twin-cylinder racing motorcycle was so designed that, if an amateur accustomed to slower starting machines tried the usual method of taking two or three running steps beside it, he was apt to find himself streaming out behind it like the tail of a kite, so quick was the getaway. If that could happen with a ten-horsepower motor what might happen with forty horses on a stampede?

On January the twenty-third Curtiss nosed out his two official world's records at Ormond Beach. With the smaller machine he did the mile in 1:02; with the twin-cylinder one he covered it in 46 2/5 seconds.

The speed carnival as a whole had not been very successful. People came expecting some event comparable to the preceding year's, when Fred H. Marriott drove a freak automobile, a special beetle-shaped Stanley Steamer, one mile down the beach in 28 1/5 seconds. This time he had only managed thirty seconds in an improved Stanley.

Then he announced that if he could get up five hundred pounds of steam pressure—normally he used three hundred—he would cover the mile in twenty-eight seconds flat. In the attempt the machine was blown to fragments and Marriott severely injured. The spectators saw the three-foot boiler fly far out to sea, sending up a column of steam as it sank.

Then Curtiss came forward with his freak go-devil. The machine was wheeled from its tent and he asked permission to make an attempt on the world's straightaway record for one mile. The officials said that they would gladly time the trial but since his machine did not conform to any known motorcycle standards, his time could not be accepted as an official record. He decided to make the trial though his heartbeat was not too steady as Tank Waters and Tom Baldwin pushed the big machine toward the starting line.

Curtiss was telling Baldwin and Waters: "For God's sake keep me up straight, if you let me go I'll fall over sure." He tightened his goggles, adjusted his toes to the pedal clips and prepared for a burst of speed.

His two friends pushed and pushed some more. Portly Uncle Tom was growing winded and they were both wondering whether he would ever decide to start the motor.

Suddenly he did slip in the clutch. They let go as the motor started with a regular rhythmical choog, choog. Curtiss turned it off as suddenly as he had started it, got off the machine and stared at it like a man in a trance.

Motors in those days spluttered and chugged, and not at regular intervals. They were never really what the man with a sensitive ear would call "sweet-running." To Curtiss's amazement the big forty horsepower motor had turned out to be the sweetest thing he had ever listened to. Baldwin and Waters shared his rapture. The sound of her told Captain Tom what he might expect when she was driving his balloon. Not so many years before Tank and Glenn would have been turning handsprings for joy at that point. Now they stood quite still for a few seconds, quietly gleeful.

Curtiss got back on the machine and was pushed again to a start-off, knowing now that the motor would work like a charm. He was still far from certain though that the machine would hold together under the strain of the terrific vibration.

But the motorcycle gained speed steadily, surely. He had no way of gauging his speed. He knew it was increasing at an enormous rate, that when he passed the starting line spectators, the bluff and the houses on it, presented a mottled blur. It took him another mile to slow the machine down to a stop.

The officials announced that he had covered the mile in 26 and 2/5 seconds, a speed of 136.3 miles an hour. The latest pink sporting broadside of the *Chicago Daily News* of January 24, 1907, carried a headline:

FASTEST MILE ON EARTH

The *News'* story pointed out that bullets were the only rivals of G. H. Curtiss. It cited the world's previous records. The next fastest mile was Fred Marriott's 1906 record of 28 1/5 seconds in the Stanley Steamer. A mile in 29 seconds flat had once been traveled by a Berlin electric car, and the best authentic time by a locomotive up to that time was 30 seconds flat made in Florida over the Plant System.

It was four years before anybody was able to travel faster in an automobile than Curtiss did on his freak motorcycle, although Barney Oldfield and other racers concentrated on beating his record.* And not until many years later, did anyone travel faster on two wheels.**

No one ever again rode the big motorcycle that did 136 miles an hour plus at Ormond Beach in 1907. The terrific strain on the light transmission had wrecked it completely.

* The record was beaten in 1911 by Bob Burman in a Blitzen-Benz. His speed was 141.732 m. p. h.

** J. S. Wright, near Cork, Ireland, made 150 miles an hour in 1930 for an unofficial record.

II

COOPERATIVE SCIENCE

With No Man Aboard

NEXT to Curtiss's grandmother, his chief mentor was Alexander Graham Bell. Both of them knew what they were about in trying to let him identify the helping wind they thought he needed.

Bell and Curtiss had in common their essentially Scotch attitude toward life and both were touched with the brush of genius. Both men had the same inward glow, the same passion for experiment. Otherwise, that is outwardly, Bell was North to Curtiss's South pole.

Six feet tall, of a fine build and erect carriage, Dr. Bell, inventor of the telephone, was what his generation called a "commanding presence." He had black hair and a full beard, both turning white when Curtiss met him. His dark eyes flashed in response to every moment of special interest. A. Graham Bell, or Graham Bell as he was better known, was as imposing as he was great; made just as striking an appearance as Glenn Curtiss didn't and couldn't to save his soul. It was Curtiss's ability to build compact power plants for balloons that brought the two men together. Bell's interest in flight problems began when he met Samuel Pierpont Langley in Washington in 1887, twenty years before his association with Curtiss. Intellectually the problem of man-flight had been an outcast. No scientist of standing had dared or cared to take the subject serious. Langley was the first to do so, and is responsible for the fact that aviation had its scientific genesis in America. From the time of their meeting Dr. Bell was one of his most sincere allies.

There was very little to be said about the subject yet, nor was Langley a talkative man. His brilliant intellect was not coupled with the gift of conversation. But he was always as ready to show his experiments to Alexander Graham Bell, as Bell was eager to go over them with him.

Inspired by Langley's enthusiasm Bell began making experiments of his own. As he became increasingly independent, thanks to the profits of his various patents, he felt economically justified in broadening his experimental work into activities conceived primarily for the pure fun of the job at hand. At the same time he would be staging a fascinating drama in pantomime for his deaf wife to follow with him. And so he began building kites of unique design.

Each man, in his way, risked his reputation as a scientist when he threw in his lot with the study of aeronautics. A man past fifty and another past forty set out to prove the impossible, each with the most infinite patience and meticulous attention to detail. Both were, in the colloquialism of the day, old enough to know better.

Samuel Pierpont Langley's important early discoveries were published by the Smithsonian Institution in *Experiments in Aerodynamics* in 1891 and *Internal Work of the Wind* in 1893. Both books were of vital assistance to other experimenters who lacked his scientific background. A characteristic reaction to Professor Langley's pioneering was expressed by the brothers Wilbur and Orville Wright in a private letter to Octave Chanute, another of the early pioneers. They wrote:

> The knowledge that the head of the most prominent scientific institution of America believed in the possibility of human flight, was one of the chief influences that led us to undertake the preliminary investigation that preceded our active work.

Langley's work up to 1893 had convinced him that a heavier-than-air machine, propelled by an engine, could be made sufficiently powerful and stable to carry a man. He concentrated on trying out many types of machine on a small scale and finally settled on a tandem monoplane with its wings set at a dihedral angle. This nearly quarter-size model measured thirteen feet from wing tip to wing tip and was sixteen feet long. Its steam boiler weighed five pounds and its engine twenty-six ounces.

As it could carry no pilot the plan was to set the controls and fly it out over water to break the shock of its fall. And on May 6, 1896, it was launched from a catapult on the top of a houseboat in the Potomac River. With its engine and propellers going full speed it rose directly into the wind and completed circles of about a hundred yards in diameter for a minute and a half. Then, its steam exhausted, it settled down gradually and gently upon the water.

Langley felt his experiments had been notably successful and that they marked the end of his efforts in the field of aeronautics. He was urged to take out a patent and reap the financial profits of his work up to that point but he refused. "Whatever I have discovered," he said, "belongs to whoever might find it useful in going on from there.

"I have brought to a close the portion of the work which seemed to be peculiarly mine—the demonstration of the practicability of mechanical flight—and for the next stage, which is the commerical and practical development of the idea, it is probable that the world may look to others. The world, indeed, will be supine if it does not realize that a new possibility has come to it, and that the great universal highway overhead is now soon to be opened."

Yet he could not get flying experimentation out of his mind. He found himself making more flights with the little model. They were always successful and of tremendous interest to those who witnessed them. Army officers attended one of the tests of the model and their enthusiasm together with the influence of Bell, who had just been made a Regent of the Smithsonian Institution, induced the Board of Ordnance and Fortification, after its members made a careful study of the model, to set aside fifty thousand dollars to enable Professor Langley to build a full-sized aerodrome capable of carrying a human pilot. The Smithsonian Institution appropriated an additional twenty thousand dollars so that the work might not be hampered for lack of funds.

Under Langley's direction Charles M. Manly built a somewhat larger model in order to try out the possibilities of a gasoline engine. The new model weighed fifty-eight pounds and its engine developed three horsepower. The first flight of this, the earliest gasoline-driven heavier-than-air craft, was made over the Potomac near Washington in the presence of a group of newspaper men, as well as official observers.

And so the work of designing and constructing the larger machine went forward. The most serious problem was to find a light but powerful engine. It should weigh no more than ten pounds per horsepower. Langley and Manly went abroad in search of such an engine but found none that was even approximately satisfactory. It is just barely possible that a man in a little town in western New York state might have been of valuable assistance to them had they known of his aptitude with motors. It is even conceivable that he knew enough in time to have prevented Langley's tragedy, but history cannot of course be written backwards. Lessons in defeat can't be unlearned.

In desperation Manly designed and built a five-cylinder, radial type gasoline motor in the shops of the Smithsonian Institution and this was installed in the aerodrome. There was necessarily a considerable difference in the ratio of its weight to the large model as compared to the ratio of the steam motor to the previous model.

The trial took place in the middle of the Potomac at Tidewater, Virginia, on October 7, 1903. Tugs and launches moved about to lend assistance if necessary, newspaper reporters and photographers lined the banks and boatsides. The aerodrome was set up on the same catapult on a houseboat which had launched the smaller models.

Charles Manly climbed into the basket seat, got the engine running at full speed and released the machine. It moved along the rails of the track with sufficient headway for normal flight. When it reached the end of track there was a violent jerk, the machine fell into the river and sank. It rose to the surface again because of the floats, which were to have been used in landing on the water, and was towed ashore. The pilot escaped without injury.

Gravely disappointed, Langley prepared as quickly as possible for a second launching. It was attempted two months later. Again the awkward form of getting the craft into the air balked the takeoff. The rear guy post was cracked as the machine moved down the rails, crippling the rear wings and the machine promptly tilted up in the front and plunged over backward into the water. This time it did not rise again but the pilot was rescued.

The newspapermen were in no mood to make allowances. They led the world in a universal outburst of derision. Professor Langley had not made friends with them. His extreme self-consciousness made him seem brusque, and he was very unpopular with reporters. Also as a conscientious scientist he felt it essential always to prove a thing before talking about it.

But this argument would not have impressed the reporters had it been offered to them. He was spending the people's money, wasn't he? Why must he be so persistently non-committal about what he was doing? First the papers ridiculed what they called the "Affair of Langley's Folly," then they blamed him for wasting public funds.

Consequently the public was not only skeptical but definitely touchy about the whole subject of flying. So much so that when nine days later the Wright brothers made their first flight at Kitty Hawk, North Carolina, accounts of it were either consigned to editorial wastebaskets or were printed in obscure corners of inside pages. They had done something which no man had done since time began, but aviation was no longer news in December 1903. The city editors regarded it as a nuisance.

To a proud and sensitive man like Langley, the storm of criticism brought pain, naturally, but his chief emotion was one of sadness. It was impossible now to obtain the comparatively small amount of money needed to restore his machine and to allow him fair opportunity to vindicate his claims. His greatest scientific venture had failed. He was an old man suddenly and all the fight was out of him. Two years later, at the age of seventy-one he died.

Alexander Graham Bell strongly resented this public conviction that man-flight was an unrealizable illusion and decided to combat skepticism with proof. A few years later he enlisted a group of sturdy young men as his shock troops in the campaign to vindicate Langley. One of the four men chosen for the group was strangely like Professor Langley in his reserve toward the press and the public. Fortunate for him also to have the sponsorship of Bell who had the gift of articulation to a degree, who faced an audience with a casual toss of his massive head and said what he had a mind to say. His talk before the Canadian Club of Ottawa was characteristic of the man as well as the way he felt about Samuel Pierpont Langley.

The subject of Bell's address was *Langley's Experiments.* He said:

"I was always interested in flying machines. I was one of the spectators of Langley's aerodrome with a fifteen foot spread of wings. This, I think, was in 1896, and the sight was presented to us then of a steam engine, flying in the air with wings like a bird. I saw it fly, photographed it in the air, and the photographs are the only record of that magnificent flight of a mile with no man aboard.

"Anyone who saw it, as I saw it, must have felt that the age of the flying machine was at hand.

"At the expense of the American War Department, Professor Langley tried to build a machine of the same type, but of a size to carry a man. The machine never got a fair test because of accidents in the launching ways, due to the ways and not the machine.

"Of course, it was no more a failure of flight than to have a ship caught in the ways in launching would be proof that she would not float. But the result was proof enough for the disgruntled newspaper men that she would not fly, and the result of this disagreement with the newspaper men was that Langley could not get more money to repair the machine.

"And it broke his heart. Not long afterwards he had a stroke of paralysis which his friends knew little about, and the second stroke carried him off. He was a man of very sensitive feelings, and I believe that the unjust criticisms of the newspapers contributed to his death.

"Before he died, by the aid of private funds, he had the machine put into condition, and it now hangs in its original form, in the National Museum.

"I speak of Langley because he was our modern pioneer and he was the scientific man who lifted the art to the plane of scientific investigation. I was closely associated with him. He was Secretary of the Smithsonian Institution, and I was a Regent. So we knew one another intimately. I knew of his work and he of mine. After his death, I pushed my work in the same line more prominently forward. Up to that time I had only played with the subject."

And Carrying a Man

G RAHAM BELL learned the advantage of tackling
a problem jointly when he was a boy in Edinburgh.
His two brothers and he divided the work and the
glory of each embryonic mechanical victory as a matter
of course. They died before he was eighteen and he moved
to America with his parents. But he had the happy faculty
of finding congenial working companions all his life.

At one period he planned to dedicate himself to the
education of the deaf, serious-minded young Scot that he
was. And he always had a great interest in the subject,
especially after he married Mabel Gardiner Hubbard of
Boston, who had lost her hearing at the age of six. But
his experiments, while teaching elocution, in producing
vibrations on tuning forks by means of an electro-magnet,
led him into inventive work. And the exhaustive study of
his telephone investigations opened up many new fields.

In 1880 when the Volta prize of fifty thousand francs
was awarded to him by the French government for the
invention of the telephone, he set the money aside for an
experimental laboratory in which he worked with his
nephew, Chichester Bell, and Sumner Tainter. Both were
young scientists.

The Volta Laboratory Association they called it, and

the profits of every patent were divided between them. The photophone, an appliance for transmitting speech over a ray of light and the telephone probe for bullets lodged in the human body were among the inventions they worked out. Bell invested time and money in the inventive genius which he felt lay dormant in the two younger men. Together they shared the profits, setting aside a portion to continue the work of the laboratory. And they had the joy as well as the practical benefits of working together and thinking together.

In 1896 the Volta Laboratory Association was converted into the Volta Bureau for the Increase and Diffusion of Knowledge Relating to the Deaf. Bell himself was up to his eyes in litigation. Bitter fights were waged by persons who both honestly felt and fraudulently insisted the telephone device was their brain child. Charged with theft, collusion and other tidy qualities, Alexander Graham Bell and his associates in the young Bell Telephone Company fought their way through an eleven-year patent war that included six hundred law suits.

After Langley's aerodrome failed to fly, Bell began conducting at Beinn Breagh, his summer home at Baddeck, Nova Scotia, on the Bras d'or Lakes, experiments with man-carrying kites towed by motor and steam launches. Careful and copious notes were made on each experiment, and all were photographed in detail. Usually it was arranged to have witnesses present. Bell had learned a bitter lesson in the possibilities of litigants to stir up trouble subsequently and was taking no chances in this new field.

He devoted himself chiefly to the construction of little "winged cells" having four triangular faces, two of them covered over with silk. These two faces formed a pair of wings raised with their points upward. Their cellular structure was calculated to keep down the weight in proportion. Because of their shape—an enclosed angle bounded by four planes—they were called tetrahedral cells and the box kites they were assembled into were tetrahedral kites. In 1905 Bell decided to build a hugh tetrahedral kite with a motor in it.

There was only one man in the country who had established a reputation as a manufacturer of aircraft motors. Glenn Curtiss had built some sixteen motors for dirigibles with notably good results. Bell learned that this young wizard of motor manufacture was to be in New York City and arranged to meet him at a hotel there.

They chatted together for nearly an hour. Bell spoke to Curtiss of Professor Langley's work and its significance and tried to awaken some interest in flying. Curtiss was much impressed by the appearance of the dignified old gentleman, with his gracious manner, but he had no belief in his cause. Like nearly everybody else in the country he thought those who worked on or believed in flying machines, including Dr. Bell, must be somewhat unbalanced.

When Bell urged him to come to Baddeck to see his experiments and to estimate on a motor for the kites, Curtiss was evasive and said he "would like to if he had the time." But for all his reserve and his reluctance, the older man was impressed with a certain quality of smouldering enthusiasm, of under cover energy, in Glenn Curtiss, even at that first meeting. A year passed before they met again. Meanwhile Bell was acquiring new assistants.

Arthur N. McCurdy had served as his secretary, assistant and photographer on most of his aeronautical experiments. McCurdy's son had been brought up to consider himself a member of the Bell family. In the summer of 1906 Douglas McCurdy then a junior in the School of Science at Toronto University, and a friend of his, F. W. Baldwin, who had just been graduated from the same school, came to Baddeck for a vacation visit. The two boys were old friends, had previously attended Ridley College at St. Catherine's, Ontario, together and had been members of the crew of the yacht *Temeraire* in an international trophy race.

"Casey" Baldwin's grandfather was the Honorable Robert Baldwin, one of Canada's most celebrated premiers and one of the men who helped found the Dominion. Casey himself, was the finest athlete Canada had ever produced.

Having read Octave Chanute's history of flying experiments, Casey had become interested in mechanical flight, to the consternation of the faculty member to whom he suggested the idea of writing his graduate thesis on the subject. He was delighted at the invitation to visit the Bell home with McCurdy because of the opportunity to see Bell's experiments.

Baldwin and McCurdy were in their early twenties, Dr. Bell was sixty and looked older because of his white hair and beard. He gladly showed the two younger men everything there was to see and urged Casey Baldwin, who was due at Cornell University summer school, to come back when he had more time to spend.

That winter Casey Baldwin returned to Beinn Breagh to direct the building of a tower on top of the mountain on which the house stood as Dr. Bell wanted to demonstrate that the tetrahedral principle he was using in his kites could be applied to stationary structures.

But they all found the idea of experimenting with the winged cell in flight more interesting and soon returned to kite building. Douglas McCurdy, stayed out of college that winter, and with Casey Baldwin, kept the work going even when their senior partner was called away to Washington or New York on business. Another ardent volunteer came to join them.

Thomas Selfridge, a first lieutenant in the Field Artillery of United States Army, was sure that flying was practical, that only stupidity, lack of persistent effort was the stumbling block. For many months he had buried himself in the Library of Congress, had, like a dry sponge, sucked up every printed word catalogued under aeronautics. Whatever had found its way into print in England or America he absorbed, and his reading knowledge of foreign languages unlocked treatises from Italy, France and Germany. The young soldier had a brilliant and a courageous mind. Some day flying would be an important military factor. The Army should find in him at least one officer who was properly informed on the subject. He reached a point where he felt he must do something more positive than studying, acquire some less vicarious experience of aeronautics. The man who had been such a firm friend to Professor Langley was still making experiments, perhaps he would let him sit in on some of them. He requested permission to call on Alexander Graham Bell.

Certainly he had chosen the most sympathetic ears in Washington, in the entire country, to tell his valiant young thoughts and beliefs. Bell immediately wrote a letter to President William Howard Taft asking that Lieutenant Selfridge be detailed to Baddeck. The President endorsed his recommendations and Selfridge was detailed to Nova Scotia "for the study of aeronautics in general and of aviation, meaning heavier-than-air craft, in particular."

Watching her husband at work with Baldwin, McCurdy and Selfridge, Mrs. Bell had an idea, which crystallized into a plan to form a group like the Volta Laboratory Association of 1880, so that "the interest of her husband's spirit" in aeronautics might remain with the younger men.

She offered to contribute as a working capital the profits from the sale of some property which her father had left her.

Dr. Bell was frankly stirred by the proposal. "You know that property was about the only thing she had," he said later, "that she didn't get from me!"

He took steps promptly to realize her ideal and to accept the offer so understandingly and unselfishly made.

In the spring of 1907 Bell made a trip to Hammond-sport to learn why the motor he had ordered more than a year before had not been delivered. He and his three associates were growing eager to give their kites a push. But he also wanted to see Curtiss's plant and to look over his airship motors. On this visit he again invited Curtiss to come to Baddeck and was met again with polite evason. The motor builder could pretend to no enthusiasm over the construction of tetrahedral kites. His factory was going full blast. There was no sense taking time out for a junket to Baddeck now. He asked himself bluntly just what there was in it for him, and the answer he found was, "Not a red cent."

Bell did manage to get work on his motor under way, though, and it was delivered at Beinn Breagh not long afterward. But it proved a disappointment from the start since it weighed twenty pounds more than the order for it had specified and had a maximum of only fifteen horsepower.

A new motor was promptly ordered. This Bell requested Curtiss to deliver in person. And he underscored his invitation with an offer to pay the reluctant motor builder twenty-five dollars a day for his time at Baddeck as well as to cover all expenses of the trip. It was obvious to Bell that if the association suggested by his wife were to flourish it would have to include an expert on power.

As a Scotchman himself Bell quite understood the justice of Glenn Curtiss's shop-keeping attitude. He could hardly be expected to give up his work in the factory for what seemed to him a silly idea. On the other hand, with that insight into character which was one of his surest traits, the scientist sensed the creative surge in the seemingly phlegmatic Curtiss. He was willing to bank on his inability to drop a thing once it had caught hold of his imagination, and he determined to play on this quality. Unable to convince Curtiss by the force of argument, he made it possible for him to tell himself there *was* something in it for him long enough to win him over to the idea.

Curtiss, of course did not dream that he was swallowing the canny Doctor's bait. He actually boasted about his own stroke of business. He told Ritchie Betts about the proposition that he was about to accept.

"Twenty-five dollars a day to lie around on the lawn and talk about flying. Sure I'll take him up on that. Easy money, that's what it is."

Glenn Curtiss made his first trip to Nova Scotia in July 1907. From the minute he walked into the big house he felt at home there. It was that kind of a household. A special feeling of intimacy between him and Mrs. Bell lay in the fact that, since Curtiss's own sister was deaf, he had learned to form his words with care in speaking. Mrs. Bell could read his lips easily and it pleased him as much as it did her. He found himself agreeing to return and become a member of the group as soon as he could make arrangements with the factory and run off a few motorcycle races.

In September he was back in Baddeck. It was a busy place. Bedwin, the shop foreman, and his assistants were covering tetrahedral cells with red silk for an enormous kite they were building. They were experimenting with smaller kites and with the *Ugly Duckling*, a raft supported upon metallic cylinders. It had aerial propellers and a small gasoline motor.

With Selfridge, Baldwin and McCurdy, Curtiss spent all day working under the direction of Dr. Bell. At night they gathered before the great fireplace to talk about flying: about what they were trying to do and what they could glean from the experience of airmen of the past and present.

What most astonished Glenn Curtiss was the fact that men like Leonardo da Vinci were practical fellows who knew what they were about, not dreamers stumbling around in a fog. And theories born of their brains, as Dr. Bell or Selfridge or Casey Baldwin told about them, became intelligible and real. Much, he learned, had already been accomplished, much that could be adapted to advantage in their own work. Even that old codger Langley, subject of so many wisecracks, was a pretty wise old bird after all.

Men like Otto Lilienthal, Octave Chanute and Professor Langley had traced a path that would not need much more traveling before they, working together with a man like Dr. Bell, should be able to really get somewhere. Then, too, the fact that the two Wrights had already done it, though the details of their method were still a carefully hoarded secret, was reassuring.

In the beginning Curtiss doubted his own ability to contribute anything important aeronautically. But as they set him to rights about the dignity of flight, he educated the others on motor practice. And soon he was suggesting along with the others, ideas of aerodynamic interest. The machinery of his mind had commenced revolving on a new set of gears. Bell's peculiar gift to make a man forget his own sense of inferiority and uncork his store of creative energy had again come into play.

On the thirtieth of September, 1907, a formal agreement was drawn up among the five men. The next day they went up to Halifax and got it notarized and attested to by the American consul. This document, having to do with the most unique and in many ways the most significant group ever formed in the history of mechanical progress, said:

> Whereas, the undersigned Alexander Graham Bell of Washington, D. C., U. S. A., has for many years past has been carrying on experiments relating to aerial locomotion at his summer laboratory in Beinn Breagh, near Baddeck, Nova Scotia, and has reached the stage where he believes that a practical aerodrome can be built on the tetrahedral principle driven by an engine and carrying a man, and has felt the advisability of securing expert assistance in pursuing the experiments to their logical conclusion, and has called to his aid Mr. G. H. Curtiss, of Hammondsport, N. Y., an expert in motor construction, Mr. F. W. Baldwin, and Mr. J. A. D. McCurdy of Toronto, Engineers, and Lieutenant Thomas Selfridge, Fifth Artillery, U. S. A., military expert in aerodynamics, and
>
> Whereas, the above-named gentlemen have all of them given considerable attention to the subject of aerial locomotion, and have independent ideas of their own which they desire to develop experimentally, and
>
> Whereas, it has been thought advisable that the undersigned should work together as an association in which all have equal interest, the above-named gentlemen giving the benefit of their assistance in carrying out the ideas of the said Alexander Graham Bell, said Alexander Graham Bell giving his assistance to these gentlemen in carrying out their own independent ideas relating to aerial locomotion, and all working together individually and conjointly in pursuance of their common aim "to get into the air" upon the construction of a practical aerodrome driven by its own motive power and carrying a man . . .

At a meeting held in the Halifax Hotel, officers were elected and the matter of salaries voted upon. Dr. Bell was named chairman of the group, Glenn Curtiss, executive officer and director of experiments in special charge of motive power. Casey Baldwin was made chief engineer in special charge of construction; Douglas McCurdy, treasurer and chief engineer in special charge of photographic experiments; Tom Selfridge, secretary.

It was decided that Curtiss was to receive a salary of five thousand dollars a year to reimburse him for time taken off from his manufacturing business. He accepted the provision, but amended it with the proposal that instead of being paid a fixed salary he would accept only half pay while not actually at the scene of operations of headquarters of the Association. Baldwin's and McCurdy's salaries were fixed at a thousand a year and Selfridge, who was under full pay from the Army, refused to accept any remuneration.

Mrs. Bell had fixed her donation to the treasury at twenty thousand dollars. If they decided to extend the time of their activities beyond a year, she stipulated that they should call upon her for additional funds.

By December the Association members were ready to try out their big man-carrying kite, the *Cygnet I*. Like Langley, Dr. Bell always favored making experiments off the water whenever possible. As he explained in an article in the *National Geographic Magazine* for January 1907:

"The inevitable accidents which are sure to happen during the first experiments are hardly likely to be followed by any serious consequences other than a ducking to the man and the immersion of the machine. If the man is able to swim and the machine to float upon water, little damage need be anticipated to either."

Since they could not manage to build water-tight floats,

the Aerial Experimenters decided to start their kite by towing it from a boat against the wind. Selfridge volunteered to go as the kite's passenger. It was a bitterly cold day and, as he lay down in the hold in his oilskins, they covered him with rugs to keep him warm. The towing boat was started and when the kite was released from the land it rose steadily to a height of 168 feet. When the wind slackened it began to slow down and sink gradually to the water.

Her pilot was snugly intact but some three thousand of the delicate cells which composed the *Cygnet I* had been destroyed as she was dragged through the water after she settled upon the Lake. Dr. Bell immediately ordered the shop to construct ten thousand more winged cells, so pleased was he with the performance of the kite.

But the man who flew in the *Cygnet I* did not feel especially excited about his 168-foot rise. As he saw it, the trip had all the buoyancy of a flight on an animated billboard. And its possible usefulness as an implement of warfare was negligible. That night at the business meeting before the logfire he put in a strong plea for experiments with craft having greater maneuverability.

Dr. Bell and the other three young men were ready, too, to branch out in a new direction. Selfridge's proposal was adopted by acclamation. It was further moved and seconded that they move their headquarters down to Hammondsport where the weather was less severe and where they would have the benefit of the facilities of the Curtiss plant. After the meeting was closed Tom Selfridge wrote into the A. E. A. Journal, in his crisp handwriting, the entry:

> Whereas, for the purpose of training the members of the Association as aviators, that they may be in position to successfully handle the flying machine the Association is to construct, Lieutent Selfridge is

anxious to make experiments with a gliding machine modeled after the machines that have been successfully flown in America and France both as gliding machines and flying machines propelled by their own power.

Resolved: that the Association aid in constructing and making such a machine in accordance with Curtiss's plans.

Moved and seconded that the gliding machine mentioned in the preceding resolution be constructed at Hammondsport under the direction of Mr. Curtiss.

Red Wing and White Wing

THE day after the Aerial Experiment Association voted to abandon the tetrahedral kite idea and try their hand at something more agile, Curtiss left for home to prepare their new headquarters. There was plenty of space available in the roomy old Curtiss house and arrangements were made to accommodate the entire personnel of the Association, as well as Mrs. Bell. The square cupola on top of the house was to serve as a conference room or office for the group.

The Curtiss factory staff had to be informed that the dirigible balloons they were still building engines for were now to have competition in Hammondsport's upper air. The head of the plant revealed his future plans to his secretary, Martha Genung, and her husband Harry Genung.

But before Foreman Henry Kleckler and his trusted assistant, Damon Merrill, arrived in the office a telegram was delivered to Curtiss from A. E. A. Chairman Bell. It said:

START BUILDING THE BOYS WILL BE THERE IN A WEEK

By the time Selfridge, Baldwin and McCurdy appeared, the Curtiss plant had made considerable headway with the construction of the framework of a biplane glider. Fabric was being stitched up for the wings. The arrival,

91

two days later, of Dr. and Mrs. Bell was the occasion for a joyful celebration at the Curtiss house.

Flying experimentation had come to Hammondsport once more, this time in a distinctly more spectacular form than that of the dirigible balloon. The entire village was astir with anticipation and pride, too, at having so distinguished a visitor as Alexander Graham Bell. Maybe Glenn was going to help put their town on the map again. He'd done it before with bikes and motorcycles. His loyal neighbors reckoned flying wouldn't stump him for very long either.

That was what they were saying over their champagne and still wines and their embroidery hoops in Steuben County. It was not many days before the townspeople noticed things actually happening. Time after time a flimsy-looking glider was seen soaring from a snow-covered slope in the vicinity. The glider would support a man if he ran and jumped from a hillside in the teeth of a fifteen-mile breeze. And if a single villager thought there was anything a mite ridiculous in their swooping and wobbling around in thin air, he kept it to himself. The sober earnestness of the thirty-year-old Glenn Curtiss and the three younger men, the magnificent dignity of the white-haired and bearded inventor of the telephone, commanded respect. Here, they sensed, was something portentous going on: a baby enterprise learning to flap its wings, but destined for sturdy flying some day.

Nor was it altogether local loyalty that made Glenn seem "better at it" than the rest. Even with this primitive craft his sense of coordination was useful in confining his quota of cuts and bruises to very minor ones. But all four of the members had their share of smash-ups, and after a few weeks there was very little left of their glider worth salvaging for further experiments.

Alexander Graham Bell's personality loomed strong throughout these days. He gave his colleagues the confidence that presently set the A. E. A. members working with enthusiasm on a motored biplane. He probably had hoped from the first that their efforts would take this direction, but had quietly left it to them to set the course.

As the association of experimenters worked "conjointly to promote the progress of aviation in America . . .," to build, according to the signed and sealed articles of their agreement, "a practical aerodrome driven by its own motive power and carrying a man," the days whirled by in a fine frenzy of creative excitement. Only the mellow wisdom of Bell or the fine articulate spirit of Tom Selfridge might have conceivably recognized this as the nature of the men's excitement.

They crammed hours full of study and work, but they were pleasant hours, for in the philosophy of Dr. Bell mental activity did not need to be abstruse or ponderous in order to be valid. Some time must also be allotted to recreation. He encouraged the members to take long cross-country rides on motorcycles borrowed from the Curtiss plant.

McCurdy returned from one of these expeditions swathed in bandages. He had a bad fall, but many a local observer thought he had earned his injuries in the heroic pursuit of aeronautics. McCurdy was a likable man, and always good humored about his misadventures. One of his weaknesses was a decided antipathy for the third of his Christian names, Douglas. But he had little success breaking the other members of the group of the habit of calling him Douglas, except with Curtiss, who held a profound and typically American belief that a man had a right to any name he wanted to be called by.

Every night the Association met in the large cupola

room, with Selfridge keeping a record of the minutes in the Notebook. They usually began with a "formal" session in the cupola, or "thinkorium," which was open to visitors. Discussion at these sessions was not limited to aeronautics!

Dr. Philias Alden, the physician who had contributed a part of his electric vibrator to the vitals of Glenn Curtiss's first working motor, frequently entertained them with talks on physical culture. Chairman Bell had a wide range of interests and gave the group the benefit of some of his researches into sociology, heredity and sheep breeding. At the close of the formal meeting, the A. E. A. members adjourned to Bell's study and delved into such subjects as the effect of "torque" caused by a revolving propeller, until far into the night.

But chiefly, even at the formal meetings, they talked flying, which was after all their major concern. Endless details of construction must be discussed and settled. And they had so little of the actual and conclusive to go on. No specific structural details on powered aircraft which had flown with passengers were available, only some general reports of experiments abroad. Besides these they had Langley's aerodynamical tables, Curtiss's experience with dirigible motors, the experiment at Baddeck with the powered tetrahedral kite and a mass of suggestions, unsuccessful, partially successful and wholly fantastic, by would-be aeronauts throughout the ages. That was all.

In solving most of their quandaries they had to rely on their own native intelligence and powers of reasoning in terms of mechanics.

The most difficult problem they had to face was how to achieve stability in the air. The principle evolved by Professor Langley, of wings set at a dihedral angle, might do in steady air, but what would happen under disturbed atmospheric conditions? After long deliberation they decided to build a biplane with rigid wings, similar to their glider but strong enough to carry the weight of a pilot and a 24-horsepower engine.

Once this point of construction was definitely determined, Glenn Curtiss proposed that they begin building their first powered aircraft. Tom Selfridge, believing they had not learned enough about how air currents react on wing surfaces, thought they should build another glider. When the question was put to a vote the majority favored proceeding without further preliminary experiment.

To avoid delays caused by too many divergent opinions it was decided that each junior member of the group was to be in complete charge of one of the four machines they planned to build with the funds available. Dr. Bell, as chairman, and the other three junior members were to offer ideas freely on all structural details, but the man in charge of the particular machine would have the final voice, be the ultimate judge in every instance.

Because Selfridge had risked his life in the launching of the *Cygnet I,* he was named the sponsor of their first effort to realize in wood and fabric and metal their dream of an aircraft which they hoped could get off the ground under its own power.

It was officially designated *Drome No. 1,* because Langley had adopted the term *aerodrome* to designate a flying machine. And because they had enough red silk left over from the *Cygnet I* for a pair of wings, the *Red Wing* was chosen as a logical familiar name for this first machine. Construction went forward briskly, but progress was necessarily slow. They knew so little and had to guess and gamble on so much.

The junior Association members were deeply disappointed when Mrs. Bell had to leave Hammondsport because of illness before the Red Wing was completed. Dr. Bell went with her. He yearned to be back in their midst, as he showed by a letter to Casey Baldwin recorded in the *A. E. A. Journal* at this time. Bell wrote:

Dear Casey:

I feel lost without any news of what is going on in Hammondsport. Won't you write me a few lines occasionally? Mrs. Bell too is waking up and wanting to know what you are all doing. Write her a nice cheery letter to bring her some sunshine from outside and a whiff of Hammondsport air.

If you haven't seen the *Illustrated London News* for February 8, 1908, buy a copy and look at the illustrations of the Wright gliding machine, taken from the Wright's English patent. There are points of construction that are new to me.

Yours sincerely,

ALEXANDER GRAHAM BELL

After seven weeks' work the *Red Wing* was ready. Dr. Bell was still absent, but the members decided they ought to attempt a flight from the ice of Lake Keuka. A consenting surface like the frozen surface of the lake, they reasoned, would be definitely helpful toward getting their aerodrome to rise into the air. Steel runners were fitted on her and everything was ready for the test, but they knew it would be foolhardy to make their flying experiment in the face of the strong March winds.

On the morning of the twelfth of March the wind died down. Lieutenant Selfridge, in the meantime, had been called to Washington on an Army mission, and the other three men dared not risk delay on his account for fear all the ice might melt before another calm day dawned. It was a clear morning, with a cold bite in the air, when the *Red Wing* was carried out of the factory on an improvised cart. A single thickness of red silk covered her two wings. The struts and beams which held them taut were of spruce. A twenty-four-horsepower, eight-cylinder motorcycle motor had been installed. The tail and front outriggers were removed and the wings set endwise on the cart in order to insinuate her 38-feet of wing-spread down the hill and through the town.

It was an imposing procession that made its way cautiously to the shore of the lake, with Casey Baldwin, John McCurdy and Glenn Curtiss as a guard of honor. Eight workmen, headed by Henry Kleckler, manned the cart with much heaving and ho-ing to avoid casualty to their ungainly, scarlet cargo. Neither horses, nor oxen nor mechanical power could be trusted to transport this precious burden.

The ice had already disappeared from the south end of the lake and it was necessary to go by boat three miles up where the ice still held. The wings of the aerodrome were deposited carefully on the flat roof of the deckhouse of a powered barge, used to haul grapes at vintage time. The outriggers and other parts were stored below.

The only outsider present on the boat trip was Tank Waters, old bicycle-riding mate of Curtiss. He inadvertently relieved the monotony of the slow trip by falling overboard, having to be rescued and thawed out. Other curious-minded lay spectators drove up the lake road and a substantial crowd was waiting near the edge of the shore where the solid ice began.

Naturally the three A. E. A. members were actually in a fever of suspense. Would she fly, this craft they had been building with such painstaking care for seven long weeks, planning for months? They resented the irony of fate that had cheated their leader, Dr. Bell, and Selfridge, the sponsor, out of this moment. But perhaps *Drome No. 1* would not take off after all that day. Perhaps it would require some structural revision. They had no way of knowing how right or how extremely wrong some of their guesses had been.

When the aerodrome was assembled, still more pictures were taken by Curtiss and the other two A. E. A. members. Harry M. Benner, a local photographer also made a number of excellent pictures. Bell had emphasized the importance of a complete photographic record of the experiment, both to aid future designs and to forestall any possible patent complications.

Then the three men drew lots and Casey Baldwin won the job of piloting *Drome No. 1*. He climbed into the seat at once and called to the mechanics to crank her up. The men who were clutching the machine heard him shout, above the thunderous din of the engine: "Let go."

The *Red Wing* skimmed across the surface smoothly, held it for 250 feet, then quit the ice and rose into the air for what to some seemed like six feet, to others as much as eight. She trembled and staggered drunkenly and gained altitude slightly, but kept on going for what appeared a tremendous distance to the men on the ice and the watchers on the shore.

Suddenly she crumpled, spun around on the ice for a second and lay in one disconsolate heap. From the photographic record it is evident that the ship gradually went into a stalling position and slid off on one wing, as the tail structure gave way under the strain.

Casey Baldwin crawled out of the wreckage, rubbing his bruised knees and elbows, and sat down in pride rather than dismay to wait for the statistical verdict. Curtiss was already walking off the space between the starting line and the finish. Then McCurdy measured it with a tapeline, and other witnesses were called in to check his result.

Three hundred and eighteen feet and eleven inches was what their creature had actually done, and to all those present at the event it seemed a stupendous accomplishment. The *Red Wing* had not only flown, she had covered more than three hundred feet of aerial distance. She had taken off under her own power from a flat surface and not from a slope where rising air currents would lend favorable lift. Nor had any outside means for launching been required to lend impetus to her start.

The spectators, having recovered from their blank astonishment at this miracle of 1908, were impressed to the point of roaring joyfully. They had witnessed the first flight in public of a heavier-than-air machine in America and they were devoutly glad they had made the trip up the lake that chilly morning.

Curtiss, Baldwin and McCurdy left Henry Kleckler and his assistants to salvage the *Red Wing* and hurried back to town. Still another experiment must be undertaken before the wind began to blow again.

The benign old typewriter manufacturer, J. Newton Williams, had been trying for some weeks to perfect a helicopter at the Curtiss shop and the A. E. A. members had been much interested in his device. They had promised to help him try it out on the first calm day. The Williams device had two sixteen-foot propellors mounted horizontally on concentric shafts and revolving in opposite directions. Below the propellors was a little platform carrying a motor and a shift-weight which was designed to tip the machine and supplement the rudder in a given direction. A turn to the left or right was to be accomplished by means of a brake.

A boy, weighing 110 pounds, rather than a full-grown

man, was selected to represent a pilot's weight aboard the helicopter. When the motor was started the machine promptly lifted the length of a short cable.

Fine! The helicopter worked too, and the A. E. A. members were delighted that the inventor had had the satisfaction of proving that his machine could get off the ground. They were not interested further in the helicopter since it could not be released for free flight, could not deliver horizontal speed—travel from place to place as their *Red Wing* had proved itself capable of doing.

Chairman Bell's reply to the pilot's account of their first flying experiment was sympathetic, painstaking and lucid. He wrote, from Washington, D. C., on March 20, 1908:

> Mr. F. W. Baldwin
> c/o G. H. Curtiss
> Hammondsport, N. Y.
>
> Dear Casey:
>
> I am much relieved to know that you escaped from the wreck of the *Red Wing* uninjured. Of course I am glad that the engine escaped too, but I don't wish to put you both in the same sentence.
>
> It is obvious that aerodromes of the type of the *Red Wing* lack the important element of automatic stability, and hence the safety of the operator and of the machine will depend in a great measure upon the skill of the operator in properly balancing or steering the machine at critical moments. The great extension fore and aft from the aviator, combined with extension to right and left, are elements of safety to life by rendering it certain that a "featherbed," as you call it, will be interposed between the aviator and the ground at the moment of landing. Recognizing the inherent instability of the form of appliance employed, it seems to me it would be well for you, as an engineer, to consider three points especially:

(1) How to improve the buffer-like qualities of the various extremities that could touch the ground first, so as to reduce the shock to the aviator of a bad landing.

(2) How to improve the lateral stability to prevent sliding off to one side—and here it seems to me that an increase in the amount of vertical surface in the wing piece (actual or resolved) is extremely desirable. I was much surprised to find that your vertical struts exposed so large a vertical surface as a resistance to side motion or tipping. If I remember rightly you had 40 square feet in all, but I presume that the greater portion of this resistance was in the center of the wing piece instead of at the ends where it would be more efficient in preventing tip.

(3) How to improve the general construction so as to permit the skill of the operator to come into play. It seemed to me that the aviator was pinned into his seat practically up to the shoulders, and I think it would be worth while considering whether it would not be well to leave him free above the waist, so as to enable him to lean to one side or the other to counter-balance a tip of the machine by a change in the position of his center of gravity, or by working rudders at the tips of the wing pieces for the same purpose.

You seem to have adopted heretofore the principle apparently adopted by the Wright brothers of keeping the center of gravity fixed, and affecting the equilibrium by means of moveable surfaces. It certainly seems to me that the front rudder, or front "control" as you call it, affords a better means of controlling fore and aft stability than the method of Lilienthal of shifting his center of gravity. But while your method of controlling fore and aft stability seems to be sufficient, you seem to have no method of controlling the lateral stability in a machine which is obviously lacking in automatic stability in the lateral direction. It seems to me, therefore, your chief thoughts should be directed to improving the lateral stability, or control over lateral equilibrium. Such control should be either automatic or voluntary. In the *Red Wing* you had neither means. Automatic control involves an increase in the amount of vertical surface (actual or resolved) at the ends of the wing piece, but such surfaces do not aid supporting power. They add mere dead load to the apparatus—a passive fault—and introduce a resistance to turning motion when you desire to steer to left or right—from this point of view being distinctly disadvantageous.

If we substitute voluntary control there are two methods to choose from, (1) shifting the center of gravity, or (2) shifting moveable surfaces at the ends of the wing piece.

The shifting of the center of gravity by leaning to one side or the other has this advantage, that it would be instinctive and not require thought, whereas the operation of moveable surfaces would involve thought.

We certainly impose a good deal upon the aviator when we require him to think of two or three different things at the same time, and it would be well to bring instinctive motions into play as much as possible. If it is undesirable to have him shift his center of gravity to any material extent it might be well to consider whether the instinctive motion of leaning to one side or the other (properly limited to previous material change in his center of gravity) might not be utilized to cause the operation of moveable surfaces at the extremities of the wing piece; thus the instinctive attempt to lean to the left to counter-balance an undesirable tip downwards of the right wing could cause the body to press against a lever which should elevate the tip of the right wing and depress the tip of the left, etc. This would render the operation of the moveable surfaces at the tips of the wings practically instinctive.

I observe that the upper surface of the *Red Wing* extends considerably beyond the ends of the lower surface at both sides, and it might be worth while considering whether the protruding ends might not be made moveable and be controlled by the instinctive balancing movement of the body of the operator. This voluntary control might be improved in this respect, that when turning movements are affected by the operation of the tail rudder—say to the right—it might be advisable to allow the right wing to dip down, in which case the aviator by voluntarily abstaining from leaning to the left could allow the tipping action to take place to any desirable extent, whereas in the case of an unexpected or undesirable tip of the machine, the instinctive action of balancing would cause the motion of the wing tips, and counterbalance the tipping effect.

These are simply a few thoughts for your consideration, and I will conclude with this thought: Would it not be wise to make a substantial model of any machine you desire to make and try it as a kite? Machines that tend to slide off the wind and come down sideways to the ground are not safe to be used as flying machines unless you can have voluntary control of lateral stability. It might be well to introduce sufficient vertical surface to enable the machine to fly properly as a kite, for the more you introduce automatic stability in the lateral direction the less will the aviator have to think of in a critical moment of danger.

Yours sincerely,

ALEXANDER GRAHAM BELL

P. S. Perhaps I am wrong in supposing that the elevation of the tip of one wing, and the depression of the tip of the other would remedy an undesirable dip of the machine. It may be that a lengthening of one wing and a shortening of the other is what is wanted in voluntary control over tipping action by moveable surfaces. If this is so it would not be necessary to change the plane of the end surfaces, but simply to lengthen or shorten them. For example: Suppose you had at the tip of each wing a moveable extension piece operating like a fan or like a bird's wing, then by opening out your fan on one side and shutting it up on the other you could increase the wing-leverage on the depressed wing and diminish it on the elevated wing and perhaps this would be sufficient.

Or perhaps instead of lengthening or shortening the wing the same effect could be produced by increasing or diminishing the amount of exposed surface at the end of the wing. This kind of action, I think, is employed by birds. I have often seen birds suddenly reef their wings, so to speak, during a sudden squall, thus diminishing the supporting area of their wings. In voluntary control by moveable surfaces what we want to do is to reef one wing and expand the other.

A. G. B."

News of the first public flight spread throughout the technical world, and warm praise for the achievement was accorded Dr. Bell at the annual banquet of the Aero Club of America. He hastened to disclaim all credit.

"I really had nothing to do with the success of the experiment," he assured the guests. "The credit for its success was due to Mr. G. H. Curtiss of Hammondsport, Mr. F. W. Baldwin and Mr. J. A. D. McCurdy of Toronto. Mr. Curtiss, who may be called the motor expert of America, produced an engine developing 24-horsepower weighing but 145 pounds.

"In this company of experimenters I must include Lieutenant Selfridge of the U. S. Army and Mrs. Bell, who supplied the capital for the scientific experiments to get the machine into the air. Although I do say it myself, I think this is the first time in America that a woman has taken an active part in making an experiment in aeronautics a complete success." *

Public interest in the work of the Aerial Experiment Association was growing. On March 21st, Ralph H. Upson, a sophomore at Stevens Institute, wrote the secretary, Lieutenant Selfridge, saying he would be pleased to be connected with the group in any way.

His letter was taken up at a meeting and it was decided that: "inasmuch as the Association was made up of men capable of handling the different phases of the problems it expected to have to solve, it was not deemed essential or advisable to enlist the services of outside talent, Mr. Upson be notified to that effect by the Secretary, but also that the Association would have no objection to his following their experiments during the next summer should he care to do so."

Still glowing with triumph over the performance record of their first aerodrome, the A. E. A. members set to work on *Drome No. 2.* The first problem they tackled was a means of achieving lateral stability, the necessity for which had been so clearly demonstrated in the *Red Wing* flight.

They had demonstrated through experiments in miniature form that, due to the curve (or camber) of the wing it was possible to warp a flexible wing down only. They therefore rejected the idea of warping the wings, for, if one wing tip was warped down in order to give a lifting action, it was regarded of vital importance that some means be devised to incorporate a downward pressure on the opposite side. By warping one side down only a turning movement might result which would tend to cause the

---

* Dr. Bell had no way of knowing at this time that Katherine Wright had aided her brothers financially in their early experiments.

machine to deviate from its course. This turning movement would offer further complications and a simpler and more reliable method should be employed.

At a midnight session in the "thinkorium" the scheme suggested in Dr. Bell's diagnostic report of moveable extension pieces attached to the wing-tips was voted the most feasible solution. One of the little secondary horizontal surfaces they devised for this purpose was designed to lift the falling wing on one side, the other to depress the rising wing on the opposite side of the machine. One of the surfaces would offset the other, and both together would lend the aerodrome—or so the experimenters fervently trusted—lateral balance.

Their next aircraft had a front elevator, a rigid rear stabilizing surface and a vertical rudder. Each wing-tip had the small hinged-on surface designed to keep the machine on an even lateral keel. A cable hooked to the rear tip was operated from a shoulder yoke: a U-shaped tube forming the back of the flyer's seat in such a way that when he leaned his body to the left or right it operated these surfaces. The function of the pilot was a perfectly natural one—if slightly strenuous—since he merely leaned in the direction in which he wished to tip the machine.

The vertical rudder in *Drome No. 2* was controlled with a steering wheel. A front elevator, controlling the up and down movement, was operated by moving the wheel-post forward or backward. The motor was controlled by a foot throttle, as it is in an automobile. To Casey Baldwin was assigned sponsorship of *Drome No. 2*. In keeping again with the color of its nainsook wings, it was christened the *White Wing*.

The ice was gone long before the second aerodrome was completed. The smooth surface of Lake Keuka would have been ideal, but they could not venture to try taking off from the water until they had found a way to build an efficient water-tight float. Others had used the rigid surface of the earth. The rubber-tired, pneumatic motorcycle wheels available in the Curtiss shop would serve, they reasoned, as a practical undercarriage for taking off. Their resiliency would also tend to soften the shock of landing.

Harry Champlin's half-mile trotting track at Stony Brook Farm, where Glenn Curtiss and his team-mates had practiced bicycle racing, was selected as a suitable flying field. An abandoned circus tent attached to the side of a barn was used to house the aerodrome when it was completed.

While the construction of the *White Wing* was still under way the Bells returned to Hammondsport and the old sociable order of things was resumed. Dr. Bell himself seldom came to the field after they started actual flying; he seemed to fear seeing one of the experimenters get hurt. And when he came he walked the two miles from the village, or drove out in a buggy. He had a curious sense of caution about automobiles, and firmly refused to ride in one down the steep narrow lane from the Curtiss house.

Lieutenant Selfridge took *Drome No. 2* off for the first time in compensation for being forced to skip flying his own *Red Wing*. He got off on wheels without difficulty, hopped a fence with slight grace but encouraging agility and landed without much damage to himself or the *White Wing*. As soon as the aerodrome had been repaired the A. E. A. members took turns flying her. Though nothing was said about a holiday, word got around the town Curtiss was scheduled as the next pilot of the *White Wing*.

"Glenn's going to fly tomorrow" was the signal for the entire student body to play 'hookey' from the village school the next day and camp on the grassy slope bordering the field. The majority of their parents managed to be there, too, which left no reason for the teachers to stay at their posts. Most of the members of the impromptu crowd brought lunches. A short flight might easily take a day in the doing.

With Curtiss aboard her, the *White Wing* barely cleared the grass. But his audience knew perfectly well what was happening; they could see daylight, couldn't they, between the aerodrome and the top blades of grass.

"He's off the ground! He's flyin'," they shouted.

An aviation spectacle of 1908 had a definite advantage over the modern version. The aircraft was always close enough to the ground so that the spectator felt personally involved. And the hazard to the pilot was also correspondingly slight.

Crashes were frequent nevertheless, but time after time the *White Wing* was put back into condition and flown again. Each flight netted fresh aerodynamic wisdom, and made it possible to make a longer flight the next time with more calculable behavior of the machine. Glenn Curtiss made the longest flight of them all, on May 22, 1908, when he flew a distance of 1017 feet. The Hammondsport *Herald's* account of the event and of subsequent A. E. A. plans is properly reverential and contemporaneous.

TO REBUILD AERODROME

THAT IS WHAT THE AERIAL EXPERIMENT ASSOCIATION WILL DO. MAY BE TRIED OUT WITHIN TWO WEEKS

The damage to the aerodrome *White Wing* from last Tuesday's flight was not repaired until Friday when G. H. Curtiss occupied the aviator's seat and made the phenomenal flight of the series.

Mr. Curtiss made some alterations in the steering and running gear which made the control of the ship much easier. After a fine start of about 250 feet the *White Wing* left the ground as gracefully as a bird. It skimmed along over the grass tops for a considerable distance, and then slowly rising to a height of ten feet, continued perhaps 100 feet or more, gradually dipping and rising at varied intervals, alighting at least 1,000 feet from the starting point, in a ploughed field, without the least breakage. The maximum height reached was not more than ten feet, showing that Mr. Curtiss had perfect control from the start.

The alighting was also a conquest, as compared with previous attempts. This flight demonstrated beyond the peradventure of a doubt that in the hands of a skilled operator the *White Wing* can fly. It was hoped that Mr. Curtiss would again direct the machine the following afternoon. This, however, was contrary to the plans of the association, arrangements having been made for Mr. McCurdy to make his first flight.

Saturday afternoon, at about four o'clock, the *White Wing* got away again in nice form, with Mr. McCurdy in the operator's seat. The flight was a very good one for 400 or 500 feet, when, 25 or 30 feet high, the machine made a sudden plunge downward and struck the ground with a terrific force. Mr. McCurdy was not injured and the engine was unbroken. The damage to the frame of the aerodrome was not great.

We are very glad to state that the association has decided to immediately rebuild the machine and continue experiments here . . . The reconstructed *White Wing* will be considerably improved . . . The reconstructed machine will also be much more easily controlled than any yet produced by the association.

Curtiss' June Bug

U P IN THEIR cupola conference room, Curtiss, Selfridge, Baldwin and McCurdy took an inventory of the findings of their aeronautical laboratory. Behind them were two aerodromes which had gotten off the ground under their own power carrying an A.E.A. member. From 318 feet, 11 inches and total collapse, they had advanced to 1017 feet and one landing at any rate "without the least breakage." Between these two accomplishments lay an interim of reluctant take-offs, disconcertingly sudden descents, with their accompaniment of broken collarbones, strained ankles and contusions. The next machine must not only fly farther; it must necessarily be more stable and controllable.

Progressive improvement was the bone and sinew of the Aerial Experiment Association's program. Even if they patched up their poor battered *White Wing* again, they were convinced that it could never fly much further than a thousand feet—which was not far enough.

A flying trophy had been offered eight months before for the first straightaway kilometer in this country, and the four junior A.E.A. members regarded it as their duty to attempt to qualify. Already longer distances had been flown abroad, and the fact that most Americans still regarded flying as a vague dream was a scurvy state of affairs which their group elected to abolish.

They would endeavor, to the best of their ability, to enlighten the unbelievers, show them flying in fact without losing any more time about it. Here was something concrete they could do to justify Mrs. Bell's investment in them.

The approach of the four men to the problem was, as usual, thoroughly scientific. Again the field was reviewed, the collective evidence of groping aeronautical design was conscientiously weighed. This evidence was then compared with their own findings and the future course determined.

They had accumulated a small library of current technical reports, with secretary "Tom" Selfridge as their chief research expert. He assimilated new data quickly, sifted out whatever was good and referred it on to his associates. John—as they had for the most part come to call him, instead of Douglas—McCurdy, in his capacity as chief engineer, in charge of photograph experiments, prepared photographs of the scale drawings of design features which were available. Among these were complete detail drawings of the Langley aerodrome of 1903, a skeleton cross-section of the Ellehammer No. 1, from Sindholm, Denmark; and skeleton two-view drawings of the Farman No. 1 and the Bleriot No. 6, from Paris. Secretary Selfridge's letter to the Wright brothers for structural information on the first successful heavier-than-air machine in the world, had met with a curt refusal.

Chief Engineer Baldwin, in special charge of construction, was particularly resourceful about putting new ideas into execution, and none of the three was lacking in imagination. But Curtiss was the best gambler of them all because his previous mechanical experience had taught him the value of trusting his own intuitions. At the same time he was always ready to entertain any fragment of a new idea. His functional optimism was infallible.

The fact that Curtiss was not an engineer made him immune, of course, to some of the caution and the preconceptions which technical wisdom entails. On the other hand, the intimate contact with their more circumspect point of view was of immeasurable help to him with his rule-of-thumb background. His own ability to visualize a detail,—"sketch-it-up" on paper—had been adequate for engines and motorcycles. But in coping with something as speculative and essentially complex as aerodynamics he required exactly what his association with the other four, over a period of months, had given him. Now, as they tackled the aerodrome which he himself was to sponsor, he was in a position to propose a number of drastic suggestions and to outline convincingly his reasons.

While their employer was acquiring a fundamental appreciation of the principles of aeronautical design, the Curtiss factory staff was being taught the importance of structural prefection. In order to fly at all it was not only necessary to pare down the weight of every part of the framework and machinery, but each part had to be flawless in its way. A minute defect might cost an aviator his life. Meantime a group of motorcycle mechanics and woodworkers was imbibing the ideology of scrupulous craftsmanship, as well as getting the feel of aircraft construction.

Except that slightly larger surfaces had been used throughout, the second aerodrome had not differed greatly from the first one. But they had made a trial horse of the *White Wing* during her month of active service. Replacement of a smashed part was always a variation upon the original, and certain design features had not demonstrated their efficacy. The forward part of the chassis—the outrigger holding the elevator control, for example, had been covered with cloth in order to lessen head resistance in both the earlier ships. But the fabric covering proved objectionable since it obstructed the view of the aviator. Because the members felt that visibility was more essential than the slight advantage gained in reduction of head resistance, they decided to omit the cloth covering from the fore part of the third machine.

John McCurdy, for all his youthful exuberance, proved to be a level headed A.E.A. treasurer. He pointed out, when they were making plans for the *White Wing,* that the cost of silk fabric was a financial hardship, particularly when one crash might render yards and yards of expensive material worthless. He proposed that they should learn about making cheaper fabrics airtight from Tom Baldwin and Charles Oliver Jones, who at that time were both building dirigibles at Hammondsport.

The idea met with general approval, and varnished nainsook was used for the wings of the second machine, while silk was used only for the tail and the control surfaces.

Since the cotton cloth had proved satisfactory, they decided to use nainsook fabric altogether in future machines. And as the cotton wings of their second machine were still whole, they saw no reason why they should not be used over again. This economy move of course had the warm approval of the thrifty treasurer.

The original front elevator of the *White Wing* was replaced with a narrower surface split in the middle to insure better visibility for the aviator. Various types; of elevators were extensively "road-tested" to determine how they would react to the moving air. The chassis of the aerodrome, equipped with motor and propeller and three-wheeled under-carriage, was the testing device on which they raced back and forth in their open-air wind tunnel. To test other control surfaces in advance, variations of the Curtiss wind-wagons of 1906 were contrived.

From the sketch, in their collection, of the Bleriot No. 6, the experimenters gleaned the idea of using a double or four-bladed propeller. The propeller for the *Red Wing* had had a framework of metal tubing covered with thin sheets of steel. The double propeller for the second machine was also metal but they did not find the four blades "convenient," and, as their first wooden propeller was ready for use, it was installed in the *White Wing*. This propeller was built up of thin strips of spruce glued together, dried under pressure, and the resulting laminated block whittled to shape and polished by hand.

Clear spruce, seasoned and free from knots and other imperfections, was almost unknown at local lumber yards. Time and patience were required in assembling enough wood that had suitable lightness and strength for the purpose. Rather than repeat the same arduous process, they cut the wood propeller from the *White Wing,* which had proved unnecessarily long, down from 6 feet 2 inches to 5 feet 1 inch. They also had the blunt ends rounded slightly. In their fourth machine a propeller with still more rounded ends was used; all part and parcel of their progressive experience.

The most radical change in the third machine was in the control mechanism. The A.E.A. Bulletin reported that: "The gearing of the wing tips was simplified by the new arrangement of wiring necessitated by the operator's seat being moved farther to the front." Control of the moveable surfaces hinged to the ends of the wing tips, which were the balancing devices, was thus made much more sure and pronounced. This vital improvement had come about quite incidentally because of the change in position of the operator's seat. Often their most essential discoveries occurred just that way.

As specific evidence of forethought and caution on the part of the aerial experimenters, two large wooden runners were provided to be used as skids in case the wheels should break down. These acted as a reserve shock absorber or bumper.

Plans for an improved aeronautical engine had been submitted to the Association by Glenn Curtiss in February. He had been working to perfect it ever since, but it was still not ready for service by the time Drome No. 3 neared completion. Their only alternative was to use the same air-cooled engine again, although its performance in a flying machine was far from efficient.

This power plant, which had been designed for use in a dirigible balloon, was built from eight motorcycle cylinders. It was rated at 24 horsepower, although sixteen or eighteen horsepower might have been a more conservative estimate. The little tank slung overhead had formerly been used in a racing motorcycle. It carried both oil and gasoline. Before every flight the engine had to be lubricated with bicycle chain graphite.

Because Casey Baldwin's wedding day was set for June seventeenth, all hands worked day and night in order to finish Drome No. 3 before that date. Baldwin left on the fifteenth, and the next day Mr. and Mrs. Curtiss and John McCurdy took a train for Toronto to be present when their comrade was married to the girl he had gone courting by motorcycle all the way from Hammondsport that spring. Lieut. Selfridge had to go to Washington but he managed to get back for the first flight of the new machine when all the other A.E.A. members were again in Hammondsport.

Keeping his promise, Dr. Bell and his wife arrived on

June nineteenth, and promptly solved the problem of a name for Drome No. 3. Their convenient system of calling a machine after the hue of its wings was disrupted because this time the wings were still white. As he looked the new machine over, Dr. Bell proposed they call it the *June Bug*, after a type of insect common to western New York, whose flight had some resemblance to that of their flying machine. Promptly it was christened the *June Bug*.

A small crowd gathered at Stony Brook Farm the next morning and applauded happily when Curtiss's *June Bug* got off without difficulty and flew 1266 feet. It was a distance record and Curtiss was sure it could do still better. It was evident that the new machine was a tremendous success, and they felt that this time they had achieved something resembling directed, controlled flight.

Mrs. Bell, warmly enthusiastic about the exhibition, was still ailing, and the emotional stress was too much for her. She returned with her nurse to Washington immediately after the flight. The strain on her would have been greater if she had been aware of the fact that a serious accident to an A.E.A member had been averted that afternoon, by quick thinking.

Lieut. Selfridge was standing in the path the machine was to take down the race track, ready to mark, for future comparison, the spot where the machine left the ground. But so swiftly did the machine gain flying speed that he was forced to do what Westerners do when they see a cyclone heading in their direction. He lay flat on the ground and allowed the impetuous *June Bug* to fly over him. Curtiss, in the machine seeing Selfridge's dog Jack scamper off through the grass, wondered why Jack's master did not make his getaway in the same direction.

Alexander Graham Bell stayed on for a few days until the weather was again favorable, and three longer flights were made by the different members. Everything looked right enough for a try at the *Scientific American* trophy, and a letter was dispatched to the Aero Club of America placing their entry on file and naming July fourth as the date of the trial.

The village had been humming with aeronautical activity all spring. Augustus Post, secretary of the Aero Club of America; J. Newton Williams, who built typewriters for a living and helicopters for the fun of it, and others were popping in and out of town to watch the flights of the *White Wing,* as well as the progress of Thomas Scott Baldwin's big dirigible, and Charles Oliver Jones' smaller one. On June tenth, Jones's *Boomerang* was floated out of the Glen, where it was built, with fitting ceremonies, marred only by the bumping of its nose into a gravel bank on the way out.

Curtiss motorcycles were still winning races regularly, and the demand for machines was heavy. What with the growing aeronautical business plans were under way to build a concrete addition to the factory buildings. The working staff was growing to such an extent that there was a local shortage of dwelling houses. Hammondsport was experiencing something in the nature of a boom, and commonsense told the city fathers that if "G. H." won that trophy on Independence Day, there was no way of telling where this aviation thing would stop.

The next six days after filing their entry were spent in frequent work-outs of the *June Bug.* Best flying times were just before five in the morning and after seven at night when the wind was at its gentlest. And bordering the wide valley where Stony Brook Farm lay were high hills and numerous ravines which could cause currents of air as steady as streams of water to pour down the valley even at those hours.

Once the *June Bug* was caught in one of those air currents and swept up so sharply that Curtiss shut off the engine. He landed safely but was puzzled by what had happened. As soon as the motor had cooled off, he went up again to investigate. This time the ascending current of air caught the machine at exactly the same point and carried it up into the air for approximately eighty feet. Curtiss allowed the *June Bug* to climb with her motor open full. In a few seconds she straightened out and together they made the longest flight yet recorded by the Aerial Experiment Association, as well as an altitude record.

The art of making turns was one which the A.E.A. men were a long time mastering. Although the trophy flight requirements did not include a turn, they knew that abroad turns had been made several times, and were eager to discover the knack for themselves.

The first half-turn was made by Glenn Curtiss one day when, with his motor badly overheated, he had to make an immediate landing. Underneath was a vineyard bristling with sharp-pointed, menacing grape-stakes. Desperately he banked the machine around far enough so that he came down just beyond the vineyard. And instead of slipping in sideways, as he had expected, he landed safely and right side up. Reason enough to be proud of their Drome No. 3.

The A.E.A. members and their chairman now looked forward eagerly to the day of the trophy trial flight. Glenn Curtiss, who had captured trophies in other fields found the idea of this new and different sort of competition particularly enticing. And, although their third machine was the result of cooperative effort with all three machines, it was fair that he should fly it in the trial because, as chairman Bell pointed out:

"Curtiss did a good deal more in relation to the *June Bug* than perhaps Lieut. Selfridge did ordinarily in relation to his aerodrome. Then it was a conjoint matter."

Many months had passed since the *Scientific American* had first published its challenge to builders of flying machines. The announcement, as carried in that magazine's issue of September 14, 1907, gives an explicit picture of the intent of the trophy offer and the motivation behind it:

"The handsome silver trophy was originated with the idea of stimulating the development of the science of aerial navigation. For many years past, and especially since the development of the dirigible balloon, the aim of all inventors in this line has been to construct a machine which would fly at a high rate of speed without the use of gas to support it. Nearly four years ago the Wright brothers, in this country, announced the successful application by them of a gasoline motor to an aeroplane, and the flight which they made upon December 19, 1903,* was presumably the first one of any considerable distance which has ever been made by a motor-propelled aeroplane carrying a man. After two years of experimenting the Wright brothers finally announced that they had perfected their machine. No public demonstration has ever been made by them, however; and although, according to their own statements and those of eye-witnesses, they have solved the problem, still many people doubt this. At any rate, it is probable that progress in the new science will be made by others, and that in time there will be several kinds of heavier-than-air machines perfected.

"It is with the idea of encouraging inventors in this line by giving them a valuable object of art worth winning, that the *Scientific American* trophy has been completed and presented to the Aero Club of America.

* The Scientific American erred in recording this date. The first flight was made on December 17.

"This club will hold annual competitions for the trophy, and, if it is impossible for an inventor to enter his machine in such competitions, he may obtain a special trial by arranging therefor with the club. The trophy is to be open to international competition, and any foreign competitor who wins it may take it to his native land, to be held by the aero club of which he is a member until it is won back by an American. In years to come the trophy may, therefore, be to aerial navigation what the 'America' cup is to yachting.

"In conducting the annual competition for the trophy, the Aero Club of America will vary the conditions of winning it, in accordance with the progress that is being made with flying machines. In view of the fact that Santos-Dumont and other French experimenters have already flown considerable distances in a straight line with aeroplanes, it was decided that to win the trophy the first time, a competitor should be required to surpass these distances; and as there have been no prizes offered for a flight of one kilometer (3,280 feet) in a straight line, this distance was determined upon as the one required to be covered.

"Arrangements have been made to hold the first competition at the Jamestown Exposition on September 14, and two machines, at least, are expected to make the trial. Should the trophy be won at this or a subsequent contest this year, the conditions next year will be changed, so that a longer flight with turns will be required. The rules under which the present competition is to be held provide that no flight need be attempted if there is a wind of over twenty miles an hour, and also that the machines should be flown against the wind, if possible.

"Thus it will be seen that every opportunity will be given inventors to make a successful demonstration of their machines. Should any competitor win the trophy three times in separate years, it will become his property."

The first of all the aviation cups in this country was an elaborate array of everything a well-dressed trophy could possibly wear. It consisted of a globe representing the firmament and carrying on one side a copy of Langley's model soaring through clouds. The North American continent was modeled in relief on the opposite side. The globe was carried on a whirlwind rising from the base at which there were six winged horses mounted on a cupped pedestal. The middle horse of each trio was mounted by a rider who held aloft an olive branch. The whole thing was topped off with an American eagle with a wreath of victory in his beak. This "Blue Ribbon of the Air" contained 218 ounces of silver and was valued at $2,500.

When the only two entrants for the competition at the Jamestown Exposition both failed to get off the ground, the Aero Club modified the conditions for the following year to the extent of allowing the contestant to choose his own time and place. The required distance was still one kilometer. The first aviator to fly the kilometer under official observation would have his name inscribed on the trophy as winner of the first of three legs.

The reluctance of some of the Aero Club officials to travel to a little town in western New York for the trophy trial sent Glenn Curtiss and Lieut. Selfridge to New York, on the first of July, to discuss it with them. Since the rules specifically provided that the contestant could choose his own site, the officials finally agreed to make the three hundred mile trip.

Traveling back to Hammondsport that night the two A.E.A. members were glad that the matter was definitely settled. At the same time there was the shadow of a doubt in their minds about the outcome of the trial. Only the preceding night the *June Bug* had flatly refused to take off. John McCurdy opened the throttle and raced over the track, but the machine declined to give any indication that it intended ever to lift again.

They were completely mystified until Selfridge discovered that the air was passing through the varnish applied to the wing surfaces instead of underneath, because as the varnish cracked, the fabric had become porous. The nainsook was completely revarnished and the machine was again in flying condition. But still . . . Curtiss and Selfridge had their misgivings. The unexpected had happened; it might happen again.

On Friday morning the four junior A.E.A. members hurried out to Stony Brook Farm at dawn for a final test flight. The weather appeared unusually fine, but suddenly Curtiss was sniffing the air, as a jack-rabbit would, and looking suspicious. He announced abruptly:

"No, it isn't right. We'd better not try it this morning."

McCurdy and Baldwin were speechless. Selfridge was surprised, but decided he was still jittery after the recent failure of the *June Bug* to take off. All three completely forgot for the moment that whenever Curtiss had said it was dangerous to leave the ground and they tried to fly anyhow, they usually wound up with a broken machine and somebody in bandages.

But the three younger men felt that failure to hold a final dress rehearsal of tomorrow's big public performance was unthinkable. And the day was apparently letter-perfect. With all the persuasiveness they could muster they urged Curtiss to make a flight that morning.

"Tank" Waters, one of the villagers who had come along to the field, knew "G. H." well enough to be concerned. He didn't think it was a good idea to drive him to do something he didn't want to.

Curtiss finally consented to go up. Perhaps he was being a little over-cautious. But when he was a little more than fifteen feet off the ground, a sudden puff of wind from a ravine in the opposite hillside caught the aerodrome and dashed it to the ground. The pilot was unhurt, but the *June Bug's* left wing was virtually destroyed. It looked as if the trophy event was automatically scratched.

Selfridge, McCurdy and Baldwin were abject in their remorse. Baldwin turned to Curtiss: Shouldn't they get New York on long distance right away, call it off? But Curtiss was too preoccupied to answer. They had not before encountered his faculty for figuring out repairs and replacements in the shortest possible space of time. Already he was rounding up every man who could be counted on in an emergency. Foreman Henry Kleckler, as a matter of fact, had his tools out as soon as the machine struck the ground. And a truck was on its way out to carry the *June Bug* to town.

At the factory, the four A.E.A. men studied the extent of the wreckage. Not only the left wing, but the front elevator had been damaged. A smaller one had to be made because there was not enough material available to duplicate the original. They worked at a furious pace all through the day, with Curtiss running around like an inspired chipmunk, lending a hand here, supervising there; performing mechanical miracles. By seven that night the *June Bug* was again airworthy.

Curtiss took off and flew a distance almost equal to the required kilometer. He wore one of his rare smiles as he landed and Selfridge knew he was particularly pleased about something.

"Everything quite all right?" Selfridge asked.

"Oh yes, everything's all right. I am just trying to figure out why she flies better now than she did before."

Next morning, by an early train, some twenty-five or thirty visitors from New York City arrived. Among them were most of the "gentleman aeronauts" of the day. Allan R. Hawley, acting president, and Augustus Post, secretary, represented the Aero Club of America; as did Charles M. Manly, of its official contest committee, who had been chief assistant engineer to Professor Langley. Stanley Y. Beach represented the *Scientific American,* and Ernest L. Jones, editor of *Aeronautics,* was the official representative of the Aeronautical Society of New York. Karl Dienstbach, popular writer on aeronautics and representative of the German government, lent an international note to the affair.

Since Dr. and Mrs. Bell were unable to attend, they had sent their daughter, Mrs. Gilbert Grosvenor, to see the flight and come home and tell them about it. Everything was in festive order that Saturday at Hammondsport—everything except the weather.

The course of the flight was officially measured and marked off with flags. Across it ran three or four barbed wire fences, a corner of a vineyard and other ground trimmings, but that did not disturb the A.E.A. members. They were sure of their *June Bug,* but they were in grave doubt about the leaden skies.

Traffic was heavy on the road that led to Stony Brook Farm and soon after lunch a crowd of a thousand or more people gathered on the slope opposite the half-mile track. All of Hammondsport was there, of course, but the neighboring villages were also well represented. Word had spread that there was a fair chance history might be made by one of the Steuben County boys that day and certain citizens of Bath and Penn Yan and Wayne thought maybe they owed it to their grandchildren to be present. Most of them were inclined to be somewhat skeptical, as were some of the New Yorkers. They had of course heard stories about what Alexander Graham Bell and the young men had been up to, but better see it first, then believe it. That was the best way.

The *June Bug* had been wheeled out of her hangar, and stood ready at the starting line. The audience was growing restive, begging for the show to start. Lieut. Selfridge carried word to the aviator that the judges and observers were waiting for him to take off. Curtiss looked glumly at the sky, moistened his finger and held it up to test the breeze. It dried too quickly. He shook his head at Selfridge. "Tell them it's impossible to make the flight with so much air stirring." A few minutes later rain began to fall, and Curtiss ordered the *June Bug* back into her tent.

Thunder showers fell throughout the afternoon and most of the crowd of visitors drifted back to town or to the nearby champagne cellars to drown their disappointment. Then, late in the afternoon, the rain stopped falling and the sun broke through. From all corners of the village they scurried back to Stony Brook Farm, where they found Curtiss had ordered the *June Bug* rolled out of her tent.

The flying machine bounced across the field, faster and faster, then seemed to rise slightly. But it was back on the ground immediately and slowed down to a stop several hundred yards away from the starting point. His helpers reached him first and kept the crowd back while he told them:

"The wind isn't right. Let's try it from this end of the field."

Carefully the machine was turned around and headed back down the valley toward the lake. At 7:30, just before sundown, the judges were notified that the flight was at last ready to begin.

Again the motor was started and Glenn Curtiss began his bumpy ride across the field. This time, to the delight of some and the amazement of others in the crowd, the machine rose slowly, steadily, from the ground. The pilot sat erect, staring straight in front of him. Then he was busy manipulating the controls as the machine wobbled crazily and seemed about to turn over. Twenty feet up it steadied, and proceeded in "straight and level" flight, crossed the flag-marked finish line. Then he flew on to the limits of the field, banked into a half-turn and landed safely.

That portion of the crowd which had followed right behind him down the field, screeching as they ran, greeted him vociferously. And other cheers from those who had remained on the sidelines echoed and re-echoed through Pleasant Valley. The visiting aeronauts were wild with delight. Some of them had studied and experimented for years without success. Now at last they had seen a power-driven machine, carrying a man, soar into the air and fly a specified distance in a given direction.

Meanwhile the lanky young motorcycle manufacturer who had performed the feat, smiling self-consciously at the hubbub, climbed out, and examined the *June Bug's* engine to see how it had stood the flight.

The official distance covered, as measured by the judges, was 5,090 feet, or 1810 feet more than the required kilometer. Although, including the turn, Curtiss had actually flown somewhat more than a mile.

While the *June Bug* was in the air a news photographer from New York City (so the legend goes) waved his arms and shouted:

"Wow! I could jump out of my skin! For two years my paper has had me chasing these alleged birdmen and I never believed they could really get off the ground!"

The gentleman áeronauts were almost equally enthusiastic. One or two, however, questioned the authenticity of the flight. Most outspoken among the objectors was Augustus M. Herring, an unusual, somewhat eccentric character, who had been identified with flying experiments for nearly twenty years. While the crowd was still cheering and congratulating Glenn Curtiss, and the other members of the Aerial Experiment Association, Herring took exception to the rulings of the judges as to the distance flown by Curtiss, although he was not an official judge or observer.

Allan R. Hawley silenced him firmly with:

"I am acting president of the Aero Club. I saw Curtiss make the flight over the required distance, and I know he made it."

To most technical men, the significance of the first measured flight under test conditions in this country by a heavier-than-air craft was obvious. At that, there was sincere disappointment that the Wright brothers, first in the world to fly, had not made this public demonstration.

The British technical paper, *Aeronautics,* commented:

This trial was really of the utmost importance, as it was the first official test of an aeroplane in America. There are but two machines in the world that have travelled farther in public, those of Farman and Delagrange. The Wright brothers have far outflown this in private, so that America is not so far behind France as might be imagined. The official flight was the fifteenth made by the machine. All have occurred under far more adverse conditions than those encountered by the French machines.

No story of that very glorious Fourth would be complete without the *Hammondsport Herald's* own account of the day:

The crowds began gathering all about Stony Brook Farm early in the day as it was not known what time the flight would be attempted. The committee of award from the Aero Club of New York and a large number of aeronautical and newspaper people arrived in the morning. They were met with automobiles and conducted to places of entertainment. It was early in the afternoon when the party arrived on the ground for the flight. The weather conditions did not meet the approval of Mr. Curtiss, the aviator, until late in the afternoon, when the big drome was brought from cover and prepared for flight.

The first attempt was a pretty flight but the machine was not on its good behavior . . . The big crowd waited for the machine to be hauled back to the track and about 7:30 the *June Bug* again soared into the air and easily and gracefully made the required kilometer, and sailed on, covering in all a mile and a quarter. The alighting was accomplished without accident.

The cheering of the crowd could be heard for miles, and Mr. Curtiss was overwhelmed with congratulations as soon as the people could reach him.

The Independence Day flight won for Glenn Curtiss not only the first leg of the *Scientific American* Trophy but later gave him Aero Club of America Pilot License No. 1.

The matter of license priority caused some debate at the time, but the first license was finally issued to him in 1911. A number of people felt that the Wright brothers, because they were known to have flown five years before 1908, should be awarded Licenses No. 1 and No. 2. But the contest committee of the Aero Club ruled that Curtiss's was the first officially observed and recognized flight in America and that he was properly entitled to the honor.

Experiments Ended

PILOTS, as such, had not been born in America in 1908. The term *aviator* was much in vogue, with *flyer* a close second, though in some circles the man who did the flying was respectfully referred to as a "professor of aeronautics."

It was still possible to say, in print, that a man *drove* an aircraft through the sky. Newspaper writers, like the people who were building and flying aerial machines, were compelled to fumble for terms until such time as the jargon had jelled sufficiently and assumed a properly professional flavor.

Because the Frenchmen were less reserved than the earlier American or English experimenters, and also because they are commonly more resourceful in the matter of speech, many aviation terms were derived from the French. In some cases they superseded our own terms, though staunch minds like Alexander Graham Bell tried to stem the tide of French terminology.

Aeroplan had become "aeroplane" (not airplane, as it emerged by official dictum after the war), and was rapidly overtaking *flying machine* and *aerodrome* in popularity. This term had not, as is commonly supposed, been coined by Samuel Pierpont Langley for his machine. It was submitted to him by Dr. B. L. Gildersleeve, Professor of Greek at Johns Hopkins University, when Langley wrote concerning a suitable name for his machine. Dr. Gildersleeve had replied:

"The word you want is made to your hand in aerodrome (plural, aerodromes)—'air runner.' No one will have anything to say against a Greek word that is found in the Lexicon."

Neither the philologist nor the scientist who gave it to the public perceived its likeness to *hippodrome,* meaning a place where horses run.

Meantime A.E.A. chairman Bell had taken a great fancy to *aerodrome,* and pointed out triumphantly that the A.E.A. members had subconsciously evolved the verb 'to drome' from it and would often speak of 'droming.' He thought, too, there should be a blanket term to include all heavier-than-air craft, and the word *aeroplane* would be inappropriate and incorrect for those machines, such as tetrahedral kites or helicopters, which had no plane surfaces in them.

Another candidate was *aerodrome-flyer,* which Maximilian Foster proposed in an article in *Everybody's Magazine.* "Although it can brag of no Greek or Roman ancestors," he said—erroneously enough—"it is a good self-made American word."

At a meeting of the Aerial Experiment Association and visiting aeronauts, held at the Hammondsport Hotel, the subject came up for discussion and they all agreed that the terminology of aeronautics required revision. Dr. Bell was pleased to learn that there was much less objection to his pet, *aerodrome,* than he had supposed, and that all those present favored its general adoption. But Bell himself later abandoned his earnest campaign in favor of the term introduced by his friend Langley, when it developed that *aerodrome* had come to mean not only the machine itself but also the shed which housed it and the inclined track along which it ran. When matters had reached a point of saying: "The doors of the aerodrome were opened and the aerodrome was wheeled over the aerodrome," it was time, he declared in one of the A.E.A. bulletins, to call a halt. Meanwhile the term *aeroplane* had taken permanent root.

All problems of aeronautical import were discussed at length in these weekly bulletins issued by the chairman, their purpose being to keep the members in touch with each other. One copy was prepared for each member and they were considered confidential, although discretional power was given the secretary to permit re-publication of material.

A file of the bulletins, which were issued every week from July 13, 1908, until March 1909, unfolds a priceless account of the period from an aeronautical viewpoint. It reveals also the spirit of congenial consecration which pervaded the group initiated by Mabel Gardiner Bell because she believed "there were great possibilities for the development of something good in aviation."

But neither she nor Dr. Bell saw any reason why the process of developing aviation should be suffered rather than enjoyed. And it was therefore a sociable group, which she mothered and which he incited to creative effort. Although his intellect was responsible for leading the men out of some of their most serious crises in design, he always insisted emphatically that: "These young men who were associated with me were acting conjointly with me and I could not say anything was my own."

They worked together well, and played together nearly as well in spite of their fundamental differences in temperament. Bell, gracious, at heart and a romantic, had for instance, a great fondness for music. Curtiss, self-conscious, monosyllabic, thoroughly disliked it because it interrupted his train of thought. McCurdy and Baldwin both had all the social graces. Selfridge was more at ease than Curtiss, though he was inclined to be extremely modest. But they managed to make an excellent go of it socially, due to the infinite tact of the Bells.

At Hammondsport, the victory of July fourth was celebrated with a moonlight ride up Lake Keuka in a chartered steamer. But before the A.E.A. members relaxed and celebrated, another flight of a semi-official nature was made in the *June Bug*.

Because it was late and because neither he nor the other A.E.A. men felt he should risk doing anything that might jeopardize their chance of victory, Curtiss had stopped at a half-turn. But among the out-of-town visitors there were some who had inquired: "Could he have turned around and flown back the same way?"

Learning how to bank a machine in the air to just the right degree for a full turn was a difficult proposition. Glenn Curtiss had had enough experience with racing motorcycles on banked tracks to have a general idea what had to be done. But he reasoned that if a 45-degree angle was enough to keep a machine on the track at sixty miles an hour, a much flatter bank would serve an aeroplane's purpose in the air.

They tried turning in the *June Bug* without banking steeply. Each time the machine would skid toward the outside of the turn, lose headway until it slowed down to the stalling point. Then it would slide off on one wing, roll over and crash. Because they flew at such low altitudes, no bones were broken and the machine was not badly damaged. But they were making no progress.

One day John McCurdy started on one of the half mile flights they were making regularly, but suddenly changed his mind about going. Down below they prepared for a crash as they saw him banking the machine abruptly and, according to Curtiss's theory, much too steeply. He did not complete the turn, but neither did he crack up, and the members were convinced now that they might safely risk a much steeper bank.

They therefore urged the out-of-town visitors to remain until the following day to witness another flight. This time Curtiss was determined to make a turn and face directly toward the starting point. His attempt to describe a circle, as attested by the account of the flight in the *Herald*, was reasonably successful:

> On Sunday afternoon the *June Bug* was brought out and the Bath and Hammondsport train ran a special to Stony Brook Farm. The crowd was made up of nearly the entire population of Hammondsport and the surrounding country. The trial of Sunday was to demonstrate to the visiting aeronautical people that the *June Bug* was under control to the extent of making a complete turn. Mr. Curtiss made a fine flight and turned the machine about with ease. It was nicely on the way back toward the start, flying rather low, when Mr. Curtiss deemed it advisable to come down rather than take a chance of a possible accident in crossing the vineyard. In alighting, the front control and left wing were slightly damaged.
>
> This was considered a very satisfactory demonstration of the perfect control of the aviator. (The final paragraph evidently refers to the turn, not the "alighting.")

Encouraged by her newly-found maneuverability, the group repaired the *June Bug* and the four junior members, made daily flights. The better acquainted they became with their third machine, the more confidence they had and the bolder they grew. Some of Curtiss's local friends thought he was growing entirely too reckless.

Late one afternoon as he was about to start the engine, the lordly DeWitt Clinton Bauder, Hammondsport's own Peter Stuyvesant, rolled up to the edge of the field in his carriage. His plump, jovial son ran up to the *June Bug*, puffing and shouting:

"Glenn, please don't fly any more tonight."

"Why not?" Curtiss wanted to know.

Jimmy Bauder did not know why not, but would go back to the carriage and ask his father. Presently he returned with the cryptic message:

"Father says to tell you just because he doesn't want you to."

"All right, fellows," Curtiss called to the mechanics. "Put the machine back in the tent. I guess one just has to respect the hunches of one's friends."

With his very full schedule, it was not easy for Curtiss to relinquish a single opportunity to fly. In addition to his routine business of building motorcycles he had worked unceasingly all spring at the baffling problem of building a new type engine. Not only the success of Baldwin's new dirigible, but the development of heavier-than-air flying depended, he was convinced, on the production of a more efficient, light power-plant.

Up at four in the morning, he would dash out to the racetrack on a motorcycle and have the *June Bug* up in the air by five. As soon as the breeze blew up, he returned to town for breakfast and to work all day in his office. Before dark he usually returned to the field for more flying. After supper he worked on the water-cooled engine, or attended an A.E.A. meeting in the cupola where plans for the fourth machine were discussed. And the best time to discuss factory problems with shop foreman Henry Kleckler and Damon Merrill was usually between one and two in the morning.

This strenuous routine was not irksome. The time which Glenn Curtiss spent experimenting, either in flying the *June Bug,* or on the design of the water-cooled motor or the new aeroplane, was not work to him. Most of his life he was able to put in eighteen hours a day without feeling any fatigue, because he spent most of that time experimenting.

Much later in life he often said: "The man who works himself down can work himself back up if he will develop a turn for experimenting."

It is an old formula, which all those men who dig deep into their minds to bring up new ore have learned. Alexander Graham Bell discovered it very early in life. Until shortly before he died, he worked long and tirelessly at his experiments. Once, when asked by a reporter to name a time for an interview, he casually named his laboratory as the place and 3:00 A.M. as the hour.

The engine for the dirigible Tom Baldwin was building for the United States Army was one of the toughest assignments Glenn Curtiss had ever had. Light, strong, air-cooled motors for gas bags had been in natural sequence to motorcycle power-plants. But this motor had to keep cool for two hours; and it had to propel the dirigible at a speed of not less than sixteen miles an hour around a closed circuit, carrying two men.

When the long awaited list of specifications for an Army dirigible first appeared in February 1908, Captain Baldwin stormed and raged. Here was the initial opportunity for American dirigible builders to prove ther military mettle and the specifications called for a particular balloon fabric of imported manufacture. Baldwin knew well enough that he could not compete with the French and German dirigible builders under the circumstances.

The pity of it was that, in the firm belief American

material should be used for the first Government dirigible, he had been experimenting to produce a first class balloon fabric. After months of effort he had succeeded in making a stuff that was as good, if not better, than any manufactured abroad. After giving the matter some thought, the wily Captain prepared a sample case and took a trip to Washington. There he displayed before the representatives of the Signal Corps his pieces of a very fine vulcanized-proof fabric, consisting of two layers of silk cemented together with seven layers of rubber. He told them it could not be affected by heat or cold and that it would stand a pressure of a hundred pounds per inch of width, and left his samples with them for testing.

The results of these tests were so decisive that the specifications were altered to call for a double-walled silk cemented together. Other American manufacturers scoured the country in vain for such material. Only one bid came in from abroad, and that was not considered. Baldwin had won his point.

He turned up at the shop one morning with a broad grin on his face and the contract in his pocket and instructed Curtiss to get started right away on a light, water-cooled engine to propel the biggest dirigible ever built in this country. It was a type engine practically unknown here, and it proved even more tricky to build than Curtiss had expected. For five months he worked with A. L. Pfitzner, a young Hungarian engineer, recruited for the purpose, and Charles Kirkham of Hammondsport, before a four-cylinder, aluminum-jacketed water-cooled engine was produced, which they hoped would function properly.

They were all tired, touchy and fearful of the outcome, as they set up the motor in a shackled plane, harnessed against a scale to measure the pull. It was of the utmost

importance to determine the results exactly and every precaution was taken to insure accuracy. A little group of
excited workmen pressed in as closely as possible, Curtiss
grabbed the switch and the test was on.

The engine warmed up, thundered, buckled to its task
and was reaching the point where its absolute qualities
must become apparent. The men gritted their teeth and
held their breath, waiting. Then they gasped; the motor
had suddenly gone dead and the propeller slowed down to
a stop.

Curtiss, still crouched beside the motor, showed no concern whatsoever.

"I shut her off," he announced, and added dryly, "If
that young man there will keep his head out of the propeller, we'll go ahead with the test."

He threw the switch and this time the test was a complete success. On the test block, of course, the motor had
an unlimited supply of cold water; and the next problem
was to find a radiator, large enough to carry sufficient
water, and light enough not to throw the big cigar-shaped
dirigible out of balance. A light aeronautical radiator was
an item not listed in mail order catalogs, but a suitable
radiator finally was located. The dirigible itself had been
finished for some weeks, and was shipped, together with
its motive equipment, to the proving grounds at Fort Myer,
Virginia.

The cabin of the airship consisted of a very light framework, with a runway made of two narrow boards. Glenn
Curtiss sat in front and kept the little 24-horsepower engine
running, while "Uncle" Tom Baldwin sprinted up and
down the catwalk to keep the ship on an even keel. In this
arduous way, the ship was kept going for the required time
over a closed circuit above the Potomac and the hills of
Virginia, on August 12, 1908.

The speed requirements had already been met in preliminary tests, and Army Dirigible No. 1 was officially accepted by the Signal Corps. Although the purchase price, of $6,750, scarcely covered the cost of producing it, both Curtiss and Baldwin were elated. They felt the ice was broken and that the first of a fleet had been launched. At Baldwin's suggestion, they gave a gala dinner at the National Press Club, which was attended by Lieut. Selfridge, Augustus Post and twelve Washington newspapermen.

Curtiss's account of the flight, as quoted in an interview by the *Hammondsport Herald*, ran:

"The endurance test of the Baldwin ship, which consisted of a flight of two hours' duration at a speed of 16 miles an hour, was made Saturday afternoon at 5:20, over a five-mile course from Mt. Myer, Va., to Clarendon and return. The entire distance covered was 33 miles, and the flight was made without the slightest hitch or trouble of any kind. The mechanical parts of the ship, all of which were built at the shops here, worked to perfection, the engine running without a miss, and the propeller developing a large amount of surplus pull. The gas bag, which is oiled silk and rubber, represents new ideas in balloon construction and it proved remarkably efficient.

"The endurance flight was the greatest accomplishment with the dirigible balloon in America, both as to endurance and speed. It could have been continued with the fuel on board for two hours more, and a trip to Washington and return would probably have been made except for the fact of darkness coming on.

"On landing, we were greeted with cheers by the Army officers, soldiers and crowds of citizens who had gathered to witness the flight. General Allen and Secretary of War Wright witnessed some of the earlier flights. The Secretary expressed himself as greatly pleased. Representatives from England, Germany and Japan were on hand to report officially to their respective countries the result of these tests."

The following month a dirigible of the same type was sold to Captain Hildebrand of the German Army and shipped on November 30, 1908. The sale was negotiated by Karl Dienstbach, who had witnessed the *June Bug* flight. It was the birth of the aeronautical export business in this country. Possibly the fact that there is no latter-day Thomas Scott Baldwin has some bearing on the fact that Germany has ceased to look to us as a source of dirigible supply.

"Uncle" Tom Baldwin exercised an enormous influence on Curtiss's professional life. His bulldog tenacity in 1904 started Curtiss building aeronautical motors. And it was he who four years later brought the United States Government to Hammondsport as a customer and persuaded the motor manufacturer to build a new sort of aeronautical engine. He was a capable builder as well as a grand showman, and one of the few men who ever broke through the wall of reserve Glenn Curtiss built between himself and the world. It was a curious friendship between them. One, genial and loquacious, the other taciturn; one, aggressive, the other retiring; each supplemented the other.

The Army dirigible was the most important of all their joint jobs, and when it had been completed, Curtiss told the reporters at Washington it was a "triumph of Baldwin's knowledge of the air," while Baldwin's bluff comment was: "Curtiss can do anything." There have not been many similar partnerships written into the record of public men.

Glenn Curtiss's own interest, now that the water-cooled engine was to hand, was in heavier-than-air flying. He was convinced that within five years the aeroplane type would, to a great extent, replace the lighter-than-air craft. Even a child knew that something light and filled with gas was pretty well bound to float off the ground if there was nothing to anchor it down. But the fact that an aeroplane left the ground at all still seemed to most people a miracle. And since it could go much faster, its flight was more exciting to watch. It stood to reason, therefore, that the aeroplane's prospects for yielding exhibition revenue were more promising.

The Aerial Experiment Association was divided after July 10, 1908, and the work carried on simultaneously in two places. Curtiss and Selfridge remained at Hammondsport to work with McCurdy on the fourth machine, while Casey Baldwin went to Nova Scotia to assist Dr. Bell on his tetrahedral structures.

The three members who remained behind in Hammondsport had made a systematic series of flights with the *June Bug* in which they accumulated a mass of data to be used in building the fourth aeroplane. Construction was begun on August 10, and the new machine was christened the *Silver Dart* after its silver-gray wings. They had decided this time to use a silk-like, non-porous balloon fabric, with a thin lining of rubber. While McCurdy and Selfridge concentrated on the new aeroplane, Curtiss, after his return from Virginia, majored in a further phase of aeronautics.

At Baddeck, tetrahedral kites had had to give way for a time to boats. Baldwin had built a hydroplane called the *Skidoo,* and they had "retackled the old problem of speed over the water in the interest of studying front and hull construction with a view to water flying. What Dr. Bell now proposed was that floats be put on the *June Bug* and an effort be made to fly it off the water. And it was to this task that Curtiss applied his energies.

The ideal of man-flight was taking hold of the public imagination in the latter half of the year 1908 Henri Farman was offered a $24,000 contract to come over from France and give a public flying exhibition. The A.E.A. members were tremendously excited over the prospect of seeing the Frenchman fly. But after the public flights at Brighton Beach, Long Island, on August 5th, McCurdy wrote Mrs. Bell:

"Farman's attempts were very disappointing indeed. The first day he flew 140 yards at an elevation of 3 feet and a rate of 20 miles an hour. He made two such flights and then wheeled the machine back to the tent. The next day there were 3000 persons in attendance, and as it was too windy he did not attempt to fly at all, much to the disappointment of the 3000. They were, however, given 'wind cheques' and told to come again the next day. We thought that we had seen all worth seeing, so Tom (Selfridge) and I left New York Saturday evening for Hammondsport."

The Aerial Experiment Association was offered $10,000 to race the *June Bug* against Farman's machine on Long Island. But the offer was not accepted since the organization was "for experimental purposes only," and their chairman pointed out that if they received money they would "lay themselves open to litigation before they were ready to defend." Though ten thousand sounded like a lot of money to the members, they appreciated the wisdom of Dr. Bell's opinion. And in any event, they decided, knowing the *June Bug* was speedier than the Farman machine, that the race would have been over before it had properly started.

Farman later abandoned the flying exhibitions because he had difficulty collecting his $6000 guarantee, nor was the $200 a flight forthcoming. It was costing him more to make the flights than he was able to collect from his sponsors.

The Scientific American trophy award to another American had served to bring the Wright brothers into public flying. And their first public flight on September 9, 1908, at Fort Myer, Va., where they were putting a ship for the Army through its paces, was a remarkable demonstration. It was smooth and graceful, the turns were competent. The A.E.A. members witnessed this and subsequent flights and found them very impressive. The cream of the capital—military, political and social—was on hand for the flights and was loud in its praises of the American inventors, who were showered with honors and invited to Dayton, their home town, for a monster welcome.

At the suggestion of Dr. Bell the Smithsonian Institution created the Langley medal "for special services in connection with the science of aerodynamics" and made the first award to the Wright brothers. On September 11, 1908, Bell sent this telegram to Orville Wright:

"On behalf of the Aerial Experiment Association allow me to congratulate you upon your magnificent success. An hour in the air marks a historical occasion."

Only in air-wise Hammondsport was the quality of admiration a trifle strained. The local paper commented:

"Hammondsport people, who are accustomed to the operation of flying machines, were not greatly surprised to hear that Orville Wright had made a flight of more than an hour at Fort Myer. With proper weather conditions an airship can stay up indefinitely. And we have every reason to believe that when the new 50 horsepower motor now being built at the Curtiss works is installed, record flights will be made."

Early in September, A.E.A. secretary, Lieut. Selfridge, had been ordered to Washington. This left McCurdy and

Curtiss to work on alone in Hammondsport, but the members were all proud to learn that Tom had been appointed a member of the Aeronautical Board of the Army. Selfridge was, of course, an official witness at the tests of the first Army aeroplane. When the Wright brothers wished to demonstrate its ability to carry a passenger, he promptly volunteered for the privilege of going up as the passenger.

During this flight a new propeller broke, and although Orville Wright stopped the engine immediately, the aeroplane pitched forward and dove fifty feet. In the fall, the pilot broke his thigh and two ribs, and the passenger was killed.

Lieut. Thomas Selfridge had come out of West Point with the profound belief that there should be at least one officer in the United States Army who had made an expert study of the whole subject of flying. He had made such a study, met Alexander Graham Bell, and, as an active member of the Aerial Experiment Association, had learned the rudiments of applied flying.

Instead of going ahead to a brilliant career in military aeronautics, he won distinction as "the first aeroplane fatality." The young flyer had died for his country in the air, which was no less nor more than he had ever expected to do. But he died too soon, much too soon to dream out his lofty dream of adequate American aerial defense.* So it seemed to his comrades in aerial experiment, all of whom attended his funeral.

On the twentieth of September the Association met at the Washington home of its chairman. They sent expressions of sympathy to Selfridge's parents, and to Orville Wright, in his grief over the death of his passenger, with

---

*Selfridge Field, at Mount Clemens, Michigan, stands as the Army's flying tribute to Lieut. Thomas Selfridge.

hopes of his own speedy recovery. Then, gravely, they took up the question of their own future course. The year was almost completed; should the life of the Association be extended or not?

Mrs. Bell proposed that if they desired to go on for another six months, until March 31st, they might call upon her for funds as they were required up to ten thousand dollars, making her total contribution thirty thousand dollars.

Yes, they would accept her offer. McCurdy's *Silver Dart* was nearing completion. And, since along that way lay greater safety, the off-the-water water experiments with the *June Bug* on floats should be carried out. And Bell decided he would proceed with his kite experiments, together with "Casey" Baldwin, at Baddeck. The tetrahedral kite did not climb high nor fly fast, but it would be very stable and safe.

The trials of the *Silver Dart* were postponed for a time while Curtiss and McCurdy finished putting floats on the *June Bug*. She was re-christened the *Loon* and, on December 2d, took very kindly to the water, but refused to leave it. They decided to hold up further experiments until after the *Silver Dart* had been flown, when they would try installing a more powerful water-cooled engine in the *Loon* in place of the little air-cooled engine which had been sufficiently powerful to take her off the ground.

Two documents on the initial performance of the *Silver Dart* appeared in A.E.A. Bulletin No. XXVI, as follows:

McCurdy to Mrs. Bell

"To Mrs. A. G. Bell, Baddeck, N. W.

"*Hammondsport, N. Y., Dec. 17, 1908:* This morning, as we have already telegraphed you (and received your very nice reply) we had a try-out, with a new propeller of much greater pitch, giving even at reduced revolutions (668 per minute) a greater pitch speed than we had before.

"The first flight was great. The balance is so good, and the controls all work so well that it is a pleasure to sit in the machine every minute of the time you are flying. She leaves the ground after traveling 150 feet exactly at the moment you want her to. She flew down across the old potato patch and then I shut her off because we wanted to look things over before trying a longer flight.

"Everything was O. K., so we ran her back under her own power and started again, this time with the intention of making a turn. I bungled it, however, and just as the turn was completed the starboard wing touched the ground and the machine spun round and broke the wheels. The brakes, however, are things that can be repaired in an hour, and so in that afternoon all the substitute wheels and sheets were prepared and tomorrow morning we will try again. I think we will be more successful.

"J. A. D. McCurdy"

Curtiss to Mrs. Bell

"To Mrs. A. G. Bell, Baddeck, N. S.

"*Hammondsport, N. Y., Dec. 17, 1908:* The two flights John made very good indeed. The first landing was voluntary on account of a new fence which we did not want to bring the machine back over. In the second trial John attempted too short a turn and was forced to land, striking one of the wings and breaking the wheels.

"A great deal of time has slipped by with seemingly not much accomplished of late. I must say, however, that nothing has interfered with the work of the Association. The entire shop has been at its disposal, and everything else has been put aside when necessary to get work out for the flying machines.

"G. H. Curtiss"

The A.E.A. chairman believed it was important always to keep the press informed as to the progress of their work in order to promote public confidence in flying. Consequently the Association received messages from all over the country asking when the *Silver Dart* would fly again. A small group of aeronautical men appeared to witness the December twentieth flights made for Dr. Bell's benefit.

These excerpts from Bell's report on the occasion are characteristic of the man, and of the time "when no good aviator would think of flying in a four or five mile wind:"

"About sundown the wind died down sufficiently to enable experiments to be made. There was still, however a breeze of, I should think, about six miles an hour blowing down the valley toward Lake Keuka. On account of the limited space available for manoeuvers in the valley higher up than the race track, it was not considered advisable to attempt flying the machine against the wind in that direction. The attempt was therefore made to go with the wind down the valley towards Lake Keuka. The engine and propeller seemed to work well and the machine made a fine run on the ground, but when McCurdy elevated the front control the machine only rose sufficiently to clear the raised side of the track and immediately came down the field beyond, running some distance over the snow before the engine stopped.

"Three attempts were made with similar results and further experiments postponed to another day.

"Poor Douglas McCurdy was much mortified at the behavior of his aeroplane in the presence of distinguished visitors, especially so because the machine a few days before had flown beautifully a distance of about a mile."

On another day, several fine flights were made in the *Silver Dart*. Her engine was switched to the *Loon* and the water experiments were again tackled. But even with the additional horsepower the suction of the water on the floats was still too great, and when damage to one of the floats caused the *Loon* to sink, the experiment was abandoned.

Drome No. 4, McCurdy's *Silver Dart* was shipped to Baddeck in January 1909, and the Hammondsport division joined the Beinn Breagh division for further experimental work. The *Silver Dart* was equipped with runners and flown off the ice. In the spring McCurdy and Baldwin made 200 flights off the ground in her, totalling a thousand miles of distance.

It was during this February visit to Nova Scotia that Glenn Curtiss suffered his only serious accident in forty years of racing and flying. With a mechanic at the tiller of a motor-driven ice-boat he set out to tune his motor to the highest pitch of efficiency. Under favorable conditions an ice boat, offering very little head resistance, can make terrific speed when driven with an aerial propeller.

Curtiss, paying no attention to his helmsman, was working on a carburetor adjustment when the mechanic approached the shore line at a high rate of speed. He forgot for the moment that the ice-boat had no reverse gear, like a motorboat. Nor had it any brakes, like an automobile. At the critical moment, when only a short distance from the boat-house, he opened the throttle wide.

They dashed through the doorway and on through the planking at the other end. The mechanic got a few bruises and minor cuts, but Curtiss, wholly unprepared for the crash, was thrown against the steering wheel with such force as to bend the iron rod forming the axis. His lower lip was nearly torn off and he sustained a bad case of shock, but no internal injuries. The only outward evidence of the catastrophe was a long diagonal cut across his lower jaw terminating near the point of the chin. He wore a little tuft of whiskers on his lower lip for a long time as well as a heavy mustache, because he could not shave.

As the end of March approached, the Association took under advisement the question of entering the *Silver Dart* for the second leg on the Scientific American trophy competition. But since making the prescribed flight of 25 kilometers (15.6 miles) would not secure the award in the event that some other entrant flew a longer distance before the close of the year, Dr. Bell vetoed the idea. He felt that an attempt to fly more than the 25 kilometers would be too much of an endurance test, and he could see no point in exhausting either the machine or the aviator or in running any risks whatsoever.

The Association also faced the very serious problem of the subsequent aeronautical careers of the three junior members. They were all convinced that there was a commercial future in flying, and the question was just what part each would play.

The ever-complicated question of patent rights had been, they believed, satisfactorily disposed of. Since the Wright brothers had never made any secret of their intention to prosecute any and all supposed infringers on their patents, Dr. Bell had taken precautions soon after the *June Bug* flight to have the machine examined by attorneys for patentable features. They were commissioned to make an examination of existing patents to ascertain whether the details they believed to be patentable were novel. As a result an application had been filed on the supplementary moveable surfaces which had been devised to lend their machines lateral balance. These surfaces had come to be called ailerons, (little wings) after they had been so labeled by a Frenchman who saw them in operation.

The aileron patent was filed in the name of the Association by its trustee and each of the members was to have the right to use it. Bell's suggestions for forming a joint stock company did not appear feasible at the time and the plan for dissolving the organization was adhered to.

The United States had been assigned to Glenn Curtiss as his commercial field on the A.E.A. designs, and he had already taken steps to engage in the manufacture of aeroplanes. Canada was assigned to Baldwin and McCurdy, who organized the Canadian Aerodrome Company. They developed important new structural features, including the first enclosed gas tanks and the first wing radiator in their *Baddeck No. 1* and *Baddeck No. 2,* but these machines crashed at the wrong time, and they were unable to induce the Canadian government to finance further work.

In 1910 John McCurdy joined Curtiss as an exhibition flyer and demonstrator, and later he organized an exhibition company of his own. During the War he was again associated with Curtiss in aircraft manufacture at the head of a subsidiary company in Toronto. After the Canadian venture, Casey Baldwin gave up aviation and devoted himself to marine engineering. He developed an important sea scout during the World War.

The first entry, under date of September 20, 1908, in the A.E.A. notebook was made by Tom Selfridge. On March 31, 1909, John McCurdy, who had succeeded him as secretary, closed the notebook with this copy of a letter to Charles J. Bell, trustee.

"Dear Sir:

"The Aerial Experiment Association, of which you are

trustee, expires tonight by time limitation and all the property, inventions, and rights belonging to the Association now pass into your hands to be disposed of as you think best in the interest of the members of the Association."

Signed:

Alexander Graham Bell, chairman
J. A. D. McCurdy, secretary."

Customer for an Aeroplane

WHETHER or not flying machines had an immediate commercial future was a popular topic of discussion in the early part of 1909. The Wright brothers were far from optimistic on the subject. Orville Wright, in an interview in England, said he did not agree with those who believed that "the aeroplane would soon come into use as a commercial vehicle."

Before Glenn Curtiss undertook the manufacture of aeroplanes, he tried to determine their market and his findings were recounted as follows in the *A. E. A. Bulletin:*

Feb. 15, 1909: Practically every flying-machine in existence has been built by experimenters and for experimental purposes. Little or no revenue has been derived from their use except perhaps the winning of a few prizes. Farman made one unsuccessful attempt at exhibition work and the U. S. Government has let two contracts. Government contracts and exhibition work seem to be the two most promising sources of revenue.

Exhibitions may and may not prove profitable according to the way in which the undertaking is handled. Farman's exploit was certainly discouraging. An experienced man would be most likely to be successful in this field, that is, one who knows how to get contracts and how to get the money after the contracts are fulfilled. There are now several cash prizes offered in America and still more abroad. But when you play for these big stakes you play against big odds and "there is many a slip, etc." However these cash prizes look very alluring. I think prize chasing and exhibition work should go hand in hand.

Of the score or more machines likely to be built during the coming year there will be nearly as many different models, and the manufacturer to get the business must, like the Voisin brothers, build anything that is wanted. Probably by another year the machines will become more standardized and a certain amount of business may be expected from private parties for machines for sport. Perhaps an Aerial Development Company could be formed to look after government contracts, prizes, etc., and get in shape to handle the large volume of business which is bound to come later.

Already back of Curtiss' mind there was a stubborn conviction that sooner or later people would fly not only for sport but would travel great distances by air. Dr. Bell had long since pictured routine journeys in a transport flying machine that would "rise vertically into the air to some considerable height at Boston and then shoot off horizontally in the direction of New York."

And Curtiss' own razor-edge imagination, whetted by that of the older man, sheared away the doubts and the years that lay between. Men would take to air travel readily; of that he was certain, since it would enable them to live faster. And although he was vague about what form the aircraft of the future would take, he had fairly definite ideas about the method by which its design would be determined. In an article, written in October, 1908 for the *New York World,* he said:

The airship which, within ten years, will carry men and freight from place to place, will be a natural evolution of the aeroplane of today and not the semi-accidental discovery of a genius. It will be the work of a man who is thoroughly familiar with the laws of fluid movement, with the effects of winds and currents and the means for overcoming the numerous difficulties which are encountered in the air. It is in the practical application of the scientific knowledge at hand that the solution of the problems of aerial flight will be found.

He had no illusions at the time about his own fitness to shape the aeroplane of the future. But the success of the ideas he had applied in the *June Bug* had taught him that he could build an aeroplane for the present. It would be vastly more exciting than the manufacture of motorcycles. He was positive flying would some day develop into an important industry, and by entering the field now, he would be in on the ground floor.

Alexander Graham Bell was reluctant to encourage the A. E. A. members to take up the commercial phase of aviation. The Wright patents were known to be very broad in scope; he was afraid that the air was too thick with imminent patent complications. It was a foregone conclusion that the first attempt at flying exploitation would be the signal for litigation to start. Perhaps the members should wait a few years. But Curtiss' mind was seething with ideas on how to improve aeroplane construction, and he yearned to try them out.

Aeroplanes as a side line in the motorcycle works at Hammondsport did not, from a practical, mechanical standpoint present much of a problem. The staff of the G. H. Curtiss Manufacturing Company, had helped build one glider and four flying machines within a year's time. From this contact with the A. E. A. experiments they had gleaned an understanding of the basic principles of aircraft construction.

A staff of nearly a hundred mechanics and workers in metal and wood had been built up around a nucleus of some eight or ten who were experts in their own line. Their engineering methods, like those of their chief, were inclined to be unconventional. The fact that G. H. could "go right out in the shop and use tools himself," and frequently did, barred any of that feeling of contempt which an expert workman sometimes has for a boss, who "couldn't do the work himself if he tried." With practically the same background as his workers, Curtiss happened to have it in him to get a new idea, sketch-it-up on paper and give it to them to build. More often than not they were good ideas that turned out to be what the world called "moneymakers." His men had long respected his ability in developing a motorcycle which was so fast that their factory had become one of the two leading motorcycle production centers in the country.

Of all the men in the shop, Henry Kleckler and Damon Merrill especially were evolving into exceptional craftsmen. Kleckler had come to Curtiss for a job in 1907. He had been made night foreman in the machine shop at the time when preparations were under way for the big freak motorcycle for the Florida speed carnival. Later on he became the shop foreman, and his close association with the work of Curtiss continued for thirteen years without interruption. His ability to follow through a mechanical idea was extraordinary, and Curtiss once summed up his talents when he said: "I'd rather have Henry Kleckler on a project than six engineers."

Soon after Kleckler joined the staff, he had persuaded Harry Genung, the plant manager, to sign on Damon Merrill. Merrill was conscientious, skillful and intelligent, and he came to be Kleckler's right hand man in the job of carrying through Curtiss' creative ideas.

Of Dutch stock, Kleckler was of medium height and stocky. He was usually known by his first name, although Curtiss called him "Henny," and Captain Baldwin always addressed him as "Heinach." He was not talkative, but he smiled more often than "Dame" Merrill, who was six feet two, had even less to say than Kleckler, and usually wore a glum expression.

Merrill gave an excellent account of himself during his years in charge of the aeroplane assembly room. He was inclined to be sensitive. Good-hearted and accommodating, he was resentful of any intrusion into his domain. Any questions about his work were apt to result in a flare-up, with Merrill hastily stumping off to the front office to find out "what in hell he was being interrupted for." But his workmanship was truly excellent, and his clever fingers could create anything mechanical. Curtiss, Kleckler and Merrill made one of those perfect triumvirates which mesh together to achieve a common end harmoniously.

Graham Palmer, another exceptional workman, was a master carver and worker in wood, and his favorite occupation for many years was making violins. Which surely qualified him for the delicate task of shaping the quaint, early propellers to perfect pitch and balance. Palmer loved the small town life of Hammondsport and he would not be deprived of his pleasure in calling off the figures at the dances in the local Grange Hall. He did this in a deep, rich baritone, while he played on one of his own violins.

Others among the early members of the factory staff were, C. Edward Clark, the first foreman of the motorcycle shop; Frank Warren, who was later in charge of the aeroplane metal work at the Curtiss Aeroplane and Motor Company; Frank Pratt, the first tailor employed to sew linen wing covers together; Robert F. Patterson, Bill Batcher, George Robinson and Harry Bailey. There was also Frank Kleckler, a fine mechanic who worked out and perfected the double-rocker-arm for the valve action for the OX motors.

They were nearly all of them local boys who had picked up a knowledge of mechanics in neighboring towns, and, under the critical eyes of Curtiss, developed into a fine group of workmen.

The Hammondsport plant became a nursery for many careers. Among those who were attracted to it after it turned its attention to aeronautics, were Tod Shriver, Blackie Fagan and Jim Lamont. They roomed together in an old resort hotel on the Lake Front.

Shriver and Fagan were a couple of roustabouts from Madison Square Garden in New York, where their duty was to push exhibits onto and off the floors at automobile shows and also to expel unruly visitors. Tom Baldwin met them first when he was staging a show at the Garden, and took a fancy to them. When Harry Genung went to New York, early in 1909, Baldwin told him that he knew two men crazy to get into the aviation business, and introduced the pair. Shriver was a long, lean fellow, somewhat sardonic looking, while Fagan was a huge Irishman with eyebrows like a hedge fence, black hair that grew down on his forehead, and a beard that covered his cheek bones. Genung hired them and Baldwin's protegès did prove very useful. Shriver developed into such an excellent aeroplane mechanic that Curtiss learned to depend on him always to tune up his motor before he started on a flight of any consequence. Fagan, however, never learned the difference between a connecting rod and a cylinder head. But when the first exhibition flights were made the custom was to house the aeroplane in a tent, where, by paying a small fee, the crowd might inspect it. Among the inspectors were many vandals eager to inscribe their names on the wings or to cut a piece out of them as a souvenir. Whenever Fagan saw anyone reach a hand towards any part of the machine, he would let out a terrific roar. The souvenir hunter would take one look and flee.

The third room-mate, Jim Lamont, was a huge fellow who had worked on steamboats plying between Penn Yan and Hammondsport. Unlike Shriver, who afterwards became an expert exhibition pilot, he never cared to fly, but he knew so much about aeroplanes and aviators, that he was indispensable. After touring the United States, Japan and the Orient, he became Ruth Law's chief mechanic, and eventually, manager of a large mid-west flying field.

Early in March, 1909, Curtiss was approached by Augustus M. Herring, who had been identified with aeronautical experiments for twenty years. He wanted to form an aircraft corporation. Curtiss, knowing him only as the big-framed, loose-jointed chap who had voiced loud objections to the rulings of the judges in the *Scientific American's* trophy award at Hammondsport, was a little dubious about the proposal.

Then something happened which galvanized him into action: a prospective customer appeared on the scene, in the form of a flying club.

Because they felt that the Aero Club of America program leaned too much toward the lighter-than-air idea, a group of its younger members had, in 1908, formed a separate organization to specialize in heavier-than-air flying. They called themselves the Aeronautical Society of New York, and among them were Stanley Beach, Gutzon Borglum, William F. Whitehouse, Hudson Maxim and Peter Cooper Hewitt. Their first exhibition of self made aeroplanes was something of a fiasco, since, although there were several on display, not one of them could fly.

The members had a session at which it was decided to make up a pool and buy the club an aeroplane that could get off the ground. William J. Hammill and Ernest LaRue Jones were appointed committees-of-one to deal with the Wrights and Glenn Curtiss, respectively. They proposed to pay $5,000 for a flying machine and free instruction to two of their members.

When the Wright committeeman reported that the answer was definitely no, Curtiss was approached. They knew that he had the factory facilities and a sufficiently experienced staff to build a flying machine at Hammondsport. Curtiss promptly accepted the order.

He was committed to building aeroplanes; ways and means would come later. He wrote to Dr. Bell:

> I accepted the order on my own responsibility, with the idea that if the consolidation was made with Herring it would be turned over to the new company. Or if a commercial organization succeeded the Experiment Association, the order could be turned over to them. If neither of these materialized, the Curtiss Company would endeavor to fill the order itself.

The hope of an A. E. A. manufacturing venture was almost negligible at this time. Curtiss knew also that his own company would incur a heavy loss if it attempted to build the machine. To produce an aeroplane involved a substantial outlay. The Association had spent some $30,000 in building four machines using the same parts several times over, while he had deliberately undertaken to build a machine for $5000 with free instruction for two thrown in. Curtiss was obstinately determined to go through with it, single-handed if necessary. Common sense told him it was a silly idea, that he would probably bankrupt himself if he tried it alone. Herring's proposition was the logical way out, so he decided to forget his prejudices. It was sheer opportunism, and it led him headlong into a lopsided arrangement that would have done little credit to a gullible school boy. His newly-born desire to build aeroplanes encouraged his quaint belief that he was a good business man and Curtiss consummated the deal.

On the face of it, the arrangement sounded alluring. A group of men headed by Cortlandt Field Bishop, president of the Aero Club, had tried to prevent inventor Herring from going abroad to finish his work, as the Wright brothers had been compelled to do. Herring reputedly had an array of aeronautical patents some of which were supposed to antedate those of the Wrights. He also had a $50,000 contract to build an aeroplane, utilizing those patents, for the United States Army. Certain "moneyed interests" had agreed to contribute $45,000 to the formation of an aircraft company headed by Herring.

Bishop was quoted as saying benignly: "We feel that if Congress will not do anything to aid Americans, we will. This matter of air navigation, especially with aeroplanes, is no longer a fad or a joke. All wide awake men in New York with means realize that fact. We are going to keep our American inventors here and give them a chance."

Herring claimed to have invented, among other things, a means of achieving "automatic equilibrium," which Curtiss only the year before had pointed to as the primary need. He had feared then that the problem would never be successfully solved. At any event, Curtiss was awed by Herring's intangible exhibits.

He wrote Dr. Bell:

> Mr. Herring showed me a great deal, and I would not be at all surprised if his patents, backed by a strong company, would pretty well control the use of the gyroscope in obtaining auto-

matic equilibrium. This seems to be the only road to success in securing automatic stability in an aeroplane.

In his ignorance and worldly inexperience it never occurred to Curtiss to ask to be shown more than "a great deal" or to have the various patents checked by a patent attorney. Instead, he not only accepted the proposition on its face value, but he made him a better proposition than the one originally suggested by Herring. Here was an opportunity he could not afford to miss, and he signed away, without a murmur, control of the G. H. Curtiss Manufacturing Company—a going concern in the production of motorcycles and aeronautical engines—in order to become vice-president and general manager of the new corporation.

All the while he honestly felt that it was something like this his Grandmother Curtiss had dreamed he might do some day. And for the moment the grown-up country boy was intoxicated with the grandeur involved in being a "big manufacturer" and part of a company backed by New York financiers.

"But," he proudly reassured R. G. Betts, editor of *Motorcycle Review,* who questioned the merit of the proposition, "I thought I'd never be anything but a bicycle mechanic."

A charter was obtained by the Herring-Curtiss Company to manufacture aeroplanes, motorcycles, automobiles, and various kinds of motor-driven vehicles. It was capitalized at $360,000. Regardless of later consequences, Curtiss took this action gladly, believing that in forming the first commercial aircraft company, he and Herring and the others were taking an important step toward the development of aerial transportation. And Curtiss was grateful to be included in the plan, as witness his telegram to Bell, March 21, 1909:

> Very satisfactory consolidation Saturday.
> Named Herring-Curtiss Co., Hammondsport.
> Interest and management retained.

Most important of all was the fact that he got what he wanted at the time more than anything else: sufficient backing to build flying machines.

From that time on Curtiss thought, spoke and dreamed of nothing but aeroplanes. He was irrevocably committed to a career of experimentation, nearly always improving on his previous efforts in one way or another, just as he had done before that with bicycles and motorcycles. When a product reached a state of commercial practicality, he immediately lost interest in it. Some of the men associated with him had sufficient business acumen to realize that it is impossible to produce costly new designs, patterns and machines and still reap commercial profits from their sale. But their earnest efforts to make a production manufacturer out of him were wasted. Like many another inventor, he could never stop inventing long enough to manufacture and sell in any important quantity the things he had invented. His restless nature could not be interested in something already built.

He had been considering a design for a new machine for months. Now he put his ideas into execution in the plane for the Aeronautical Society. He made it smaller than the *June Bug* in the interest of greater speed. Instead of hinging the ailerons on as tips of the main wings, he mounted the balancing surfaces on the struts between the wings. This was the first appearance of the inter-wing aileron idea.

One day Curtiss announced: "I think this taper stuff is just a lot of expensive construction for nothing." So the wings in the new plane were straight and uniform in width instead of tapering, as in the A.E.A. machines. A front wheel was added in addition to the two wheels underneath the chassis to prevent the plane from toppling forward. A more efficient rudder control was worked out. The wing covering was unbleached linen with a filler, or Niad cloth, which looked like gold in the air.

On the sixteenth of June, 1909, the first commercial aeroplane ever bought and sold in this country was delivered into the hands of the Aeronautical Society at Morris Park Race Track, New York City. Curtiss made three short flights, which the new aeronauts considered a satisfactory demonstration of their machine. This year, they boasted, the people who bought tickets to their second annual exhibition, scheduled for June 26th, would see an aeroplane in the air.

But a 26-mile wind almost blasted their hopes. While the crowd waited a wind-organ raced around the track at high speed. Glenn Curtiss made two very short hops. There were balloon ascensions and a parachute drop; and at 6:30 Tom Baldwin flew his dirigible in the teeth of the gale, although it was damaged in landing. Most of the audience had gone home discouraged when the wind died down sufficiently for Curtiss to make one complete circuit of the course. The Aeronautical Society felt that its face had been saved, and granted permission to Curtiss to borrow their *Gold Bug* for an attempt to win the second leg on the *Scientific American* Trophy.

Morris Park Race Track had proved unsuitable for flying since there was no place to land except on the track itself and the winds always blew crosswise over the track. The local papers announced that a new flying field was to be selected for the Aeronautical Society. With some of the members, Glenn Curtiss drove out over Long Island, and chose Hempstead Plains, east of Mineola, as a "nice flat place."

There in the early morning hours of July seventeenth, a small crowd of enterprising scientists, engineers and sportsmen arrived to watch Curtiss fly. He went up first for the President's Cup, offered by Cortlandt Bishop of the Aero Club for a flight of one kilometer. Then he took off on the *Scientific American* Trophy flight.

The minimum required was 25 kilometers or 15½ miles, and it was by far the most exacting test of the aviator and his craft up to that time. The air conditions were good and his motor was in excellent form as he took off and swung the machine around the posts that marked the turns in the triangular course. He banked steeply for the turns and flew on mile after mile at a steady pace. As he approached the twelfth and final lap, the crowd waited tensely. He completed it, and there were loud cheers. Knowing, however, that the trophy award would be made for the 25 kilometers only if no one else made a longer flight during the year, Curtiss flew seven more laps, and landed when his fuel was exhausted. He had covered 24 7/10 miles and, since it was the longest flight, the second leg on the trophy was awarded to him at the end of the year.

The members of the Society chosen to take flying lessons from Curtiss—in accordance with the terms of the sales contract—were Charles F. Willard and Alexander Williams. They flipped a coin to see who should be the first student. Williams, who won the toss, was given minute ground instruction about what to do in the air. But he became rattled soon after he left the ground and pulled the controls back so far that he stalled the machine and crashed. He was injured only slightly, but the machine was badly damaged.

When the *Gold Bug* was repaired, after almost two weeks of feverish work, Curtiss taught Willard to fly it.

Then he hurried back to Hammondsport, where he had been building, mostly by long distance, a machine for the international air meet scheduled for August 22-29, at Rheims. He had previously abandoned any thought of the meet because it was understood that the Wright brothers would represent America. They had sold their patent rights to a French syndicate and made a series of sensational flights at Auvors, Pau, and Rome. All Europe was excited at their feats and took it for granted they would be at the meet. Then Wilbur Wright cabled the Aero Club president that neither he nor his brother would compete. The rules of the contest, he said, permitted an aeroplane to touch its wheels on the ground during a race; but since the Wright machine was equipped with skids instead of wheels* the rule would be likely to operate in favor of the wheel-machines. Therefore they had decided not to enter.

Offers to modify the rules did not serve to alter their decision, and, with the thirty day limit for filing entries almost at hand, it appeared that America would lose by default. As soon as Bishop, who was in Europe, heard of the showing made by Curtiss in the *Gold Bug* he cabled urging him to enter the Rheims meet. Curtiss replied:

> I am not a professional aviator and fear that I would stand little chance with the great flyers of Europe. Besides I have only one machine completed and that is not built for great speed.

The Aero Club president cabled back an offer personally to reimburse Curtiss for all expenses incurred in case he failed to win any of the $40,000 prize money. Curtiss cabled his consent and was registered at the last moment as America's official entry.

---

*The Wright machines were launched on a mono-rail by means of a weight in a tower.

Upon his return to Hammondsport a few days before the fifth of August, when he was scheduled to sail for France, he found the factory in a frenzy of preparation. It would have to be the best possible aeroplane the factory could turn out if he was to win the five thousand dollar prize in the Gordon Bennett Cup speed race.

The new machine was almost a duplicate of the *Gold Bug*, except for certain changes made in the interest of greater efficiency. The diameter of the propeller had been increased from six to seven feet, which involved lifting the plane structure higher above the ground so the propeller blades might swing clear. A new position had been found for the outriggers supporting the elevators and for the rudder control. The wings had been built in separate panels for the sake of portability. The ailerons were again operated from the struts.

Curtiss decided his *Golden Flyer* looked promising enough, with its trim tan linen wings. He was taking two propellers in case one broke, and he found Graham Palmer and "Baldy" Davison affectionately putting the final touches on them in the quiet of the wood-working room. The two artists were resolved that "G. H." should have a propeller more beautiful than any of those Frenchmen's.

The chief concern, of course, was the motor. News had just been flashed of Bleriot's triumphant Channel flight, and there was a rumor that he was getting an 80 horse-power engine ready for the meet. Curtiss and Kleckler and "Tod" Shriver worked all night over the 8 cylinders of the water-cooled engine, until they were reasonably sure it would develop 50 horsepower on the test-block. Better than that they could not do.

There was no time left to test the aeroplane and see if it would fly, although there was no reason to suppose that it wouldn't. While the train was being held, the motor was taken off the block, packed and rushed to the station, where it was shoved into a box car besides the packing box containing the aeroplane. Hammondsport's entry was started on its journey across the Atlantic.

The Fastest Man

Mrs. Curtiss and Martha and Harry Genung came to New York to see America's representative off to the international flying tournament on the steamship *La Savoie*. To France with him went his favorite mechanic, Tod Shriver, and Ward Fisher, who was the agent for Curtiss motorcycles in Rochester, New York. It was Curtiss' first ocean voyage and he dreaded it, but before they reached France he sent a triumphant wireless message to his wife assuring her that after five days out he had not been sea-sick. He had enjoyed the trip, although he was far from optimistic about winning the speed cup. He thought a little ruefully of his motorcycle racing days; of how he had made it a rule not to enter an event if he knew he was "licked" before he left the starting line. Still the speed qualities of his motorcycles had not always been responsible for his victories. On occasion he had out-maneuvered his opponents when he knew he could not out-ride them.

Tank Waters and he chuckled when they recalled how they had performed a major operation on the course of the Waltham hill climb. Curtiss didn't know just what type of strategy would help a man to win an air race if he could not out-fly his opponents. Still, Tod Shriver, busy at the moment trying to accommodate his long frame in a deck chair, was a wizard at pampering a motor.

It was barely possible, too, that some of the French planes were not as good as they were reputed to be. Besides, somebody had to represent America, and since his expenses had been personally guaranteed by the Aero Club president, he couldn't lose any money. On the other hand, if he should happen to make a good showing, it might be the making of him so far as manufacturing aeroplanes was concerned. In the meantime he would have an opportunity to see what Europe was like.

Thirty-eight flying machines, all of them having given "proof of their ability to fly," were entered for *La Grande Semaine d'Aviation*. The tournament was scheduled for August 22-29, 1909.

The continent was greatly keyed up over its first competitive flying spectacle. A wire service correspondent reported:

> The excitement registered already over this coming Aviation Week can scarcely be comprehended in America. It is as though there were to be a week about New York which would include the Vanderbilt Cup Race, the Futurity, a Yale-Harvard boat race, a championship series of ball games between the Giants and Chicago, and a municipal election.
>
> There's that much excitement.
>
> *Tribunes* (grand stands) to accommodate 50,000 persons are in place on Bethany Field, the great plain outside the portals of Rheims. Thousands are already crowding the hotels and boarding houses. As much as $500 for the week had been charged for a suite. One American owner of magazines has paid $600. Tiny bedrooms in humble houses rent for $10 a day. Good weather and absence of high wind are the only requisites for a stupendously successful affair.
>
> It is expected that no less than 250,000 spectators will be on hand at the beginning of the great week at the old champagne town.

Curtiss was greeted at the station in Paris by Cortlandt Bishop, one of the best-groomed and most suavely cosmo-

politan men of his day. He took the American contender
who looked anything but dapper in his ill-fitting, slightly
rustic clothes, to call on the sponsor of the major speed
event at the Week of Aviation. Bennett, of whom Don
C. Seitz said, "no man did more to stimulate interest
in the costly sports," was eager to meet Curtiss. He received him cordially and complimented him on his fine
sportsmanship in entering the meet. But when he learned
that his aeroplane had fitted nicely into a compartment of
a passenger car on the way to Paris, and that his reserve
equipment consisted of one extra propeller, he whistled
and looked out of the window. He was not quite sure
whether the American contender for the Bennett Cup was
courageous or slightly mad. His guest was equally staggered
when he learned that Bennett's chief hobbies were his
porcelains and his cages full of canaries.

Curtiss cut short his stay in Paris to hurry on to Rheims
to prepare for the meet.

James Gordon Bennett was not alone in his surprise at
the limited amount of equipment, as a news cable sent to
the Hammondsport *Herald* reveals:

> The diminutiveness of Curtiss' machines as-
> tonished both aviators and laymen. For sev-
> eral days various aeroplanes have been passing
> through the streets of Paris enroute to Rheims.
> They have been packed in huge boxes; two of
> them, abreast, blocked the wide avenues. The
> Parisians naturally expected something like this
> from Curtiss.
>
> "Where is your plane, M. Curtiss?" they
> asked him.
>
> "Here," said the American, pointing to a
> couple of small flattish boxes which a man could
> carry without great difficulty. Then he had to
> explain that his apparatus, with its 50 horse-

power motor and all, weighs less than two hundred pounds.* "I have been carrying it with me as personal baggage, so that no harm would come to it," he told them. And it was true.

At Rheims lodgings had been arranged for Curtiss and his party at the home of a Catholic priest. They were grateful for the welcome their kindly host extended, but they hurried out to the flying field at the first opportunity.

Bethany Plain was alive with aeroplanes, parts of aeroplanes, aviators and mechanics. On the outskirts hovered a fringe of curious, respectful citizens who had squirmed past the guards or climbed over the fence which separated the vast field from the outside world. At one end was a row of wooden structures to house the aeroplanes, at the other, three *tribunes* had been erected for the spectators.

Originally the meet had been scheduled for the month of March at Monte Carlo. But since the area available was so limited that the contestants would have been obliged to fly out over the Mediterranean Sea, the flyers did not care to take the risk. The project was therefore transferred to the ample bosom of Bethany Plain. By moving the date of the meet up to the end of August, the list of prospective contestants was considerably lengthened. Louis Paulhan, for example, had not learned to fly until June of that year, nor would Glenn Curtiss have been in position to enter by March.

Most of the planes already assembled or on their way to the field were monoplanes. And it was these which offered the greatest threat to Curtiss. He knew his biplane was speedier than any of the other biplanes, mostly Wrights, Voisins, and Farmans. But since the recent feats of Louis Bleriot and Hubert Latham, the monoplane-type had demonstrated definite points of superiority. Bleriot

* A case, of course, of journalistic undersight.

had five of his planes at the meet, while Latham had three Antoinettes. The dopesters were convinced that the big speed event would be a contest between these two French-men, and their monoplanes.

Bleriot had recently topped off his long list of impressive achievements by making the first flight across the English Channel. He was the darling of France and the favorite to win the Gordon Bennett Cup. The picturesque new flyer, Hubert Latham, also occupied a warm place in French hearts. Shortly after the *London Daily Mail* had announced a prize of $5,000 for the first flight across the Channel, Latham had proceeded to Calais. He started on July nineteenth, but his motor balked when he was only six miles out, and he came down safely on the water. He was picked up, nonchalantly smoking a cigarette, by the destroyer detailed to follow him, and was ready to make another attempt when Bleriot took off on July 25th and landed safely near Dover, England.

There were other Frenchmen at Rheims, who had won flying fame since the South American Santos-Dumont, in August 1905, first flew a heavier-than-air plane off European soil. Henri Farman, who had made exhibition flights in America, was there with his Farman biplanes; Louis Paulhan, who had already captured one of the Wright brother's records in his two months of flying tenure, was preparing to enter the events in a Voisin biplane. Santos-Dumont's Damoiselle, and Leon Delagrange's special craft were too light to offer any serious competition in the speed events. Comte de Lambert, a pupil of Wilbur Wright, and Lefebre entered Wright biplanes; De Rue was flying Voisins, of which there were seven at the meet. Alfred Leblanc, another Wright pupil, had entered a Bleriot monoplane.

Since each type aeroplane had a hangar assigned to it,

one hangar was reserved to house the Curtiss machines. It still looked alarmingly empty after the single American plane was unpacked and assembled. Glenn Curtiss and his two assistants had taken off their coats and gone to work. It took them some little time to realize that the stares and excited gestures of the French mechanics who gathered about were caused not by the sight of the aeroplane, but by the sight of the Americans working in shirt sleeves, rather than the traditional French workingman's blouse. Even more confusing for their sense of fitness was the fact that the American aviator pitched in and worked on his own plane, and that he did not affect the conventional flying togs of the day.

Very strange people, these Americans. And very queer people these French, who insisted upon calling Curtiss, "Koor-tees." Tod Shriver and Ward Fisher conceded a point and purchased jaunty berets for themselves, so they might feel less conspicuous. But Curtiss continued to wear his visored cap. On it was pinned the only luck token he ever used: a little swastika emblem from a flying school at Hempstead Plains, called Triaca's Aerial Garage.

The American flyer had sprained his ankle soon after arriving at Rheims, much to the concern of his Catholic host, who insisted upon presenting him with a walking cane. The priest and his lodger seemed to understand each other beautifully without the bridge of a common language.

The week before the opening of the meet was spent by the contestants in trial flights and some of the aeroplanes, which had proved their ability to fly, also proved their ability to fall. The total number of planes entered was decreased from thirty-eight to thirty before the meet opened.

Curtiss made several flights in his machine on August

nineteenth, and found its performance satisfactory. Tod Shriver pointed out gleefully that Curtiss was the only flyer who always landed back at the place where he started, in front of his own hangar. This was due in part to his eagerness to avoid a long tramp across the field on his injured ankle.

On one of the flights a collision was narrowly averted when, for the first time in history, three planes were in the air at the same time. M. Dumanest, in an Antoinette monoplane, approached the *Golden Flyer* at right angles and on the same level. "Quick as a flash," according to the newspaper report of the incident, "Curtiss realized the danger. He elevated his plane and his machine instantly shot upward and soared safely over the Frenchman." Observers below applauded wildly. The third machine in the air was flown by Paul Tissandier.

The opening day of the meet, Sunday, August 22nd, brought bad flying weather. It had rained heavily the night before and gusts of wind were blowing across a sodden field. Nevertheless, two hundred thousand persons bought tickets of admission. All the gentry of Europe were there, with a goodly smattering of America's sporting bloods. The citizens of Rheims and the surrounding country made up the rest of the audience. Myron T. Herrick, on his first term as French Ambassador, came from Paris and brought his family. From Berlin came Ambassador Andrew D. White. Helen Cannon, daughter of "Uncle Joe," speaker of the House of Representatives; Mrs. Theodore Roosevelt and her daughter Ethel and her sons Quentin and Archie, were on hand. Also in attendance from the Embassy at Paris were Commander F. L. Chapin, Naval attache, and Captain Bentley, Military attache.

Cortlandt Bishop and his brother, David Wolfe Bishop, did the honors at the Curtiss hangar, and introduced a steady stream of countrymen anxious to meet America's lone representative. Among the visitors were Mr. and Mrs. George Gould, Mrs. William K. Vanderbilt, William H. Crane and Nat Godwin; R. D. Chapin of Detroit, and Mr. and Mrs. Lewis Kitteridge of Cleveland. Curtiss although he intensely disliked this sort of thing, was called upon frequently to pose for pictures, including one with Anna Held.

The first day's weather was little more conducive to successful photography than it was to sightly flying. It looked as though the President of France, who had come to assist at the formal opening of the meet, might have to go back to Paris without seeing a flight. But Louis Paulhan was too patriotic a citizen to let this happen. He took off and flew around the course in his clumsy box-kite Voisin. It swayed and tilted drunkenly, but the honor of France was saved.

The elimination contest of seventeen French aviators which was the routine business of the opening day, had to be postponed until late afternoon. Then, in the face of a twelve-mile wind, Bleriot, Latham and Lefebre won the right to represent France in a Bleriot, an Antoinette and a Wright biplane, respectively, in the Gordon Bennett Cup event, scheduled for August 28th.

The *Coupe Internationale d'Aviation,* and a $5,000 cash prize that went with it, was created by Bennett as a companion-piece to his *Coupe Internationale des Aeronauts* for balloonists. The new trophy, valued at $2,500 was the highest honor any flyer could win at the meet, and it was to be awarded to the victor in the speed race of twenty kilometers (12.42 miles)—or twice around a course with sharp turns.

Other prizes, with valuable purses also offered were: the *Gran Prix de la Champagne,* with a total purse of

20,000 francs to be divided into three prizes, for the fastest single lap of the 10 kilometer (6.2 mile) course; the *Prix d'Altitude* for the aeroplane going highest, and several other smaller prizes, as well as awards for "the now antiquated" balloons.

Curtiss had come to France especially for the Gordon Bennett Cup, and the flying fans commended his caution in entering no events on the first two days of the meet. After all, the man had only one plane to risk while the other leading contestants had several.

On the second day, Latham and Paulhan battled it out for the altitude prize, with Latham the winner at 155 meters (503.75 feet), an unprecedented height. The figures according to a current account, didn't "mean a thing . . . It was necessary to see the machine way up there to get the impression." Louis Paulhan made duration and distance records.

The *Prix de la Champagne* was scheduled for the third day and Curtiss was much interested, as Bleriot took off. Tod Shriver, who was timing all the contestants with a stop watch, reported his time at 7 minutes, 47 4/5 seconds for the 10 kilometers. The gifted Frenchman had clipped 15 seconds off Lefebre's record of the previous day. But Curtiss had done nearly as well on one of his trials before the meet, and just as the time limit for starting in the event was expiring, a cry went up that the American was taking off. His countrymen were delighted that the Frenchmen, Englishmen and Italians in the audience should at least learn that the American aeroplane could fly. And they were proud to note that he won second place in the event. His time for the lap was 7 minutes 51 3/5 seconds or 3 4/5 seconds behind the winner, Bleriot.

The next three days were filled in with lesser events and balloon contests. The Americans, confident now of the

stamina of the *Golden Flyer,* earnestly wished Curtiss
would resume his policy of hugging the ground, as they
looked down the course to the "graveyard," a spot over
which air conditions were especially rough. It was littered
with the wrecks of a dozen machines. Curtiss however,
entered several of the smaller events to get in better shape
himself and break in his still green aeroplane.

In preparation for the main event he had removed his
large gas tank and installed a smaller one to lessen head
resistance. His French competitors were greatly interested
in his wooden propeller, but they were convinced of the
superiority of metal propellers. It was for this reason that
M. Chauviere, who supplied propellers to Bleriot, had
built a metal one for the American's plane. It was a
thoroughly sportsmanlike gesture, but Curtiss, after trying it out, decided to continue using his own home made
propeller.

The Saturday morning of the Gordon Bennett Cup race
dawned clear and stifling hot. The flags of all nations
which decked the *tribunes* drooped and the Americans re-
joiced because it looked like "Curtiss weather." They knew
he always avoided windy days. But the manner in which
the machines that were in the air early rocked and pitched
indicated deceptive air conditions. The entrants for the
speed cup race were called together before the committee
and heard the rules explained. Flights for the prize must
be made at any time between the hours of 10 and 5:30.
Each entrant might make as many trial laps as he wished,
but he was instructed to notify the judges, when ready to
start the official flight.

There was great activity in the hangars of the leading
contenders: Bleriot, Latham, Lefebre, of France, and the
Englishman Cockburn. But Curtiss made the first move.
Having decided the weather was not likely to improve, he

ordered his machine out of the hangar before ten o'clock and immediately took off and circled the field. He rose to 45 feet and crossed the starting line at full speed, went around the course and crossed the finish line at twelve feet. Immediately a white ball was hoisted on a pole at the timer's stand, indicating that a lap record had been broken.

The air conditions over the "graveyard" were unusually bad, but the system of starting high and diving down had proved its merit. Curtiss ordered the fuel tank re-filled and sent word to the judges he was ready to start.

On the first lap he throttled down in the area where the uneven heating of the ground caused heat waves that made the *Golden Flyer* wobble and drop several feet. But throttling down meant loss of speed, and seconds might cost him the race. On the second lap he employed his diving strategy and rode down hill right past the finish line. Time had also been gained on his turns by banking the machine steeply. He landed with a feeling that he had done his best with the machine.

The two Bishop brothers led him away to their automobile to watch the remainder of the race. They felt confident his speed of 46 miles an hour in time of 15 minutes and 50 seconds, could not be beaten. But Curtiss, remembering Bleriot's 80 horsepower engine was doubtful.

Cockburn started next, for England, but dropped so low over the bad area that he crashed into a haystack and was out of the race. Early in the afternoon, Hubert Latham took off in his graceful, long-bodied, Antoinette. There was a rumor that he was going to bring out reserve power in his motor. But his speed was five miles slower than Curtiss'; his time 17 minutes 32 seconds. Lefebre, in a Wright biplane, flew the two laps in 20 minutes, 47 2/3 seconds. None of the other four starters averaged better than 35 miles an hour.

The race had narrowed down to a contest between Bleriot and Curtiss. The Frenchman made a trial flight in his big No. 22 at noon. He changed the propeller and went up again at 2 o'clock; at three he made a trial with a four-bladed propeller.

Shortly after five, Bleriot started on his official flight. The French crowd was optimistic. Nervously the Americans watched him whip his plane around the course. The weather had changed and he did not pitch and roll over the "graveyard." As the time for his first lap was posted, the crowd was in a tumult of joy. He had beaten Curtiss' best lap by 5 2/5 seconds. Then the big monoplane seemed to slow down; there was an agony of doubt as the results were tabulated.

Cortlandt Bishop left Curtiss in his automobile and hurried with Bennett to the judges' stand. There they found Tod Shriver clutching his stop-watch and muttering wildly. He had an idea one of the judges was preparing to hoist the French tri-color. He was afraid they were going to announce a victory for Bleriot. "Tell them we win!" he pleaded hysterically, when he saw Bishop. Then the time for the lap was marked up and he felt reassured. Bleriot's total time for the 20 kilometers was 15 minutes, 55 and 3/5 seconds.

Bishop returned to the automobile shouting triumphantly: "America wins! The judges find you have beaten Bleriot's time by 5 and 3/5 seconds."

A crowd of hysterically excited Americans rushed over to Curtiss. In front of them was a Frenchman in flying clothes. With tears streaming down both cheeks, Louis Bleriot embraced Curtiss and congratulated him on his victory. Eighteen years later the same redoubtable sportsman was on hand at Le Bourget to greet Lindbergh, with the same genuine warmth when he arrived in France on Glenn Curtiss' birthday.

Next to offer congratulations was Ambassador Herrick, who also did the honors when Lindbergh landed at Le Bourget. The tall diplomat shook Curtiss' hand and said heartily, "I came to see you win and you have done it. We shall give a dinner in your honor at the Embassy tomorrow."

Overcome with embarrassment, the aviator climbed down out of the big red motor car. But the resolute ambassador took firm hold of his arm and said: "Why, my dear fellow, you can't run off now. I'm taking you out on the field to meet the official representatives of the Republic of France." This prospect staggered Curtiss. Searching frantically for an excuse, he muttered something about getting off a cablegram to his wife. But the newspapermen assured him that the news had already been flashed to the ends of the world.

He was led protesting to the base of the tall pole in front of the *tribunes* on which the victor's national colors were run up after each event. The American flag was hoisted and the band played *The Star Spangled Banner*. There followed an elaborate ceremony during which the victor was only a little less uncomfortable than he would have been had he understood what the French officials were saying about him.

The newspapers had an orgy of superlatives in telling the story of that day's victory. France applauded, despite her disappointment; and Hammondsport, which felt its name had been "writ large in the history of flight," was beside itself for joy. The *Rochester Democrat and Chronicle* announced that the event "should remind critics that it is not the habit of Americans to march or fly in the rear of the procession."

On the last day of the meet Curtiss proved to his own satisfaction that his victory was not accidental by winning first place in the *Prix de la Vitesse* with the fastest three-lap flight of the course, although he was penalized one-twentieth for making a late start. His time for the eighteen miles was 23½ minutes. And for the three major events his total winnings were $8,000. Technically his three victories were regarded as evidence of the superiority of the biplane type.

Few among those who were fortunate enough to be there questioned the historical import of the international week of aviation. A dispatch to American papers reflected the popular reaction in saying:

> A week of miracles has ended. In this con-course of men of a new epoch, marvel has suc-ceeded marvel, all so breathlessly impossible until now. We have to rub our eyes to allow our-selves to reach a realizing sense that what we have actually seen in the air here above Bethany Plain, above Withy and Bourgoyne, against the ancient towers of Europe's lovliest cathedral, has been no dream but a veritable fact. Never since history began have there been witnessed such scenes of wonder, scenes pompous with human accomplishment and so presagent of a change in the life of man upon earth.

There followed for Curtiss, the ordeal of the Embassy dinner. The *New York World* correctly estimated his sentiments when it said: "Curtiss fears ceremony more than he fears the most perilous flight. He was not intending to go to the dinner, but when he had been solemnly prom-ised that no one would call upon him to speak, he came."

As Bleriot walked in, arm in arm with Curtiss, followed by Latham and Paulhan, the five hundred dinner guests rose and gave each flyer an individual ovation.

The Europeans at the dinner were impressed with the singular indifference with which Curtiss accepted applause, not realizing that his apparent poise was actually embarrassment. When he was back home Glenn Curtiss told his own story of the banquet. "I could eat off the gold plates all right," he said. (He was deeply indebted for tactful hints on gold-plate problems to Miss Helen Cannon, seated next to him during the dinner.) "But when they wanted me to stand up and make a speech, I was lost. If only they would let a fellow talk sitting down it might not be so bad."

Paris was filled with aviation delegates from most of the cities of Europe, and they besieged Curtiss with invitations to fly at meets which were being planned in several countries. He adopted Cortlandt Bishop's counsel that the really important one was the invitation from the Royal Aero Club of Italy to a meet at Brescia, scheduled for the second week in September.

He accepted Bishop's invitation to drive him there. Ward Fisher and Tod Shriver went by rail with the *Golden Flyer*. It was a memorable ride across the Alps to Italy. Bishop drove the big French car to which he was so devoted that he had nearly worn out the brakes and gears. Curtiss sat on the back seat with the chauffeur, and Bishop never realized that the intrepid aviator had the door of the car open a dozen times ready to leap for his life. Like many good drivers he was a craven passenger.

In Italy he was received with such enthusiasm that Curtiss decided the French people were phlegmatic compared with the Italians. No flights had previously been made in that part of the country and when the first contestants took to the air there was vast excitement. Policemen and soldiers sweated and swore in the effort to keep people in the grandstand. When a flyer nosed down for a landing they rushed out on the field to acclaim him, oblivious of the danger. One day Curtiss had to rise five times from an attempted landing. Finally he came down in some rough acreage outside the grounds with an empty fuel tank. After that he never thought of landing within bounds.

The crowds adored him, not only because he won the *Gran Prix* and other flying awards, but because he typified their idea of what an American citizen should be. Here was a man who could do great things without seeming to attach any importance to them. The Wright brothers, their own Calderara and Savoia, had made a tremendous impression by their flights, but this "Koortees" was a hero extraordinary. His reserve and his timidity were interpreted as the outward signs of superhuman qualities.

Moreover, Curtiss took Gabriele d'Annunzio for a flight, and clinched his place in the heart of Italy. When the poet first saw him fly he begged to be taken up. Knowing his machine would stand the burden of one additional man, Curtiss consented. A board was wired to the top of the lower wing, and Curtiss's as well as Italy's first flying passenger clung precariously to the struts and wires.

The crowd below shouted and waved ecstatically as Curtiss landed in a bumpy field nearby. D'Annunzio declared he had never lived until that hour, and that he would commemorate the occasion in the best poem he knew how to write. Enterprising mechanics at the field, seized upon the narrow board on which d'Annunzio had perched, chopped it up, and auctioned off the pieces.

Twenty years after that day a citizen of Hammondsport who was visiting Pompeii was amazed when, having signed the hotel register, the inn-keeper remarked:

"Io conosco un uomo da Hammondsport." (I know a man from Hammondsport.) . . . *"Oh si, si, il grande signor Koor-tees."*

Back in Paris, Curtiss found cataclysmic news. He and his company were being sued for damages in an amount far in excess of all his prize money. He embarked immediately for America, with a feeling of weary distaste for the financial difficulties ahead.

In New York he was warmly hailed as the "Fastest Man of the Earth and the Skies." His mile in 26 2/5 seconds in 1907 had not yet been beaten in any ground machine.

Members of the Aero Club met him at the dock with a gold medal. They dragged him off protesting to a dinner in his honor, though Curtiss was in no mood for social functions. The Wrights had threatened before, now they had acted. He was a thoroughly frightened man. All his pretenses of understanding big business were washed away, and he faced the future gloomily. But before he could settle down to try to find some way out of his difficulties, there was one more essential formality to be disposed of.

It having been officially decided that "it would not be right if there was no one from his home town to shake him by the hand when he landed," a party made up of Mrs. Curtiss and Henry Kleckler, Charles Kingsley and Joseph Friedel had come down to New York to meet him. That pleased Curtiss no end, but he was distressed to learn that a monster welcome was in preparation and that a special train had been chartered for him on the Bath and Hammondsport Railroad.

He was in poor form for the brass bands and the bunting that greeted him when he stepped off the train at Bath into a fine drizzle. There were speeches before his train was permitted to leave for Hammondsport, where it arrived at seven o'clock. There almost the entire population of the village awaited him, ankle deep in mud, apparently oblivious to the downpour of rain.

The "champion aviator of the world" was not permitted to ride in an automobile, for a twenty-man-power team had been appointed to draw him up the hill. Before he could get into his coach of honor several hundred people rushed up to shake hands and tell him how proud they were. Then they pulled him through the mud up the hill to the Curtiss homestead. Sky rockets were fired from under umbrellas. Electric welcome signs dotted the landscape. The citizenry had worked all night and all that day for the occasion. Hammondsport was obliged to give Curtiss as good a welcome as Dayton had earlier in the year given the Wrights. There was no time to have a gold medal made or to get a government official for the reception, but whatever custom, and local patriotism could devise had been done. For the first time since Theodore Roosevelt was elected president, the big village flags had been taken out and dusted. A fresh supply of bunting was ordered in from Rochester, and the local gun squad had shined up the brass cannon. Subscriptions were taken for the gold medal, and a suitcase bought for Curtiss' mechanic, Tod Shriver.

It was a relief to the marchers to find that their triumphal arch in front of the factory had not been washed away. They drew the carriage through it, and led Curtiss into the big factory room, which had been cleared and decorated with flags. No formal program was planned, but Judge Monroe Wheeler delivered a splendid oration.

At least two of the villagers had committed poetry in honor of the victor. Professor Z. L. Parker, of Bath, declaimed:

> *Then Ho for Glenn Curtiss!*
> *Just down from foreign air,*
> *He travels at his option,*
> *And Europe pays the fare.*

While Penelope Gleason Knapp expressed herself in this fashion:

> *He's a lion now and a great big gun,*
> *Jest what t'other feller'd been if he'd won.*
> *An' the Stars and Stripes were histed up,*
> *'Cause our Glenn won the Bennett Cup.*

After that the flying wedges got in their team work and the hero was forced into a corner from which there was no escape until he made a speech.

There were calls for quiet and a tense silence followed while Glenn Curtiss blurted out desperately:

"Ladies and gentlemen, I'm back from France. Had a very nice time. Had a whole lot of luck and a little success. As you know, I just had a common school education and I didn't learn any words big enough to show you my appreciation of my welcome home."

Showing America

Having learned quickly and easily how to fly the *Gold Bug*, Charles F. Willard, New York City's pioneer aviator, proposed to the members of the young Aeronautical Society of New York that they organize an exhibition team. Having had the enterprise to purchase the first commercial aeroplane built in this country, he saw no reason why they should not capitalize on their property. That master showman, Tom Baldwin, had assured him that there were millions of people who would gladly pay to see an aeroplane fly.

Willard's suggestion was adopted and the *Gold Bug* leased by the Aeronautical Society to the Aeronautical Exhibition Company. That was how aviation came to lose its amateur standing in America.

The professional flying careers of the Aeronautical Society members were nipped in the bud by an injunction charging that they were about to destroy a large source of revenue which the Wright brothers would otherwise receive. They were restrained from exhibiting the *Gold Bug* and required to cover damages for exhibitions already held.

The bill of complaint, executed in Washington on August 16, 1909, set forth that the Wrights as "the true, original, first and joint inventors of new and useful improvements in flying machines" had created an invention of "great value."

It was the first tocsin. Aviation's defection into the ranks of commerce was destined to be a painful process. Consciously or unconsciously Willard had thrown the aviation controversy into the fire. He had raised the question of whether anyone in America other than the Wright brothers, and the company which acquired their patent rights, was entitled to build or fly aeroplanes for profit.

The suit against the Aeronautical Society was quickly followed by another, filed on August 25th against Curtiss and the Herring-Curtiss Company, who had built the *Gold Bug,* asking injunctions in the sale and manufacture of the Herring-Curtiss aeroplane. Since Curtiss was still abroad at the time, the papers were served on Mrs. Curtiss and L. D. Masson, secretary of the Herring-Curtiss Company. Both the company and Curtiss still had a leg to stand on in the Herring patents which were supposed to antedate those of the Wrights. Judge Monroe C. Wheeler, counsel for the company, immediately issued a statement that the suits would be defended . . . "by patents taken out by Mr. Herring and associates . . . before the Wrights applied for patents."

Theoretically Herring was the best possible person to

depend on in building an answer in the case. He had a background which included association with Samuel Pierpont Langley, whom he left to join Octave Chanute. Chanute, next to Langley, was the most prominent pioneer in this country. At that time he had twenty-five thousand dollars which he was willing to devote to aeronautical experiment. With Herring's assistance he built several very successful biplane gliders, although they had no recorded success with a power machine. After Chanute abandoned his experiments and turned over the results of his studies to the Wright brothers, Herring claimed to have assisted them until their success in 1903, and to have witnessed their early flights. Moreover, he said he had made a powered flight (as others have since endeavored to prove) before the Wrights.

Backed by the patents which he allegedly had, the Curtiss defense in the suit brought by the Wrights should have been very nearly invincible. But the Herring-Curtiss Company was a house divided, with Herring assuming an aggrieved attitude. He resented Curtiss' conduct in "arbitrarily" withholding certain company profits. Of the total sum of $4,500 plus the sum of $150 for repairs to the plane, collected in payment from the Aeronautical Society, Curtiss had deposited only $3,000 in the company treasury. It seemed a "fair amount" to Curtiss since he had delivered the machine and done the exhibition and instruction work on it, and also since the motor in the machine had been partly built by his company before the Herring-Curtiss Company was created. This situation, of course, gave rise to a "latent hostility" between the two men.

Before Curtiss returned, Herring had contracted to exhibit the *Golden Flyer* for $4,000, which amount, he held, should go into the company proceeds together with all Curtiss' European prize monies and any further money he might earn in exhibition or prize flights. Curtiss, on the other hand, insisted his position was that of demonstrator and advertiser for the firm; that, as such, he was entitled to his salary and savings and any prizes he might win individually.

Herring still insisted that all such monies should go back to the company. Then Curtiss lost his temper and suggested that Mr. Herring should have the privilege of risking his neck for like gains. He realized perfectly by now what a grievous mistake he had made that spring and recognized how feeble were the weapons with which he had armed himself to combat the Wrights' patent suit.

Herring had offered a great many ideas, but none of them proved of value and few were ever tried out. The factory staff, accustomed to looking to Curtiss for ideas, of course resented his suggestions. Although control stock in the company had been issued to Herring principally in payment for his patents, he had never turned them over to the company. These patents included features which it was expected he would utilize in the machine he was to deliver to the U. S. Army for $50,000. After numerous postponements the Army contract was cancelled in September, 1909.

Glenn Curtiss, finding himself in an unhappy dilemma of his own creating, turned to the company directors for help. Luckily his good friends, Baldwin and Judge Wheeler, of Bath, were the other directors. Wheeler who was also counsel for the company and a shrewd attorney, found a way out of the muddle for the time being at least, so that Curtiss could proceed unhampered with his flying plans.

Later, with the company affairs still in a tangle, action was brought in the State Supreme Court to compel Herring to turn over his patents and other property in the company, and an injunction was obtained to restrain him from disposing of any of his stock. But when notice of the action was served on him, at a directors' meeting, he and his lawyer mysteriously disappeared.

With the entire village tracking down the clues to what the *Hammondsport Herald* called "a sensational getaway," the story was pieced together.

Young Rumsey Wheeler was hired at Bath by an unknown third person, who obviously did not dream his driver was Judge Wheeler's son, to drive to a hotel in Hammondsport and call for a stranger, evidently Herring's attorney. Then the boy was directed to proceed cautiously down the west side of the lake where the huge frame of a man—who was undoubtedly Herring—popped up out of the bushes. At this point the driver decided he was involved with a sinister band of criminals and, in a panic, dumped the last two by the roadside while he fled back to Bath with the man who had employed him. The two stranded men apparently walked to a house in the next village, said their car had broken down and were driven to a New York train the next morning.

Locally the somewhat eccentric Herring was cast in the role of villain, especially after the papers reported that he had gone into the enemy's camp and given testimony in support of the Wrights' claims. It was generally conceded though that "Glenn should've had better sense than to take him in as a partner." Nor is there any doubt that Herring really believed in himself, and his personal honesty was unquestioned.

When an opportunity was finally provided to examine Herring's alleged patents, it developed they were all old patent applications dating back to 1895, none of which had ever been allowed. An involuntary petition in bankruptcy was filed by the directors and the assets sold, after

Herring had brought suit against Curtiss and others charging fraud. The technical verbiage of court procedure had it that "because of his difficulty of adjusting his attitude of mind to the requirements of a corporate business which was not solely his own, as his old company had been," Curtiss had been guilty of a "breach of his fiduciary duties" toward Herring as a stockholder. The suit was originally brought also against Cortlandt Bishop, but in his answer he united with the plaintiff, whereupon the charges against him were withdrawn.

Curtiss had a serious quarrel with Bishop, who felt even more bitter about Curtiss' "thick-headed" determination to enter professional flying than he did about his arbitrary attitude on the subject of his corporate "fiduciary duties" to the "only stockholders who had contributed actual capital to the enterprise." He felt, too, that it was most unethical of Curtiss not to stick to his bargain. Accordingly he aligned the said stockholders, who were himself and his brother, on the side of Herring.

Herring's complaint was dismissed when it came to trial in the lower court, but the case was appealed and dragged on through the courts until long after the Wright infringement suit, which had precipitated the situation, was disposed of. The resentment of Bishop, the New York social lion, who was known to loyal Hammondsport only as "that mean old man," did not unbend until years after both the principals had died, when the case was finally settled out of court.

Out of the welter of legality one fact emerges: the Herring-Curtiss Company broke up, and from the wreck sprang more than twenty years of harrassing litigation. Curtiss naturally felt he had been badly fooled, while his former partner went out of the company in a fury. "Charley" Strong, one of Curtiss' old factory assistants, summarized the patent controversy as it appeared in the eyes of the staff and most of the population of Hammondsport:

"Herring came along and said, 'Oh you don't have to worry about patents, I've got a lot of patents.' But when they came to unpack his suitcase he didn't have a thing. Of course the reason G. H. got into this mess was because the Wrights tried to stop him from building aeroplanes. But to my mind it's always been a question who really invented the aeroplane."

During 1904 and 1905 the Wright brothers had carried on experiments in secrecy, although it was known that they had made at least 45 flights in 1905. Because they vigorously resented prying intrusion at the scene of their experiments, they were regarded as mysterious hermits of the air. They were probably acting upon the advice of their patent attorney, H. A. Toulmin of Dayton, who no doubt warned them of the danger of allowing their machine to become public property before their patent rights were adequately covered. In 1906 they obtained patents on what was believed to be a "fool-proof" combination of specifications. Eighteen claims of their patent application, filed March 23, 1903, were allowed.

The Wright brothers had struggled against great obstacles in inventing their aeroplane and had performed untold sacrifices in order to carry through their experiments, only to find that other men all over the world had also been experimenting with a degree of success. Most of these experimenters, in their opinion and within the wording of their patent, as they proceeded to endeavor to prove, were copyists pirating their invention. They therefore launched a gallant attack to establish their exclusive rights in the air.

At first they fought alone and voluntarily, but later

they had to continue the contest since they were bound to sustain the validity of their patents under terms of contract with the Wright Company, formed in November 1909. They had to go on fighting whether they liked it or not, and it seemed rather certain they did not like it. It was in the nature of a nightmare for both sides, and the result of constant litigation was bad financially as well as morally. Even in the early years of the suit defendant Curtiss said it cost him $40,000. It may have cost the Wright brothers even more.

Nor was it, after the Wright Company was organized and capitalized at a million dollars, a legal battle with two men of Curtiss' own financial status. Rather it was a highly professional contest with an invincible group, strong, not only financially, but in social prestige and publicity influence. On the board of directors, together with Orville and Wilbur Wright, were Robert Collier, August Belmont, Russell A. Alger, Edward J. Berwind, Howard Gould, Morton F. Plant, Allan A. Ryan, Theodore P. Shonts, Andrew Freedman and Cornelius Vanderbilt.

The patent injunctions caused discussions all over the country. Whatever any man did in an aeronautical way, beginning August 16, 1909, required plenty of determination and courage. It was the era popularly known as "flying in spite of the Wrights." Nor was this condition limited to the United States. The Wright brothers had filed patent claims in most of the civilized countries in the world and they were prepared to prosecute infringement anywhere under the sun.

The Voisins in France were the only aeroplane builders in the world who had adopted a method of balance which could not possibly be construed as an infringement. They simply built their huge "flyers" like a cellular box-kite with closed or boxed ends. When rocking in the ordinary air currents these vertical surfaces supplied the increase or decrease necessary in maintaining lateral balance.

Any newspaper of the day reflects the patent turmoil. A copy of the *New York World* for March 6, 1910, has this item in a cable dispatch from Paris:

> There seems to be much indignation in France about the attitude of Wilbur and Orville Wright over their patents. Some of the adverse opinion is real, some manufactured. On the other hand there is much public sentiment in the Wright's favor. This is voiced in *La Liberte,* an evening newspaper, which says:
>
> "The Wrights ask only for royalty which certainly is due them. They have a perfect right to protect their patents. Sympathy should go out to them as inventors and pioneers, not as mere chauffeurs or mechanicians who learn to pilot aeroplanes."

(The point about professional distinction for the Wrights probably goes back to a remark made by Orville Wright to the effect that "We are no mechanics, we are scientists.")

However unfounded the Wright brothers' sense of abuse may have been, it was very sincere. They felt personally responsible for the birth of flight and thought ill of anyone who sought to encroach upon their financial rewards. And they were extremely successful in arousing burning sympathy in their favor. It was dangerous to broach the subject in any gathering.

Octave Chanute issued a dispassionate enough statement on the subject, which was, however, labeled rank partisanship for the "Curtiss crowd."

"Wilbur and Orville Wright," he said, "are entitled to a reward for their efforts, that is to say, for the things they actually performed. I know that they thought, at the end of the year 1908, that they were so far ahead of the rest of the world in aviation that they could not be caught up with for from three to five years. Suddenly they discovered that their world's records for speed, duration, distance, altitude, and carrying capacity in the air were not so far in advance that they could not be duplicated or surpassed.

"Now, as to the wing-warping patent, under which they claim damages from others for alleged infringement, this is not absolutely original. On the contrary, many inventors have worked on it, from the time of Leonardo de Vinci. Two or three have actually accomplished short glides with that basic warping idea embodied in their machines.

"Mouillard, a Frenchman, in 1898, tested his machine near Cairo, Egypt. He found at first that his machine was not big enough, and he altered and enlarged it accordingly. He made one successful glide, using the warping wings principle as a basis, but he suffered two consecutive strokes of apoplexy shortly afterward.

"Now, it is one thing to suggest an idea and another to put it into practice. All that came before the Wrights' accomplishments were suggestions or conceptions. It was up to them to put these conceptions into practice, and they did. Probably forty men preceded Bell in conceiving the telephone, but it remained for his master mind to make it practical. Joseph Henry of the Smithsonian Institution was probably the real idealizer of the telegraph but it remained for Morse to put the conception into practice.

"When the Wrights wanted to start, they wrote to me that they had read my book on gliding and asked if I would permit them to use the plans of my biplane. They said that they did not desire to enter aeronautics for financial reward but for pleasure or sport. Indeed, it was only a year ago they felt almost the same way about it.

Instead of hunting or fishing or playing some game during the summer, as other men do, the Wrights took their pleasure in working on aeroplanes.

"I turned over all my data and made them free of it. I was glad that someone wanted to continue the work, which, because of my lack of mechanical ability, I had been compelled to leave off.

"There was money enough to be made, I think, without lawsuits. But regardless of the merits of the controversy, which must be left to the courts for adjudication, it does seem to me as if it was just a little bit too early in the game for the Wrights to shut off experiments—which are perhaps best carried out by public competition—in the way they have tried to do."

Under injunction not to sell or manufacture planes, Curtiss' only asset was his reputation as a designer and flyer. He had available for exhibition purposes the machine which had been built at the factory while he was abroad. While the Rheims machine was still on display at Wanamaker's store in New York City, it would be at his disposal again later.

If aviation was to progress beyond the impasse created by the infringement suits, the public would have to be educated through nation-wide demonstration. Few people in 1909 had any sound conception of how a man could fly through the air without a balloon attachment. Shrewdly enough, Curtiss realized that showing the aeroplane to the people of America might be a step toward bringing popular sentiment to bear on the tangled patent situation. A public aroused to a first hand knowledge of flight might demand that the Wright Company bans be lifted.

On the other hand he was, aside from all selfish considerations, a hopeless proselyte in the cause of aviation, the only cause which seemed to matter to him at the time.

He was bitterly disappointed because most people regarded the aeroplane merely as a wonderful plaything rather than as something that might eventually take its place along with such agents as the telephone and the electric light. So, following in the footsteps of Charles Willard, Curtiss became aviation's first consistent promoter, the chief salesman of commercial flying.

And until the lawyers had arranged with the courts for the building of aeroplanes under bond, there was nothing else for him to do unless he wished to devote his time again to designing motorcycles, which were still being turned out in quantity in the factory.

No sooner had word of his success at Rheims reached America than Curtiss was flooded with cablegrams and letters. Apparently millions of people wanted to see him fly, dozens of promoters wanted to exploit him, and hundreds of ambitious young men wanted to learn to fly aeroplanes. Two exhibition contracts had been closed while he was still in Europe. Curtiss had agreed to exhibit his machine and his flying ability at the Hudson-Fulton celebration in New York during the last week in September, and to do as much at the St. Louis Centennial.

The Wright brothers, too, had departed from their previous policy and agreed to participate for the first time in a public exhibition. The idea of an aeroplane flight in the advanced 1909 manner seemed to give just the proper fillip to New York's monster tribute to two prominent river navigators. It appealed strongly to the popular imagination and people waited impatiently to see the flyers soar overhead. They felt flying had reached a stage where a man could ascend at will as high as he pleased and snap his fingers at the weather.

As a matter of fact there were only three flyers in America who could fly more than a few yards: the Wright brothers and Glenn Curtiss. They were encamped on Governor's Island, waiting for weather.

The fall of 1909 was the windiest in years, and the wind played havoc with the river route. Curtiss, under contract to fly at St. Louis on October 4th, was in a quandary. If he attempted the flight in the face of the wind, he risked having his only available machine wrecked. The public was growing bored with waiting. Just a little flight up the river and a swing around the Statue of Liberty, they said, and everyone would be satisfied.

But the wind persisted and Curtiss, half crazy because the machine performed poorly on two short hops, decided to call Hammondsport. The machine had been built in his absence and it was possible that Henry Kleckler could catch a train and arrive in time to get the plane into flying shape. But long distance reported that everybody in town had gone to the fair. Curtiss afterward said, reproachfully: "It looks like somebody would've stayed at home."

The next day he decided to evacuate, while Jerome S. Fanciulli, a Washington newspaperman whom he had engaged to serve as intermediary between himself and the press, announced that Curtiss had made a flight around the Statue of Liberty at four o'clock in the morning and had then had to pack up and leave, in order to fill his St. Louis engagement. The newspapermen were furious, and felt that whether the flight had actually been made or not, Curtiss had treated them very badly. A few days later, the weather calmed down and Orville Wright made a magnificent flight to Grant's Tomb and back. In addition to the journalistic chill toward Curtiss, another Wright-Curtiss controversy had been born; and one in which Curtiss, by condoning what looked like a shabby ruse, had earned much of the hostile criticism that was heaped upon him.

After the exhibition at St. Louis, Curtiss made two flights

in Chicago. From there he went to Detroit, where he was the guest of R. D. Chapin, general manager of the Chalmers-Detroit Company, whom he had met at Rheims. During this visit he "explained aeroplane building" to the members of the University Club. But it was no speech, as he hastened to explain. He was constantly having to issue denials of fantastic reports that he was going on a lecture tour or even into vaudeville.

At first the flying exhibitions included only two machines. Charles Willard, having taken up his flying career where it was broken off when the Wright brothers enjoined the Aeronautical Society, flew the *Gold Bug,* and Curtiss flew the machine built during his absence, which was a duplicate of the Rheims plane.

When he returned from the Middle West, he found a small mob of would-be flyers awaiting him. He discouraged as many as possible, but some of them hung on in the face of refusal. Most tenacious among them was Bud (J. C.) Mars also of the Aeronautical Society of New York, who was made a member of the exhibition team.

In the formation of this group of flyers, Curtiss had definitely embarked on his professional flying career.

But flying exhibitions at Hammondsport began properly in the absence of Curtiss and under the auspices of a lively young fellow who had previously thrilled New Britain, Connecticut, and other points on the globe. Little red-headed Charley Hamilton, who barely tipped the scales at 103 pounds, had had the world by the tail almost since he could walk. He had traveled extensively as a balloonist, parachute jumper and operator of dirigibles. On the day Bleriot flew across the English Channel, he was in Japan making a record flight in a dirigible across the Bay of Osaki. But when news of Curtiss and his Rheims victory reached him, he sailed for America.

Hamilton was the most prominent of all the young men who wanted to take flying lessons, but Curtiss informed him there was no machine available and that he could not take him on as a student. Then Curtiss left town. Meantime a new aeroplane was completed and hauled out to the hangar at Stony Brook Farm. Without consulting anyone, Hamilton drove out to the field one day when there was nobody about and flew the plane by means of his personal ingenuity, his dirigible experience and his indestructible nerve. He made several short flights before the men at the Curtiss plant realized what was happening. They were greatly relieved when he set himself and the aeroplane back on the earth, unbroken. The next day he was at it once more, unbeknown to them. But Curtiss had returned to town and he was greatly astonished, when Harry Champlin telephoned to say:

"Hey, Glenn, you'd better come right over here. Charley Hamilton has your aeroplane in the air. He has flown fifteen times around the field and doesn't know how to get down."

Curtiss rushed out to the race track and found Hamilton having the time of his life, going out for an endurance record. Up twenty-six minutes altogether, he circled the field nineteen times, made two cross-country flights and negotiated a total of twenty miles. It was obvious from the way he handled the machine that he was an instinctive flyer. Curtiss remained to watch in admiration. In a few weeks Hamilton was an expert aviator and a member of the Curtiss exhibition team. He was daring and lucky always, and a stickler for fulfilling contracts. If their team was billed and the weather was so bad nobody else was willing to risk it, Hamilton usually would save the day. Once in a small town in the state of Washington a blizzard was blowing up just at the hour set for the show to begin. Ham-

ilton explained to the committee that it would be hazardous to fly. The chairman, however, pointed to a determined
group of men watching quietly at one side.

"See those fellers?" he asked. "Well that's the constable
and a lot of special deputies, duly sworn in and armed.
The folks here mostly believe that flying is just a fake.
They think you get their money and then don't get off
the ground. They got the officers here. So make sure you
do fly, or else trouble will come."

Hamilton looked at the sheriffs and then at the sky.

"Looks like I get killed if I go into the air, and get
killed if I don't go. Altogether I believe I'd rather die
in the friendly atmosphere than at the hands of this crowd;
so just tell them the weather conditions are perfect and
that I'll be off the ground in ten minutes."

The wind buffeted his machine and almost upset him as
he raced down the rough field, but he picked up flying
speed and got off successfully. With his life in peril, he
gave some sort of an exhibition, which delighted the crowd.
And the committee prided itself on its firmness in refusing
to "let any lazy showman fall down on them."

Some of the exhibitions given by Curtiss, Willard, Hamilton and Mars were disappointing. Promoters filled with
enthusiasm for gate receipts, neglected to fill the terms of
their agreement. They failed to provide large fields, smooth
and free from obstructions, and expected the flyers to take
off from the town baseball park or from the center of a
half mile race track, surrounded by grandstands, horse
and cattle sheds and high fences. Finally, when "Bud"
Mars landed on top of a parked automobile and Willard
cracked up in the rough enclosure of a track at Memphis,
Curtiss decided to limit the exhibitions to exactly what the
terms of their contracts called for. These did not demand
circular flights, nor flights of any special altitude.

Curtiss with the higher-powered "Rheims motor" ship, as they always called the *Golden Flyer,* decided to undertake the tricky work himself. He saw to it that the crowd got a thrill, even when the conditions of the field were so bad that the less powerful ships could not attempt anything out of the ordinary. He made quick starting records and altitude records. Accurate landings were his specialty and it is a question whether any man ever landed in smaller space with greater delicacy.

Though he never did stunt flying, Curtiss always caught the crowd. Because of his victory at Rheims and also because he had made the world's fastest mile on the ground, his name signified a great deal. But there was something more to it. People seemed to regard him as a blazer of trails through the air, over which they, too, might dare to travel some day.

American sportsmen meanwhile looked to Cortlandt Bishop, still president of the Aero Club and vice-president of the Federation Aeronautique Internationale, "to check the aerial showmen."

And this champion leaped into the fray. Aviation was a gentleman's sport and he wanted to keep it so.

"Soon," he said, "we shall have the best people in the world interested in flying machines." He felt that every effort should be made to combat "the ruthless destruction of a great enterprise and a delightful sport" through an excess of promotional vigor. "The ambition to make money in the show business," he stated with contempt, "has reached the stage where the average flying machine constructor builds more for the road than for the air. In several instances builders have purchased a show tent before they knew their machine would fly, and engaged a press agent before procuring a motor."

Bishop also resented the aviation stock promotion

schemes which were flooding the market, and pointed out
that one company in New York was informing the public
that it was capitalized at fifty million dollars. The indignation of the blooded aeronauts raged on and they were
joined by the Wright brothers who also felt that exhibition
flying was a menace. Wilbur Wright explained their position:

> It was not in scientific experiment that Bleriot
> was injured * and Delagrange killed, nor was
> it for such purposes that Farman and Paulhan
> came to America. We have always encouraged
> real development of this art.
>
> The so-called marvelous advance of French
> invention in the last year has consisted almost
> entirely in copying more and more closely the
> main features on which our patent is based, and
> that is exploited sensationally in money-making
> shows. We think the advancement of this art
> will not suffer greatly if these imitators are com-
> pelled to do some real experimenting and invent-
> ing instead of step by step bringing their method
> of lateral balance closer each day to an exact
> copy of ours.
>
> The pretense that we are endeavoring to pre-
> vent others from doing anything to advance the
> art of flying is absolutely untrue. We have never
> taken legal steps against any man unless he even-
> tually tried to make money for himself by pa-
> rading our particular invention without compen-
> sation to us. No man who confined himself to the
> development of the art has been molested by us.
>
> We really do not know, what the future of
> human flight will be. It will depend upon how
> much money will be available for experimental
> purposes. If the profits resulting from the pres-
> ent public enthusiasm are awarded to individuals

* Bleriot crashed in December, 1909 during an exhibition flight at
Constantinople.

who are interested in flying only as a show business, and who have no intention of spending it or any part of it in developing "the art for art's sake;" the advance will be slower than if the profits are put into the hands of people who are interested in the future usefulness of flying machines more than in immediate spectacles and who will spend a large part of the receipts in experimenting for the purpose of making flying something more than a mere show business. We think the profits of flying ought to bear the burdens of such experiments. The greatest problem in this art today is to find a satisfactory method of conserving the financial floods of today in such a way as to make irrigation possible when the dry season comes again.

The argument was well reasoned but unfair to a number of men whom the patent prosecution measures had deprived of the means of experimenting decently, promoting decently, and manufacturing legally. Bleriot and Delagrange, Paulhan and Farman were none of them greedy sensationalists. Nor was Glenn Curtiss. He stated his own case very simply:

"I had to accept some of the offers to give exhibitions with the flying machine. Up to that time the aeroplane had been seen in but few places in the country. That was one reason. Another was that I could not afford to reject the offers. There was no commercial demand for aeroplanes at the time, and such as we had were useful only as show machines."

The Wright brothers nevertheless had excellent grounds for urging restrictions on exhibition flying, although they themselves later felt compelled to enter the exhibition field. The prizes offered for special flights and exhibitions had resulted in a flock of self-taught professional aviators. Their machines were usually indifferent copies of successful types and were responsible for giving aviation a worse name than it deserved. Very few careful students of aviation lost their lives.

Curtiss, knowing how dangerous flying was, never dreamed of having inexperienced laymen on his exhibition teams. It was his object to educate people, not to frighten them off with broken necks and wrecked machines. He actually did more to give flying a good reputation than men who sat by and pointed out the pretty obvious truth that exhibitions were all wrong. In a sense they were. But in their curious roundabout way, through the showman, the circus sky-rider, they served to raise capital to enable men both here and abroad to continue experiments for the purpose of producing sturdier, better aeroplanes. And it was, at the time, the only way.

Every city of any size felt impelled in the winter and spring of 1909-1910 to stage an air meet. St. Louis, Cincinnati and other cities staged meets of national importance, but it remained for Los Angeles to hold an international air meet in America in January 1910.

It was the first grand conclave of flying folk, and there was much fraternizing, as well as a volume of publicity on the flying events. The Wright brothers were not represented, but Louis Paulhan had brought two Bleriots and two Farman planes from France and there were several Curtiss planes. There were also some fairly successful machines built by enterprising experimenters, including a multiplane, with no less than five wings, built by Professor J. S. Zerbe. Lincoln Beachey and Roy Knabenshue in their dirigibles and the U. S. Government dirigible were frequently in the air; and eighteen balloon ascensions were made.

The sky at the meet was resplendent more than once

with a variety of aircraft, all cavorting above the excited crowds. Huge rectangular tents, instead of the extravagant wooden hangars of the Rheims meet, were provided to house the aeroplanes.

Paulhan captured nearly all the heavier, slower machine prizes, while Curtiss and his team won those for lighter, swifter craft. Many records were broken during the meet. Altogether the Frenchman, who was the particular darling of the audience, won some $19,000 in prizes, while the winnings of the Curtiss team amounted to $6,500, although Curtiss' own prize money only amounted to $3,000. When Wilbur Wright was approached for an opinion on the two stars of the meet he said, accurately enough:

"Aside from Curtiss, Paulhan is probably the most skillful aviator in the world, and really more daring than his American rival."

The statement tends to indicate an absence of personal animosity on Wright's part toward either of the two men who had been compelled by Wright injunctions to post heavy bonds in order to be able to fly at Los Angeles.

Partly because of their joint patent problems, the volatile Paulhan and the taciturn American flyer became very good friends at this time. Curtiss said afterwards:

"Paulhan appreciated all the good and bad features of engineering workmanship, and we had a good time pointing out all the things we did not like about each other's aeroplanes. He did not speak English and I did not speak French, so we got along very well together."

Glenn Curtiss made the opportune discovery at this time that he could manage to fill an aching void in a public speech with a joke. At a dinner during the "brilliant aviation week" at Los Angeles he drafted one of the current favorites:

"A man learns quickly and easily to fly. Ten to one there are here tonight future record-breaking aviators who are as ignorant of aviation as Mr. Rockefeller used to be of golf. Mr. Rockefeller, you know, was asked some years ago if he liked golf.

" 'Golf?' he replied. 'I have never seen the game. I wouldn't know how to hold my caddie.' "

There was much issueing of statements during the Los Angeles meet at the instance of members of the press, according to time-honored custom, on the "future of flying," the advantages of lighter-than-air over heavier-than-air craft and similarly weighty subjects. Curtiss said "for the papers:"

"There are two things at present which are retarding long-continued high flights by aeroplane. The first is the nerve of the operator; the second, the fear that the motor will suddenly stop or develop other troubles that might make a quick descent from a high altitude dangerous. With the going of the motor troubles, will come the greater nerve of the operator."

The Aeroplane Goes to Court

The original injunction in the infringement suit against the Herring-Curtiss Company and Curtiss was vacated at the end of 1909 by Justice Coman of Utica, New York, on the grounds that the terms upon examination, were inconclusive and indefinite. But the rejoicing of Curtiss and other designers was short lived.

On January 3, 1910, the first opinion in the history of jurisprudence directly involving the aeroplane was issued by Judge John R. Hazel of the United States Circuit Court at Buffalo, New York. According to his ruling, the Herring-Curtiss Company was restrained from the manufacture and sale of aeroplanes infringing on patents "for improvements in a flying machine granted May 22, 1906, to Orville and Wilbur Wright and subsequently assigned to the Wright Company."

H. S. Toulmin, patent attorney for the Wright brothers, succinctly phrased the reasoning on which the decision was based:

"Although men have been experimenting since 67 A. D., the Wright brothers discovered the secret whereby aeroplanes, or sustaining surfaces, could be steered and controlled through the air."

The two inventors had found out that by increasing the lift on one side and decreasing it on the other, simultaneously using the rudder at the rear, they could control the center of balance under the machine and keep it poised safely while flying in choppy winds or making turns. Their patent was worded so broadly as to include any method of crosswise balance in which the rear rudder was used in conjunction with the balancing surfaces, whatever their nature.

The burden of the argument for the Wrights was directed against the aileron as a method of obtaining lateral stability. First used in this country by the Aerial Experiment Association at the suggestion of Bell, the supplementary surfaces were hinged to the tips of the main supporting surfaces. Beginning with the *Gold Bug*, Curtiss located the ailerons, or "little wings", between the main wings, first attaching them to two of the forward struts, then to two of the rear struts. Today they are universally used at the trailing edge of the wing.

It was the contention of the socalled infringers that the aileron differed radically from the wing-warping method, since when the wings are warped, or bent, the rudder must be used simultaneously, while the ailerons and the rudder are not interdependent. It was this existence or non-existence of an essential link between the two structural features which was the subject of long and bitter controversy.

The aileron method, the defendants argued, also tended to lend greater strength to the machine, since a wing which might be warped was necessarily weaker structurally. Bleriot, for example, had used the wing-warping method in his earliest planes, but had practically discarded it for this reason. The Aerial Experiment Association had considered using this method but had decided against it because they were convinced that the hinged supplementary surfaces, as they used them, would offer a more dependable means of obtaining lateral stability.

Louis Paulhan, in order to avoid patent complications, had had the stabilizing surfaces which ordinarily hung from the rear of the upper plane removed from his Farman machine. He had installed a non-infringing stabilizing device of his own in the Farman and in two of the other machines he brought to America. These machines, both Bleriots, had crashed, probably because of the improper functioning of the device. But Paulhan's foresight was wasted. He was served with an injunction upon landing, allowed to fly only under bond, and was restrained from any further flights in this country on February 29th. His contract with a promoter, rumored to be for $24,000 a month, therefore had to go by default.

Curtiss, who had been frightened by the prospect of patent difficulties, was strangely unruffled now. And having lost his first terror, he was amazingly resourceful in the matter of contriving evidence. Time after time when the attorneys were ready to give up, he found new ammunition. He issued a statement on the aileron to the Associated Press at Los Angeles on January 10th:

> In the arguments of their lawyers the Wrights
> proved theoretically to Judge Hazel in the Fed-

eral Court at Buffalo that my machines depend on the vertical rudder to maintain equilibrium. I will demonstrate by actual flight that they do not. That will end the action for injunction, for the Wrights' patents hinge on what is called the warping surface.

Their machines have to depend on the vertical rudder to help them maintain their balance. The warping surface of the planes give the machines a turning tendency which the rudder has to overcome.

The rudders on the Curtiss machines have no such function. This demonstration will prove what I say. We are going to take the decision of the judges before the courts.

To prove his contention, Curtiss made a flight with the rudder tied and sealed, but he was far too optimistic in thinking that such a demonstration would end the suit.

While the case was under appeal from court to court, Curtiss was able to continue manufacturing and flying only by posting heavy bonds, which would be forfeited to the Wright Company in case it won the suits and succeeded in its attempt to wipe out competition by law. Most of the aeroplanes in operation at that time were frankly copied after those Curtiss was building. Some were sold openly as "Curtiss-type" planes. But Curtiss paid no attention to the copyists; his hands were full defending himself in the Wright suit. His only retort was to produce each time a better machine than the one the copyists were building. Other than that, he himself had all the orders his factory was prepared to fill.

In January, 1910, the Paris agent of Wyckoff, Church, & Partridge, sent an order for an aeroplane for F. L. De Riemsdyke, a Dutchman, living in France, who had attended the Rheims meet. It was the first Curtiss aeroplane

sold to an individual. Orders had also been received from
Europe for the type motor used in the *Golden Flyer*. Another order for an aeroplane for individual use was placed
with Curtiss in the spring of 1910 by Clifford B. Harmon,
New York City sportsman. A. P. Warner, of Beloit, Wisconsin, who had for years been manufacturing anemo-
meters (wind-registering instruments) for the United
States Government, ordered the third privately-owned
machine from the Curtiss plant. It was set up entirely in
accordance with Warner's printed instructions, and he
made fifteen flights in it the first day.

Since no one was about to instruct him, Warner simply
took the plane off and flew it. This was pointed to as proof
positive that a cool headed amateur could quickly learn to
operate an aeroplane which was properly rigged and which
had been properly tested beforehand.

Free instruction was, of course, included in the purchase
price of the machine, which was usually between $4000
and $5000. Even so, the aeroplanes were sold at a loss.
They cost the Curtiss plant more than that to build, even
if no charge was considered for overhead and engineering
expense and Curtiss' personal time and service. The total
cost per machine was actually about $20,000. But most of
the aeroplanes were sold in the early years between 1909
and 1911, at the expense of other departments of the
factory in the hope of a larger future business based on
volume production.

Production costs of other manufacturers were undoubtedly equally high or even higher, and few were able to
charge more than $5,000 per machine. Expenses were high
at this period because each individual part of the aeroplane
had to be manufactured, and no jobber could supply the
parts required. Most of the patterns had to be designed.
Whatever the mechanics wanted they made, and then

named it. The shop had to supply its own brazing, welding, enameling, wood-treating and doping experts. It had to manufacture its own wire bracings and turnbuckles. Some of the hardwood required was cut on the neighboring hillsides and seasoned, but the bamboo for the outriggers had to be imported from Japan.

A visitor at an exhibition performance looked over a plane one day and then asked Curtiss who stood nearby:

"I suppose you fellows can pretty nearly piece one of those flying machines together from the parts you can buy, can't you?"

Curtiss replied guardedly, "Well, we don't have to make the magnetos."

J. A. D. McCurdy, another former Aerial Experimenter, built a machine that March at Baddeck and sold it to Gardner H. Hubbard, of Boston. A number of sportsmen became pilots during the spring of 1910, and attempted to make flying firsts, and Anthony J. Drexel, Jr., pupil of Bleriot, opened a school of flying abroad.

Aeroplane designing was one of the favorite avocations of the day. It was the initial era of the back-yard aerodynamic laboratory. Some of the machines built were worthy of notice. W. T. Thomas, an Englishman who lived at Hornell N. Y., and was a former employee of the Curtiss plant, built a very successful biplane. E. R. Thomas, Buffalo automobile builder, fitted a flying machine with a Thomas taxi-cab motor, and it flew along the street and above it at a terrific speed. Among the more important American designers were Roger Sommer, who beat the duration record of 2 hours and 21 minutes with which Wilbur Wright won the Michelin Cup, and M. B. Sellers, of Kentucky. This wealthy young Southerner ransacked the world for suitable materials and worked for ten years building an aeroplane with four planes. It was the smallest machine in the world, smaller even than Santos-Dumont's Damoiselle, and was the type of soaring-machine which had been forecast by Lilienthal, Langley and Chanute. It had both wheels and runners. Patents were granted to its builder on July 6, 1909, and he flew it successfully. However publicity was distasteful to him, and he never exhibited it or entered production with his machine.

The Hammondsport factory took it for granted that G. H. would find some way out of the patent tangle. Suppose the courts decided that the aileron could not lawfully be used; in that case it was up to their chief to devise a new machine that would be in every way as good. Curtiss, too, was inclined to look for the inventor's way out.

Many persons trooped to Hammondsport in 1910 who were seeking the help of his versatile plant to give their ideas mechanical expression. Curtiss allowed the shop to take orders for all sorts of strange aerial devices, but refused to build devices which people wanted to pay for but which were obviously impractical. And there were frequent calls for that sort of thing. A Chicagoan, for example, was eager to build a fantastic device which was patterned after the action of the human lungs. Taking in and expelling air, it was supposed to gasp its way across the sky. Curtiss tried unsuccessfully to discourage the man, and finally built him a small model to demonstrate the flaws in his idea. A Buffalo inventor, ordered an ornithopter with an enormous pair of wings like an albatross. He was extremely jealous of his invention and would only practice in the dark, so that no one could pirate his idea. The machine flopped up and down the length of the pasture many times before its designer could be persuaded to abandon the experiment.

These inventors were prepared to pay whatever they

were asked, and sometimes the asking price was large. Their machines therefore constituted a better source of profit than the standard aeroplanes.

The real business of the shop was to discover a substitute for the aileron. Idea after idea received a fair and unprejudiced trial. A machine was built similar to Langley's, with the wings set at a dihedral angle. In flight the wings swept backward and rotated en masse around a vertical shaft mounted on ball bearings. It resembled a monstrous butterfly. They tried Dr. Bell's idea of a vertical fin set over the center of the upper wing, and they also tried attaching a small vertical plane surface to the rear spar at the extremity of each wing. They placed a pair of tiny dihedral wings above the upper wing with a lever to give them a slight rotary motion; they divided the elevators so that they worked separately on either side of a wide tail.

A friendly group of designers cooperated in this work at Hammondsport. Yet each was trying to solve in his own individual manner the problem of a practical balancing device which would be of immeasurable benefit to them all.

Among them was Lieutenant Alexander L. Pfitzner, the Hungarian engineer who had come to Hammondsport to help design the water-cooled engine. He built one of the first successful American monoplanes, a trim, coal-black, low-wing machine similar to the Curtiss biplane, but very different from the European monoplanes. He controlled cross-wise equilibrium by means of sliding panels at the ends of the wing. They were adjusted so that one pushed in as the other pushed out to increase or decrease the wing surface for banking. His persistence and courage in building the monoplane were amazing. Six times he crashed in the trials. Each time he patched up his machine and on January 12, 1910, made a really successful flight. After that he flew it many times.

As generous as he was gifted and tenacious, he announced that all those who were interested in his invention were free to copy it. He wanted only the credit for having done what he set out to do.

While Pfitzner's machine was one of the fastest per horsepower built up to that time, another experimental plane constructed at the same time was one of the slowest. Although its top speed was only thirty-two miles per hour, it could fly in more turbulent winds than faster aeroplanes. It was a tractor biplane with wings of red silk, and was intended to alight on two wheels and a tail skid, but it had an extra front wheel to prevent nosing over in a bad landing. The designer was the most seasoned and picturesque airsailor of them all, Captain Tom Baldwin. He called it the *Red Devil* and entered exhibition work. Although he was nearly sixty years old, he flew it around St. Louis and under the Eads' Bridge spanning the Mississippi, and then took his first heavier-than-air craft to the Orient for exhibition purposes.

Baldwin used the vertical fin overhead for balancing, which was conceded to be clear of infringement claims.

Another balancing method was that devised and patented by Israel Ludlow, who was one of Louis Paulhan's counsel in his contest with the Wrights. He used permanently fixed small dihedral planes, placed between the main plane surfaces at each extremity. Ludlow was badly crippled while experimenting with his device, as were other similarly courageous men of the time.

The net result of all the balancing device experiments was that they all would allow a machine to fly on an even keel, but not one of them were good enough to take the place of the aileron, and those that approximated efficiency would no doubt be called equivalents and still be subject to infringement allegations. Curtiss therefore decided to go on building aeroplanes with ailerons while the patent suit was being fought out in the courts.

With all this heated aeronautical activity in its midst, Hammondsport and most of Steuben County was aero-mad. Almost every day prominent men from many parts of the country visited the Curtiss plant with a view to purchase flying equipment. Sales, both in deference to the patent suit and to limit competition, were being confined to private individuals, and the factory had refused to take orders from professionals. Nevertheless, ten aeroplanes, all on order, were in various stages of completion. Here was mass production. And the item of $1,250,000 to be expended for aviation in the budget of the Minister of War of Russia held out prospects of lucrative foreign business.

The entire village was conversant with all this which augured so well for its industrial future. The citizens not only knew the dry commercial facts about local aviation, but they were on intimate terms with most of the technical developments. A *New York World* writer sent up to report on the various balancing device experiments was amazed at the all-for-aviation spirit that prevaded Hammondsport and its environs. His impressions of the village read:

> In order to reach Hammondsport, you take a typical up-State branch line railroad at Bath. On your way you are quite certain to hear the conductor discuss some of the Curtiss affairs with a passenger. Indeed within a radius of ten miles around Hammondsport Curtiss and aeroplanes are the staple of conversation. Contrary to the rule he is the hero of the community. Everybody in town calls him "Glenn" and feels a proprietary interest in his career. The pride of the village in the young man who patched bicycles and

soared to fame on a flying machine is thrust at
you everywhere.

Hoyt's pharmacy displays a portrait of Curtiss with the legend, "He's Good Enough for
Us." Even in the postoffice the only decoration
on the wall is a portrait of Curtiss. The fact that
Barney Oldfield failed in his recent effort to beat
the "fastest mile on earth" made by Curtiss on a
motorcycle in 1907 serves as fuel to the flame of
their loyalty.

The town was once known as the centre of the
wine aristocracy. But now it is absolutely domin-
ated by the air kings. When you point up the
hill and ask what that group of buildings is, they
tell you with conscious pride, "It's the Curtiss
factory." If you hope to escape the flying industry for a while and wander down into the Kingsley flats you discover two or three buildings
flanking the road on either side which are known
as "the annex" and "the aerodrome." Both are
owned by Curtiss. If you happen to hear the
throb of a powerful motor, somebody is certain
to tell you, "that's Curtiss in his automobile."

The most astonishing experience of the visitor is to hear an eight-year-old child talk about
the virtues of flat surfaces as compared to
curved surfaces with the glib sureness of an expert . . . Or to engage a charming young
woman in conversation while waiting for Pfitzner to fly, and have her give a learned disser-
tation on the thrust of propellers. Everybody in
Hammondsport has an expert's familiarity with
aeroplanes. Boys begin building them when they
are eight years old. Steadily and surely the community is producing a specialized class of mechanics who will probably be the best airship
craftsmen in America.

The academic interest in aeronautics was not confined
to Hammondsport. Cornell University had organized an

Aero Club with 54 members, while the Amherst Aero Club had a membership of 25 members, which was said to be a "strange combination of daredevil collegians and sedate professors." They were making frequent glider flights and balloon ascensions. Notre Dame also had an active Aero Club, and the Harvard Aeronautical Society had 240 charter members. This group's avowed reason for existence was "to do its share for the advancement of aeronautics and particularly to make information accessible to Harvard men." Their program included lectures, model building, glider and volunteer experiments. The Society invited Curtiss to Cambridge for a reception on December 23, 1909.

And erudite Boston, from February 16 to 23, 1910, held the first national aeroplane show in America. The Aero Club of America had had a small exhibit at the New York automobile show as early as 1906, and there had been aviation sections at other indoor shows, but this was the first "decisively aeronautical" exposition. The Boston show, held at Mechanics Hall, boasted exhibits of eighteen heavier-than-air machines, while the recent Paris show had only eight planes on display.

August Herring's biplane was pronounced the best constructed exhibit at the show. Although it had not yet demonstrated ability to fly, its six triangular fins were supposed to form an ideal means of obtaining automatic stability. This award was salve to the feelings of the disgruntled Herring, who had lost the first skirmish in his suit against the Herring-Curtiss Company. He took occasion to point out with considerable scorn that "Curtiss was merely a skillful aviator."

Most of the larger American cities and some of the medium-sized ones, such as Dayton and Hartford and San Diego, had local aeronautical organizations during this period. The exhibition flyers who roved the country from end to end were largely responsible for this civic urge to spread the gospel. A number of states had aero clubs and there was a New England Aero Club, as well as a Pacific Aero Club. These groups were all eager to have the international competition for the Gordon Bennett Cup held on this side of the Atlantic in 1910.

But since the Wright Company had won the preliminary contest over patents, the outlook for the international meet had been dubious. Cortlandt Bishop, as president of the Aero Club of America, had received a steady stream of letters from European aviators who, remembering what had happened to Paulhan's plans earlier in the year, wished to know what guarantee would be offered that they would not be prevented from flying if they brought their machines to this country. Curtiss and other American flyers were in the same position. To settle the question a committee from the Aero Club met with Wilbur Wright and Andrew Freedman, of the Wright Company executive committee, and drew up an agreement which was hailed as an assurance that the next Gordon Bennett Cup Race would be staged in this country. According to the terms of the agreement, the Aero Club recognized the rights of the owners of the Wright patents under the decision of the Federal courts, and refused to countenance infringement of those patents so long as the decision remained in force.

In order to encourage aviation, in the meantime, both at home and abroad it was agreed that the Aero Club of America, as the American representative of the Federation Aeronautique Internationale, should approve only such public contests as were licensed by the Wright Company, and that the Wright Company, on the other hand, should encourage open meets wherever approved by the Aero Club by granting licenses to such promoters as made satisfactory arrangements with the company for its compensation for use of patents. At such licensed meets any machine of any make might participate freely without obtaining further license or permit.

But the early exhibition flyers of this country were a stubborn lot. Widespread and intensive experiment had demonstrated that the aileron was the only balancing device for the fast, maneuverable type machine necessary for competitive or exhibition purposes. Therefore they continued for the most part to fly aileron-equipped machines, and without licenses from the Wright Company—as prescribed in the official dictum of the Aero Club of America.

Down the Hudson

Early in 1909, Joseph Pulitzer conceived the idea of a flight between New York and Albany as a climax to the Hudson-Fulton pageant. The dramatic contrast of an aeroplane flying over the course of Hendrik Hudson's sailing vessel and Robert Fulton's steamboat, so fascinated the publisher that he forsook his entrenched position in respect to one, at least, of the two pet follies of the day: expeditions to the North Pole and flying. He cabled Don Seitz, business manager of the *New York World,* an order to post a ten thousand dollar prize for the man who should fly over the distance between Albany and New York City during the two weeks of the Hudson-Fulton celebration.

It was a revolutionary step. No newspaper had ever made an effort to foster aeronautics in this country. The American press had until 1907 been inclined rather to sneer at flying, particularly after Langley's aerodrome sank, instead of soaring. Little effort had been made to direct public interest toward the Wright brothers, who had, on December 17, 1903, accomplished the concededly impossible.

In England, Lord Northcliffe, publisher of the *London Daily Mail,* had consistently encouraged aviation. His initial prize offer of ten thousand pounds for the flight from London to Manchester met with considerable derision when it was first made in 1906, and it was not claimed until 1910. But in the meantime other *Daily Mail* prizes had been offered, including the one of a thousand pounds which inspired Bleriot to make the first Channel flight. Gordon Bennett, owner of the *New York Herald,* had donated an annual cup for aeronautics and one for aviators, with cash rewards attached. But the *New York World,* at Joseph Pulitzer's behest, was the first American newspaper to follow in the *Daily Mail's* footsteps.

A non-stop flight over the 150 miles lying between New York and the state capital was not as preposterous a conception in 1909 as the Manchester flight of 186 miles was in 1906, but it was still relatively improbable. Hendrik Hudson had been dependent only on the wind to propel his sailing vessel; the *Clermont* could carry enough coal to make steam for the entire journey. But an aircraft was unable to bear the weight of sufficient gasoline. It must return to the surface of the earth enroute for a fresh supply of fuel. The fact that 24.6 miles was adjudged the longest continuous flight in this country during 1909 is an indication of cruising range.

The prize competition as officially announced for the *New York World* by the Aero Club of America on February 4, 1909, was open to lighter-than-air as well as heavier-than-air craft. But although dirigibles had remained aflight for more than 30 miles, nothing comparable to the required distance had been negotiated. Nevertheless, many a builder of aircraft, professional or amateur, swallowed hard at the breath-taking possibility of answering the *World's* challenge, and proving that he could fly that historic stretch. The whole country was wondering how soon this first aerial highway would be opened.

Hendrik Hudson in the *Half Moon* had required five days to explore the river down to Manhattan Island in 1609. Robert Fulton brought Albany and New York within thirty-two hours of each other in 1807 on the first trip of the *Clermont*. In 1835, the steamboat *Champlain,* "raced from New York to Albany", in nine hours and thirty-one minutes. The Empire State Express of the New York Central Railroad made a record run of two hours and forty minutes in 1909. And in April, 1910, that hardy pedestrian, Edward Payson Weston, startled the country by walking from Albany to New York in the same length of time it took the *Half Moon* to sail down the Hudson. The question was: how will aircraft measure up against the other pace-makers?

Although no aviators came forward to compete for the ten thousand dollar prize during the Hudson-Fulton celebration, three balloonists pluckily served notice of entry. On the 26th of September, Tom Baldwin and George L. Tomlinson took off from 119th Street and Riverside Drive, which spot had been renamed Fulton Flight Square for the occasion. Tomlinson, was a wealthy sportsman from Syracuse and inventor of a rifle cleaner, as well as an enthusiastic aeronaut. He was forced down almost immediately by a leak in his gasoline tank. Baldwin, because of his heavy load, fell into Spuyten Duyvil Creek when one of his gears broke. Neither flyer was severely injured. John Roeder, an electrical engineer from Germany, was unable to get off the ground.

There was no everhead convoy for the flotilla of gaily decked steamships and sailing vessels that voyaged up the Hudson. It was, after all, Robert Fulton's and Hendrik Hudson's fortnight of glory, except for Orville Wright's twenty-mile flight from Governor's Island to 122nd Street and back.

Curtiss had never been one to miss competing for a good prize offer, if there was a fair chance to win. This time his equipment was too far below the par set by the conditions of the contest. He had taken a bad enough gamble in entering for the Gordon Bennett Race. That, however, was a question of being able to fly faster than the other fellow. This was a question of being able to fly far enough, and of flying over rugged country and water. Some day a trip of 150 miles would be nothing at all, but just now they weren't ready. There was so much to be learned; that matter, for instance, of flying off the water. If he could do that, it would be possible to make an emergency landing on the Hudson.

When the Herring-Curtiss Company was incorporated, less than two months after the prize award was announced on February 4, 1909, there was a provision in the charter specifying: "A machine will also be built to operate over water." It pointed to a smouldering resolution to tackle the Albany flight during the Hudson-Fulton Celebration. But instead of continuing the hydro experiments undertaken the previous year, Curtiss went to France. On his return, his exhibition work, law-suits and experiments with balancing devices left him little time, but he made many fruitless efforts to solve the off-the-water flying problem.

Although the *World* prize offered for the Albany flight was immediately renewed for another year, no contestants presented themselves until May 1910 when the conditions for the flight were modified. The new conditions were liberal enough. They called for a flight to be completed within twenty-four hours, with two stops allowed for re-fueling. The start might be made from the metropolis or the capital at the option of the contestant. It was necessary merely that he should take off from within the limits of one city and make his final landing within the limits of the other. Glenn Curtiss' eyes widened as he read the announcement of the new rules in the Sunday *World*. A number of planes and flyers would now be in a position to qualify. It would be wise to get started as soon as possible.

But when the family learned of his intention, there was considerable discussion. Mrs. Curtiss was frankly opposed. She was afraid of the terrain rather than of the aeroplane, as she had flown with Curtiss several times. Harry and Martha Genung took part in the debate; Martha Genung favored the attempt, while the others were dubious. But Curtiss had made his decision. If he could satisfy himself that conditions were right, he would attempt the flight.

The next morning he stepped across the driveway to his office and hastily looked over the mail. Then he went to the door leading to the factory and called:

"Tell Kleckler and Merrill to come here."

When Kleckler got the message, he pulled his oilstained cap down tighter over his forehead and said: "Come on, Dame, I guess G. H. has another one of his ideas."

They found him out in a corner of the old motorcycle shop. Merrill perched on a high stool, while Kleckler found a squatty one, and Curtiss stood leaning against a wall and shuffled one foot as he talked. (If he happened to be out of doors he always kicked at the sand with that foot).

"Why can't we get something ready right away to fly from Albany to New York? I'd like to take a crack at that prize and I see they've fixed the rules so it can be done with two stops."

Kleckler's guess had been right. He asked doubtfully: "But where are you going to find two places to stop at? How do you figure getting across the Catskill Mountains?"

"I figure on stopping only once, and I'll follow the river."

Merrill squinted. "What'll you do, tie a canoe under you like Orville Wright did when he flew up to Grant's Tomb?"

Curtiss scowled, remembering his own unsuccessful attempts to get a plane to take off from the lake.

"Well, I thought maybe we could rig up that one you're working on now so it won't turn over if I have to come down. What do you think of something like this?"

He turned around and sketched his idea on the wall. They talked it over in a preliminary way, as the three of them always did on a project. Then usually Merrill whittled on a little wooden model of the completed ship until they were satisfied with it. But in this case, it was just a matter of reinforcing one part or paring down another, and building the flotation gear. The time element was important because Curtiss wanted to get started in a few days.

The requirement was for a plane fast enough to cover the distance within a reasonable time and yet stout enough to carry the equipment necessary to keep it afloat in case of a forced landing in the water.

A slender sausage-shaped tube of rubberized cloth, filled with ground cork, was attached to the fore and aft member of the landing gear for its entire length. In front of and a little below the axis of the front wheel there was attached a small hydro-vane which was supposed to keep the plane from somersaulting. A pair of cylindrical metal tanks was carried, one on each side of the center section, under the lower wing. This flotation gear, together with the fuel and passenger load, brought the total weight to 1,004 pounds, which was the heaviest load per square foot carried up to that time. The machine measured thirty feet fore and aft.

In order to test the equipment, Curtiss flew over the lake and landed near the shore where the water was shallow but still deep enough to determine whether or not it would somersault. The result was very satisfactory, and he knew it would be a tremendous comfort to feel that he could alight safely on the river and probably salvage the plane.

Having flown the aeroplane for forty minutes over the lake, he concluded his chances for the prize were better than even if he got a head start on the other contestants. Albany, he decided, was less hazardous to start from than New York, since there were possible landing places in case of an early forced landing. He ordered the plane crated, and shipped to Albany. Then, accompanied by Mrs. Curtiss and his manager, Jerome S. Fanciulli, Curtiss made a trip down the Hudson on a dayline boat in order to get the best first-hand data on atmospheric conditions along the route. Questions about air currents received full and explicit answers from the captain of the boat. He thought Curtiss was just making conversation and cordially invited the party up to the pilot house where they might have a good view of the country along the route.

Suddenly the Captain grasped the fact that this passenger was seriously debating whether to fly under or over the bridge at Poughkeepsie in the course of a flight from Albany to New York. Curtiss, he concluded, was mentally irresponsible. Thereafter, his chronic reply to all queries was: "Oh yes, I guess so." But fortunately, he had previously revealed certain facts about air currents which Curtiss needed to know.

As soon as Charles Hamilton, one of the Curtiss exhibition flyers, received word of the new provisions, he wired his entry to the *World*. He was still in the South, where he had made some notable flights, and had beaten Curtiss's quick start record of 5½ seconds by getting off in a space of 70 feet in 3.9 seconds. Since Hamilton represented competition of sorts, and had notified the *World* he would be ready to start from Governor's Island on June 3rd. Curtiss lost no time in mailing his entry notice, in compliance with the stipulation that a formal notice must be filed at least twenty-four hours in advance.

He also sent the following letter to the sponsors:

Gentlemen:

I have today sent my official notification to the Aero Club of America, announcing my intention to try for the *World's* $10,000 prize for a flight between New York and Albany, and making an official entry for that prize. It is my intention to start from Albany on Thursday morning, May 26, 1910.

For over a year I have made exhaustive experiments with the object of perfecting a machine which would start from and alight on the water. It was my intention to give such a machine its first practical test by attempting to fly from Albany to New York over the Hudson River, with the hope of obtaining the *World's* most commendable Hudson-Fulton prize.

While my experiments have proved very successful, they have not been completed. It is my belief that the incentive offered by the *World* to aviators and experimenters has been responsible for considerable activity similar to that in my own case.

If I should be successful in winning your prize, I would have only one regret; that is, that there would be no further inducement for other aviators to make the same flight.

Yours very truly,

G. H. Curtiss.

As the news of the prospect of an early take-off in the ten thousand dollar flying contest became known, public interest skyrocketed. Hamilton was expected daily; the Wright exhibition flyers had sent in an entry notice, although it had not been decided who was to fly the plane. Sixteen-year-old Cromwell Dixon announced that he would enter with a four cylinder dirigible. James E. Plew of Chicago, former Western agent for Curtiss motorcycles, notified the *World* he was building a machine to compete the week of June sixth.

The next morning after sending in his entry, Curtiss drove to the northern end of Manhattan Island. He was fairly sure he could complete the trip to Governor's Island with one refueling stop, but he wanted to acquaint himself with that territory in case he felt the need of landing there. He found such a place at Inwood, where the Harlem and the Hudson rivers meet, and just within New York City limits.

On the 25th, Curtiss and his wife and Augustus Post, who had been appointed official timer, caught an early afternoon train for Poughkeepsie which was 87 miles south of Albany. Four hours were spent scurrying about the countryside in an automobile, looking for a suitable landing place. Their first choice was the lawn in front of the State Hospital. Superintendent Taylor beamed and said:

"You might as well land here as anywhere. All the crazy people land here eventually."

But Curtiss decided, notwithstanding, to go elsewhere since there were too many trees and rocks. The Vassar lawn was equally impracticable, and Curtiss was beginning to think he might have to land in the river, tow the machine ashore and take off again from the dock. But there were no docks large enough, as he needed at least a hundred feet, and there was a further danger of getting his magneto wet. It was essential that a place be found to land at Poughkeepsie, as he dared not risk flying further than that on the first lap.

Three miles south of town, at Camelot, they found a fairly level piece of ground near the river and not too closely bordered by trees. The owner, F. W. Gill, readily agreed to the use of his meadow as a landing field. A Poughkeepsie dealer promised to be on hand with a supply of gasoline, oil and water.

At Albany they found the *Albany Flyer* at the Rensselaer's Island mud flats, ready to start the next morning. But Henry Kleckler insisted that the ends of all bolts should be painted with shellac after the nuts had been screwed up so as to make sure that no nut would slip. The search for shellac and the process of applying it caused a three hour delay. Then it was necessary to wait for favorable weather, and Curtiss was compelled to postpone his start until the next day.

Previously, he had taken one further precaution. Within certain limits, Curtiss had confidence in the efficiency of his motors, but he knew that to save weight they had been trimmed down to the limit. At Los Angeles that January, Hamilton had been forced down on a cross-country flight, after fifteen miles, when a crankshaft snapped. He was none too certain that his engine would fly the required distance.

The Elbridge Engine Company at Rochester was turning out a small 40-horsepower engine that seemed to be standing up very well. Irwin DeLong, their engineer, was greatly surprised when motor-builder Curtiss walked into his office and said:

"I'd like to see one of your engines on the test block."

"You sure can," DeLong announced with enthusiasm. "I didn't suppose you were interested in anything but your own motors."

"To tell you the truth," Curtiss told him, "I don't feel any too sure the motor will stand up through the New York flight."

They put a motor on the block for him and gave it a long, hard run. Curtiss checked the diameter and pitch of the propeller, and with an old fashioned tachometer counted the speed at which the motor was able to turn it. It did not have the power and speed of his own engine, but it would do in an emergency. Better yet, the crank case flanges were of such dimensions that the motor, if necessary, could be quickly substituted for his own.

He arranged with DeLong to have the motor thoroughly broken in and then crated and sent with a mechanic to follow him down the Hudson by rail.

With the *World* ballyhooing the event and other papers doing likewise scores of seriously interested and merely curious people flocked to Albany on May 26th. *The New York Times* chartered a special train consisting of the New York Central's fastest locomotive and four cars to carry the official observers and *Times* reporters and cameramen down the river abreast the *Albany Flyer*. The stage was set for a train-plane race and the *Times'* first big aviation news-beat.

The pace-making train was under steam on a siding with the right of way to New York, reporters were plentifully on hand, and the crowds were waiting. Everything was in readiness for the start, everything apparently, except the aviator and his aeroplane.

By Friday, the 27th, the *Albany Flyer* was ready, and Curtiss eager to take off, but the unsettled weather continued. To set out against a stiff, adverse current of wind would mean certain failure. The United States Government weather bureaus at Albany and New York kept him in touch with conditions along the route.

Hundreds of persons visited the tent which housed the aeroplane. Among them was Ezra Benedict, young Albany flying fan. He begged Curtiss not to take off before Saturday because it was his fourteenth birthday. To add weight to the argument, he produced a scrapbook of clippings about his youthful exploits. Curtiss kept Ezra with him the entire day much to the boy's delight. His efforts to promote a postponement of the flight's start were, as it turned out, beside the point.

Curtiss was up before four o'clock daily and out at Rensselaer Island, studying the air, hoping for a let-up in that steady wind from the south. Henry Kleckler was on duty by three every morning, ready to call Curtiss if conditions seemed favorable. They killed time puttering around on the machine, while Curtiss tried to dodge the interviewers who all voiced the same petulant note:

"When are you going to fly . . . ?" "Do you really intend to fly . . . ?" "Do you think you can make such a flight . . . ?"

While the newspapers bickered and scolded, the engineer of the special train growled his resentment of the delay. Each morning at daybreak, crowds came out to the mud flats from Albany and went back disappointed. The adventure was rapidly losing caste.

Saturday at first promised well. The aeroplane was rolled out of the tent, then the south wind blew up once more and grew steadily stronger. A larger crowd than ever was up before breakfast time and flocking to Rensselaer Island. The weather forecast had read: "Fair; light winds."

Neither the crowd nor the reporters made an effort to conceal their disappointment when the aviator announced that no start would be made that morning. Curtiss gritted his teeth, forced a weak smile and then reiterated: "No flight." Had he started that morning he would have run into a small gale long before he reached New York.

The *Albany Flyer* was ordered back to her tent and Curtiss returned to the Hotel Ten Eyck. There, in the morning papers he read the disquieting news that Charley Hamilton was in New York, preparing for flight. He had just announced that regardless of weather conditions, with one exception, he would start not later than Tuesday, the 31st, to fly up the Hudson to Albany. The one exception he made was in case of a strong wind from the north. In the face of that he knew he would be at a great disadvantage if Curtiss came down the river with the wind, while he flew against it.

"I shall do it sure enough," the little flyer had vowed gamely. "The *World* can get that big check ready. If I can, I will do it without a stop at all."

According to the news story of the contest, Dr. William Greene of Rochester, former dirigible flyer, had ten mechanics working day and night on a plane in which he would attempt the flight if Curtiss failed.

Curtiss tried to shrug off the tidings, but his nerves were tense to the breaking point, and he spent a most unhappy day.

The third postponement brought a storm of indignation. The attitude of the New York newspapermen at Rensselaer Island was already far from friendly toward Curtiss. They had not forgotten the Hudson-Fulton celebration hoax and some of them were not sorry of an opportunity to retaliate. In their opinion, Curtiss was just looking for free advertising, and they placed bets among themselves that he would not even make a start. His silent reserve seemed like indifference and they were angered by his dogged "leave-it-to-me-I-know" manner.

Crowds had waited for three days along the river banks,

and a Poughkeepsie editor gave vent to the general reaction when he raged in print:

> "Curtiss gives us a pain in the neck. All those
> who are waiting to see him go down the river
> are wasting their time."

The next day would be Sunday, and the aviator stated gravely: "I'm not right anxious to make the flight on a Sunday. I wouldn't like to offend anyone, and many perhaps might think it wrong. But if there is a good chance, I don't think I ought to miss it. Real good chances are so rare, I daresay people will forgive me."

Sunday morning was ideal, and the weather reports from all stations along the Hudson River were favorable. Curtiss reached Rensselaer's Island at five o'clock in the morning and Henry Kleckler reported joyfully:

"Everything is good and ready."

"Well, let 'em sleep a while," said Curtiss, referring to the mechanics.

When he got back into the automobile and started for town, some of the bystanders thought the flight was off. As a matter of fact, he was dashing back to the hotel to tell Mrs. Curtiss and her party to get ready to take the special train. He also wanted to delay the start, long enough to make sure the wind would not come up with the sun.

Having officially notified the New York *World* representative and the observers for the Aero Club that he was ready to start, he returned to the Island. As soon as Kleckler saw him, he hurried over to the special train which was scheduled to start at the signal of a flag raised on a tall building when the motor was warmed up. Into his pockets he had stuffed a hammer, a screw driver, a brace and bit, a little wire and some tire tape.

While Tod Shriver tuned the motor, the *Albany Flyer's* pilot knotted the twine that supported his fisherman's long canvass waders around his neck. These were worn for warmth rather than for their waterproof qualities. He had found them the best idea for a flying costume. He put a chauffeur's leather jacket over them, reversed his cap, slipped over his goggles, and climbed into the seat.

The motor was running perfectly. Curtiss took off at three minutes past seven o'clock, and without so much as a farewell wave, headed due south at an altitude of 500 feet.

Down on the ground the crowd of a hundred people waved their hats and cheered, while some, according to a contemporary account, "in a delirium of excitement wrung each other by the hand." Jacob L. Ten Eyck, who was the official starter, said with quivering earnestness:

"Whether this flight is successful or not, there is the fact that because of a few sticks, a number of bits of wire, some widths of cloth, a motor, and a superb courage, none of us will ever forget this day."

As the pre-arranged signal flag appeared, Engineer "Charley" Lewis gave a happy war-whoop, sprang into his cab, and sent his iron horse thundering down the east bank of the river. He was still wrathy because someone had chaffed him about being unable to keep up with the flying machine. Curtiss watched the railroad tracks and when he caught sight of the train, slowed down until it caught up and then flew along with it for miles.

The river craft all along the way gave rousing toots and the crews waved their caps as the *Albany Flyer* flew above them. Arrangements had been made in some of the towns along the river to signal the news of Curtiss' departure to the outlying inhabitants. In this manner, word traveled quickly downstream. He could see people hurrying to both

shores and people straining out of windows waving hand-
kerchiefs.

The train, traveling 49 miles an hour, kept up until
the city of Hudson was past, then the tracks swept inland
for a piece while Curtiss stayed with the river. At 8:10,
he passed Staatsburgh, cleared the arch of the Poughkeepsie
bridge and picked out the American flag which Farmer
Gill had run up to guide him. He saw Gill in the middle
of the meadow in his shirt sleeves, flagging him down
with his coat.

Curtiss glided in above the trees at the edge of the pasture, and landed safely one hour and 24 minutes after
leaving Albany. But the man who had agreed to bring oil
and gasoline had not considered Sunday as a possible flying day.

Five hundred automobiles from Poughkeepsie in the
meantime raced out to the field. The motorists rushed over
to the *Albany Flyer* and, in the exuberant vernacular of
the day shouted, even bellowed: "Oh you Glenn Curtiss!"
and "I guess maybe you're not the class!" They congratulated the aviator and begged to be allowed to shake hands
with him. Two of the first arrivals drove off to find the
necessary supply of fuel.

Poughkeepsie was tremendously excited, and the Reverend William K. Hubbard, pastor of the Mill Street Bap-
tist Church announced that conditions had come to a
"pretty pass" when church members should so far forget
themselves as to allow such a spectacle to draw their
thoughts away from the proper observance of the Lord's
day. That morning at church, he preached:

> "It seems strange to me, that this man could
> not have picked out one of the six other days
> of the week in which to make his trip."

But most of the members of his flock forgave Curtiss, just as he had hoped they would, and one of the deacons of the church joined in the cheering, and congratulated the Sabbath violator, before he hurried back to town for the services.

The escort train had arrived at Gill's Mill Dock station, and the passengers clambered up the embankment to the meadow. Kleckler checked over the machine while Curtiss gave the reporters such impressions of the flight as he could muster. He had noticed particularly that when flying several hundred feet above the water, he could see to a much greater depth than when flying close to it.

It took the volunteer searchers some little time to locate the needed fuel supply, and Curtiss was beginning to get restless when the accommodating motorists returned. The tanks were filled, the field cleared, and Curtiss took off on the second lap of the flight.

Henry Kleckler and Fanciulli, who failed to respond promptly to his warning signal, were summarily left behind by train engineer Lewis. He was already convinced of the superior speed qualities of the flying machine, and did not want to lag any further behind than he could help.

From Poughkeepsie down, the going was harder because of the mountain drafts. It was so rough that Curtiss tried descending, but found the air even more turbulent closer to the surface. He started climbing and found steadier air at between five hundred and seven hundred feet. It was his first lesson in the wisdom of flying high.

Then Curtiss sighted West Point and recalled what the boat captain had told him about the treacherous air currents between Storm King Mountain and Dunderberg. A down draft from the gorge caught the machine, and tossed it about as if it were a paper kite. He thought the flight was ended, but the *Albany Flyer* weathered the awkward current somehow and steadied. Then another gust from one of the gorges tossed him into a bank so steep that the machine side-slipped to within a few feet of the water before he could recover. By sheer strength and determination he righted the machine, regained his lost altitude and proceeded on down the river. The crowds along the Palisades watched him and marveled at his skill.

Before long, Curtiss sighted the Metropolitan Tower and below it a fringe of skyline, and decided to land at Inwood. The oil supply was running very low. He thought he had been too enthusiastic about using the oil pump lever, until investigation the next day disclosed a bad leak in his oil tank.

Curtiss flew across the Harlem River and landed on the grassy lawn of the Isham estate. Finding more of an incline than he had anticipated, he jumped down and held the machine to prevent it from rolling down the slope. Three boys appeared almost immediately to relieve him while he ran to a telephone. It was necessary to notify the *World* of his arrival in New York. The metropolis was eagerly expectant. New Yorkers had been watching for days the flag-staffs of the Pulitzer Building, the Singer Building and the Hotel Astor for the pre-arranged signal. The Hotel Ansonia at 73rd Street and Broadway displayed from the fifteenth floor balcony the banner which in December would tell New York that the ice on the ponds in Central Park was navigable. But this was May, and the citizens knew the white flag with a red ball in the center meant that Glenn Curtiss was on his way.

All morning New Yorkers followed the progress of his flight by means of bulletins posted frequently in front of the Pulitzer Building and at United Cigar stores throughout the city. The large hotels and clubs also were advised regularly of his progress by bulletins in the main lobbies. At the Hotel Gotham the night clerk called every guest in the hotel, by request, to let them know that Curtiss had left Albany.

When the bulletin that he had passed Yonkers went up there was a grand exodus to the roofs. His stop at 214th Street put a damper on the crowds, who began drifting downstairs again. But they rushed back when the news was flashed that Curtiss was off again. All those who were up high got an unobstructed view of the *Albany Flyer* from the moment it passed Grant's Tomb. Then those who could, hurried down to Governor's Island, while others clustered around the Pulitzer Building, where he would have to go, of course, to get his ten thousand dollar check.

The terms of the *World* contest did not demand that, having crossed the city limits, the contestant should fly on down to Governor's Island. But Curtiss knew well enough that he had disappointed New York once before; this time he would make it up to them and show his critics that he was not a faker. So he refueled and took off again from Inwood, and as he came flying by, Riverside Drive and the wharves and docks of the Jersey shore echoed with the shrieks of the crowds. Every steam whistle in the vicinity blew, the boats on the river kept up a steady tooting, and cannon boomed a welcome.

He circled the Statue of Liberty and set his plane down on the sandy parade ground at Governor's Island at 11:58, having completed the trip two minutes ahead of time, since he had planned, if all went well, to make it by noon.

The officers and men of the garrison rushed to the parade ground with Colonel John Van Rensselaer Hoff, Surgeon-General of the Department of the East, among the first to welcome him. Curtiss' leading rival ran up, out of breath, to shake hands and assure him:

"It was beautiful, Glenn. No one could have done better and very few half as well. There is nobody I would rather have seen win, but I think I would have got it if you hadn't."

Hamilton had left breakfast as soon as he heard of Curtiss' departure from Albany, and spent the morning in the neighborhood of the Pulitzer Building reading the bulletins of the flight. He watched the plane pass over the city and then hurried to Governor's Island to greet the victor.

The *Albany Flyer* was rolled into a shed, while Curtiss doffed his flying outfit, and proceeded to the offices of the *World*. There the aviator became so engrossed in the original cartoons lining the walls that his attention was with some difficulty brought back to the presentation ceremonies. After an introductory speech by William Johnson, one of the Sunday editors, J. Angus Shaw, secretary of the publishing company, presented the check. And then began the serious business of the day: interviews, all shapes and sizes.

Page after page came off the presses that day acclaiming the achievement. The *New York Times* devoted six pages to the flight, which was record space for a single news event. They virtually took the champion apart to see what made him run in the assiduous effort to satisfy the public curiosity. Typewriters turned out dripping encomiums.

It was not easy to dress up this unassuming person as a super-hero, and for the most part the interviewers were so impressed with his sincerity and simplicity of manner that he defeated any desire they may have had to make him appear glamorous. A *World* reporter however, gave an honest impression of Curtiss, the man, rather than the conquering aviator:

"Glenn Curtiss speaks quietly, looks constantly to others for suggestions or amendments and is not at all forward. But there lurks within him the element of enthusiasm that goes to make up great adventurers, and it speaks out from his eyes, which are the most expressive part of his face. A well trimmed dark mustache covers his lip, and back on a high forehead thin, black hair is carelessly flung. His fingers are long and shapely, his feet small.

It was so difficult to get colorful copy on the flight that the reporters labeled him the Sphinx of Aviators. He was willing enough to talk, but he never made orderly mental footnotes when he flew, for subsequent quotation. And the reporters, knowing well how newspaper readers adore learning what went on inside the hero's mind during the journey, exactly how he felt when he knew he had won, labored fruitlessly to draw the little human interest touches out of him.

When his wife rushed from the Grand Central Terminal to meet him, she said: "Glenn, you did splendidly!" Instead of saying something affectionate and quotable, his reply was an abrupt, "You bet."

Only for the same *World* reporter who described him so understandingly did he unbend enough to admit shyly:

"I couldn't hear the blamed old steam whistles that greeted me as I neared the city and as I flew down the Bay, but I could see the escaping steam that marked the blow-off. And every time I saw one blowing, I let go one hand to wave to that little cloud of white steam. I knew they couldn't see me, but I felt I had to do it, and once, when I noticed I had passed one saluting boat without responding, I turned around in my seat to wave my hand. Funny thing, but it seemed as though all the success of my finish depended on replying to the salutes."

Every member of the Curtiss party was interviewed at length. And Mrs. Curtiss confessed, in the coy manner of the period, that Mr. Curtiss had promised to buy her "a dandy little runabout" with part of the prize money.

The story of the day as told by the New York press drew this comment from a *New York Evening Mail* writer:

> In every newspaper that you picked up yesterday you read a thrilling account of the great achievement of Glenn H. Curtiss. The detailed description of his wonderful flight stirred every emotion in you. Chills ran up your spine and tears of joy came to your eyes as you read on and on of the courage of the man who had propelled his airship* at a speed of fifty-three miles an hour at a height of a thousand feet above the earth. He realized all of the time a broken bolt or some little thing gone wrong might dash him to death.

With the name and the statistical details shifted ahead seventeen years, it might be a verbatim quotation from a newspaper of the day after Lindbergh's solo flight across the Atlantic.

According to the official report, Curtiss actually covered a total of 150 miles in two hours and 51 minutes flying time, at a speed of about 52.63 miles an hour. The distance to the city limits from Albany was 137 miles, and the time two and a half hours. The average speed of the escort train was 49.6 miles.

The interest of the Metropolitan papers in the flight re-echoed all over the country. The CURTISS AVIATION BOOK, published in 1912, gives an excellent digest of the newspaper comments. The *Birmingham News,* for example, remarked at the extravagance of the *World* in paying $10,000 for a trip, when the train fare for the same distance was only $4.65. The *Houston Post* offered this:

The wonder is that Curtiss did
Not pass New York and onward whizz
Southwest by south, half south, until
He got where Houston, Texas, is

One month earlier, Louis Paulhan claimed the *London Daily Mail* prize for a flight from London to Manchester. *Aeronautics* magazine's comparative comment on the two flights read:

"Paulhan took four hours and twelve minutes elapsed time to cover 183 miles when he won the *Daily Mail's* fifty thousand dollars, and made it in two stages of 117 and 66 miles each. The 117 miles were covered at the rate of 44 miles per hour. On the following day the 66 miles were done at the rate of 48 miles per hour. The average speed for the trip was 44.37 miles per hour. Paulhan could have landed at almost any time and started again, whereas Curtiss could not have started if he had had to land in the water, and for the whole distance there was scarcely a suitable space for landing on the ground."

The evaluation of the two achievements by the European press paralleled that of the American flying magazine. Curtiss' first leg of 87 miles also won him the third leg and permanent keeping of the *Scientific American* Trophy.

In all the excitement following his landing Curtiss forgot for several hours that he had come to New York bearing a letter to Mayor Gaynor from Mayor McEwan of Albany. He hastened to repair the oversight and personally delivered the letter. Other famous airmail caches have included several items. Curtiss carried only the one letter.

Many luncheons and dinners were given in honor of the

* Airship still signified heavier-than-air craft in 1910.

aviator who stormed the Palisades, the most important of them being the dinner given by the *World* at the Hotel Astor on the night of May 31st. Mayor Gaynor presided, and the distinguished company of guests included Brigadier General Walter C. Howe, James M. Beck, Adolph S. Ochs, Don Seitz, Hudson Maxim, and Colonel John Jacob Astor.

As soon as the guests were seated, Mayor Gaynor announced that the *St. Louis Post-Dispatch* now offered a prize of $30,000 for the first successful aeroplane flight between New York and St. Louis. It was the first of a series of valuable newspaper prizes that were posted during the next few days "to inspire," the mayor explained, "the brave and heroic pioneers, in air travel to still greater feats."

Hudson Maxim prophesied in his speech: "As that warless era of which we catch glimpses in our dreams of a distant future is unquestionably yet far away, we must, in our prediction, look to the flying machines which war, as well as sport and commerce, is to build and perfect.

"We shall not have to wait a hundred years for the staunch, wind-defying machine with automatic equilibration. Very soon automobiling of the air will be as safe as automobiling upon the earth now is. Neither shall we have to wait a hundred years for that spectacular eventuation— a fight between aerial navies—for those are bound to come."

Glenn Curtiss, himself, as he told the guests, had "planned everything about the flight in advance except the possibility of making a speech." He arose, as commanded, and spoke for a period generously estimated at "less than five minutes." Commenting on the Hudson flight, William Howard Taft, President of the United States, wrote:

"I am intensely interested in what Mr. Curtiss has done.

It seems that the wonders of aviation will never cease. I would hesitate to say that the performance of Mr. Curtiss is an epoch, because tomorrow we may hear that some man has flown from New York to St. Louis ...... His flight will live long in our memories as having been the greatest."

For its time, the Albany flight had great significance for America. It was, for example, the first inter-city flight of any consequence, and the first recorded evidence that flying was not just a stunt, but a means of transportation. No wonder, therefore, that up until that May 29th New York had not seen such an excited crowd since the day of Halley's Comet.

The *New York Times* headline: CURTISS FEAT CAPS EFFORTS OF AGES was merely conservative journalism in 1910.

IV

ALL THAT GOES UP

Bolts from the Blue

HUDSON MAXIM was not alone in his belief that aerial navies were bound to come; the newspapers had already labeled the flight down the Hudson River as an object lesson in the potential menace of the skies.

Consider the aeroplane, said the New York *World*. Might not 6600 aeroplanes be purchased for the price of one battleship? Yet a single aeroplane could utterly destroy a dreadnought. It could also demolish cities, bridges, arsenals, bodies of troops. Sane preparedness demanded the inclusion of this new weapon of offense and defense in modern armaments.

Curtiss and Charles Hamilton heartily endorsed the suggestion. Curtiss was quoted:

> It is certainly true that I could have thrown explosives upon anything which lay beneath my path on the flight from Albany. Presuming that

my aeroplane could have carried 300 to 500 pounds of excess weight composed of an air gun and picric bombs, I could have scattered destruction all along the route between here and Albany.

I think also that I can hit a target within a reasonable radius. Experiments abroad have proved that a missile thrown from a moving airship can strike within twelve feet of a given spot. Think what this means. I could have blown up the bridge at Poughkeepsie, set fire to the homes of the wealthy along the Highlands, destroyed the railroad tracks on both shores, and cleared the river of its shipping.

An aeroplane flying like mine over the length of the North River could have demoralized its busy commerce. Transatlantic steamers, ferries, battleships, all are equally vulnerable from above.

I could have touched them without danger to myself or to my machine. By swooping down low and darting up again at great speed before their cumbersome guns could be brought into play, I could escape unscathed.

The *World,* in an effort to promote military aeronautics, suggested that Curtiss prove with dummy bombs that it was possible to gauge speed and wind deflection correctly. And on June 30, 1910, he gave a series of demonstrations at Hammondsport. The bombs, dropped from altitudes of 500 to 800 feet, were lead weights with colored streamers attached, and the target was a raft anchored in Lake Keuka. The representative of the *World* found his accuracy relatively good. But Curtiss's own opinion of the attempt at aerial bombing, as quoted in *Aeronautics,* was that in order accurately to drop bombs in actual warfare, one man would have to be carried for the purpose of dropping the bombs, since it was impossible for the pilot to make accurate calculations of angle and speed.

The Army and Navy officials invited to witness the demonstration were not impressed by it. United States military officials were burned children. They could not forget the public blame which had followed the fruitless expenditure of $50,000 for the Langley experiment by the Bureau of Ordnance and Fortifications.

When, in October, 1905, the Wright brothers offered their plane to the Government, their claims of successful performance were not taken seriously. Just how it might have altered our whole aeronautical picture if the Army had given encouragement to the Wright experiments at that time, is an interesting subject for speculation. Quite possibly Tom Selfridge, the Army's earthbound lone eagle, would have found wings without turning to Graham Bell. There might have been no reason for the existence of an Aerial Experiment Association, and Glenn Curtiss might have become a builder of automobile busses.

It was a moody destiny that shunted the inventors of the aeroplane outside their own land to peddle their patents. Like all the pioneers, the Wright brothers realized that their logical production field was military. In 1905, Wilbur Wright told Octave Chanute it had dawned on him that there was some money to be made by selling the invention to governments for war purposes. It was by order of President Roosevelt in 1907 that the War Department investigated the Wright brothers' plane, and in September, 1908, the Army's first heavier-than-air craft was delivered at Fort Myer, Virginia. On July 30, 1909, all the official tests were completed and United States Army Aeroplane Number One—and the world's first military aeroplane—was officially accepted. Army Dirigible Number One had been accepted in August, 1908.

Both Curtiss and his lighter-than-air colleague, Captain Baldwin, were convinced that the governmental market was the most promising one for aircraft. They were always ready to give demonstrations designed to attract the attention of the military mind. At New York, in June 1909, Baldwin dropped a shell-like object from his dirigible in the teeth of a gale to show what could be done in time of war by dropping a projectile on an enemy camp. And in August, 1910, Lieut. T. E. Fickel, of the Army, first demonstrated the possibilities of sharp-shooting from an aeroplane in flight in a Curtiss machine at Sheepshead Bay, Long Island. At the same time and at the same place the first wireless messages were sent and received in a Curtiss aeroplane by J. A. D. McCurdy.

Aero clubs all over the country cooperated to urge government support of the development of areonautics. In February, 1910, Glenn Curtiss went with a committee representing the Washington and Baltimore aero clubs to urge the President of the United States to recommend appropriations for the equipment of the army with aeroplanes. President Taft regretted that owing to the economy policy such a recommendation would have to wait until the next session.

The United States Navy first took official cognizance of aviation in September, 1908, when Orville Wright demonstrated the Army plane at Fort Myer. Lieut. C. G. Sweet and Naval Constructor McIntee were detailed to act as observers on the occasion when a world's duration record of an hour and two minutes was established. The two naval observers immediately suggested that an aeroplane be equipped with pontoons in the interest of adaptability for naval use. Although the Wright brothers offered to construct such a plane, the Navy decided against investing funds in aeronautical equipment, due again to the economy policy.

Two years later, Captain Washington Irving Chambers, who was on duty in the Bureau of Equipment of the Navy Department, acted as official observer at the aviation meets in Belmont Park and Halethorpe, near Baltimore. Impressed with the skill of the pilots and the maneuverability of the planes demonstrated, he decided that the Navy needed aviation. But the Navy Department on the other hand, decided to the contrary.

Why not demonstrate that an aeroplane could be launched from a battleship? Captain Chambers wondered, and went immediately to the Wright brothers with a proposal that they fly one of their planes from the deck of a ship. When they declined to make such a flight, Chambers went to Curtiss, who received the idea with enthusiasm. It proved to be the first skirmish in a campaign which eventually won him the resounding title of father of naval aviation.

After The *World* published a story on the plan suggested by Captain Chambers, the Hamburg-American Steamship Company came forward with the sporting offer of the afterdeck of their S. S. *Pennsylvania* for the experiment. A large platform was built at a right angle to the ship on its stern. McCurdy, the Curtiss exhibition flyer, was scheduled to travel fifty miles to sea on the *Pennsylvania*, and fly off her and back to shore. Just as the ship was preparing to sail, the aeroplane's propeller was smashed by an oilcan accidentally left on one of the wings. Since it was too late to secure another propeller, the plane was lifted to the dock. The ship was forced to sail without it.

But the Navy was curious enough now to want to find out whether the thing really could be done, and offered to let Curtiss build a platform on the deck of the cruiser *Birmingham* at Hampton Roads. Eugene B. Ely, another

Curtiss flyer, waited all day on the improvised platform, hoping the weather would improve. A strong wind was blowing and later a heavy mist came up off shore. Ely decided to take off before the mist closed in altogether. He went down the short runway under full power and dropped off the planking. Just as he touched the water with his landing gear, the plane lifted and he flew ashore.

The Navy officials were profoundly impressed, but did not accept Ely's ship-to-shore flight as convincing evidence in the case Captain Chambers was trying to build up. They were not yet ready to list aircraft as essential naval equipment. If the Navy was not sold, Curtiss was. The fact that the problem of getting an aeroplane to take off from the water was still baffling did not discourage him. He had been working at it intermittently ever since the winter of 1908. That year he said: "Even if a suitable device for launching and landing on land is secured, a water craft will still be indispensable for war purposes."

After two years' work, he had been able only to land on the water, but he believed he was close to the solution of the water take-off. In the meantime, he had another idea that might help to break down military resistance.

The first Army air squadron came into existence in 1909, when Wilbur Wright gave flying instruction to Army officers at College Park, Maryland, the first Government aviation field. But the Army air force was still in an embryonic stage, although the large European countries had already organized military branches and were actively instructing men to fly. Since there were no funds available for the purpose in this country, Curtiss sent an invitation to the Secretary of War and the Secretary of the Navy, offering to instruct without charge one or more officers of their respective departments in the science of aviation.

Because California had suitable year-round flying weather, Curtiss had decided to open winter headquarters at San Diego. The Spreckels Company had turned over North Island in Spanish Bight as a camp site. When he arrived at the island early in January, 1911, he found his first flying recruit there ahead of him.

Lieut. Theodore G. Ellyson, U.S.N., was profoundly pleased with his new assignment and delighted to learn that his first opportunity to help prepare a demonstration to overcome naval skepticism on the subject of aeronautics was already cut out for him. Together Curtiss and he land plans for the undertaking.

In San Francisco Bay, ten miles from the scene of the San Francisco air meet, part of the Pacific fleet lay at anchor. Rear Admiral Barry, in command of the fleet, learned that Glenn Curtiss wished to complete the experiment begun at Hampton Roads in November and sent word that his flagship, was at Curtiss' disposal. The equipment required was outlined and the big battleship, which, by coincidence was also a *Pennsylvania,* proceeded to Mare Island Navy Yard. In due time it returned, wearing a slightly inclined wooden platform, thirty feet wide, on its stern.

Greatest caution was used to prevent the aeroplane from crashing against the gun turret at the end of the runway. Twenty hemp ropes were stretched at intervals across the platform, which was 125 feet long, and a sailor's duffle bag containing a hundred pounds of sand was tied to each rope-end. The hooks underneath the plane would, they hoped, catch on the ropes and the weight of the sandbags would gradually bring the machine to a stop. These hooks acted ordinarily as double brakes to stop the plane by digging into the ground. Two wooden rails extending longitudinally raised the ropes several inches above the boards. Tarpaulins were attached to either side of the platform and at the upper end to catch the aviator if he missed the runway or was pitched forward in landing.

Curtiss, who had supervised all the preparations, was called to San Diego at the last minute and could not witness the flight about which he was so deeply concerned. In spite of the elaborate precautions, a landing of extreme precision must be made in order to land safely on the narrow platform and avoid almost inevitable disaster. Eugene Ely took off from Camp Selfridge, where the aviation meet was under way, at 10:45 the morning of January eighteenth. The air was clear and fairly calm. He flew up the peninsula, over the city and headed for the warships. The U.S.S. *Pennsylvania* with the apron of new lumber aft was readily distinguishable from the air. A fleet of launches stood by to rescue the aviator if he missed the runway. Ely circled the battleship and headed for the stern. Officers and enlisted men of the fleet watched him. They saw him dip a little more sharply than for a regular landing. Just as his wheels touched the planking, he levelled off and sped up the incline. Within sixty feet he came to a standstill, with the aid of the ropes and the hands of a number of sailors who ran down from the gun turret.

It was a truly skilful piece of flying and Ely's audience applauded vociferously. The harbor ships tooted, the ship sirens shrieked, and the din continued during the forty-five minutes Ely was lunching with the officers of the Pacific Squadron.

The machine was turned around and the ropes across the platform pulled away. The aviator shook hands with Admiral Barry and Captain George F. Pond and took off, dropped almost to the water again, rose and flew back over the admiring crowds at the air meet and landed at the camp of the 30th Infantry, which put the flight on record as an official link between the Army and the Navy.

Ely's skillful flying, Curtiss's initiative in undertaking to demonstrate that it was possible to land on a cruiser, even fly back to shore again from it, were widely hailed as irrefutable evidence that the aeroplane was a practical instrument of war. Other demonstrations of a military nature had been made during the San Francisco meet, at the scene of which the 30th Infantry was encamped to participate in the maneuvers. Lieut. Paul W. Beck of the Signal Corps, had sent messages by wireless from a Wright plane. He carried a 32-pound wireless set in a box on his lap with an aerial hanging from the tail of the aeroplane. Charles Willard, with a small receiving set installed in his Curtiss plane, successfully received instructions to turn and land. Real bombs, not oranges, had also been dropped during the meet. They were bombs of two types —a percussion shell bomb which exploded on contacting the ground, and a time bomb, both inventions of Lieut. M. S. Crissy.

The newspapers were sure that the time had arrived for Government action, when flying could dramatize naval, reconnaissance and attack possibilities all within the space of a few days. But despite the rather impressive demonstrations, despite the ground display of uniforms, the military officials were of a different mind. They had no intention of being swayed by newspaper histrionics, and were inclined to question the practicality of Ely's demonstration in one respect.

"You have done what you hoped to do, Mr. Curtiss," they propounded, "But don't you see that a battleship could not reduce its efficiency by sailing with a platform stretched from gun turret to rudder?"

In reply Curtiss suggested that the landing platform might be set atop the turret, allowing it to extend out over the guns. Such a platform, he added, might be made to swing about so that the plane could land against the wind. But Secretary of the Navy Meyer countered:

"Your ingenuity seems never to fail you, but before you can convince us that the aeroplane is a weapon in which the Navy Department could officially interest itself, you will have to show us that you can land your plane, not on an interfering platform on a fighting ship, but on the sea alongside. When you have invented an aeroplane that can be picked up by a boat crane and dropped over the side to the water, so that the flyer can go off on an errand and later return to the water alongside, get picked up by the crane and brought back to the deck . . . well, then I shall be ready to say that the Navy Department is convinced."

Obviously there was to be no naval aviation until there was marine aircraft. And the logic of Secretary Meyer's position was incontrovertible. Whereas an expert like Eugene Ely could make a perfect landing in small space, disaster might easily overtake less skillful flyers. Curtiss himself was no less convinced now than he had been three years before, that water craft was indispensable for war purposes. He chuckled as he read the communication from the Navy Department chief because he was reasonably sure that he could take the challenge in his stride.

The first officer detailed to the camp at North Island was Curtiss's chief collaborator in making an aeroplane over into a hydro-aeroplane. Lieut. Ellyson was a congenial, gifted young Southerner with a mop of curly red hair and a great fondness for two articles of food—chocolate candy and potatoes. Curtiss had liked Ellyson on sight and was soon calling him by his nickname, "Spuds." The twenty-six-year-old officer and Curtiss, who was then thirty-three but looked forty, worked tirelessly trying out various types of pontoons. Then one day Curtiss got off the water, and the thing was solved: they were ready to convince the Navy.

Word was sent to the Captain of the U.S.S. *Pennsylvania,* now in San Diego harbor, of the desire to pay him a visit aboard ship. Captain Pond was one of the few ranking naval officers who was willing to bother with flying experiments. He replied without hesitation, "Come on over."

On February 17th, three weeks after the hydro-aeroplane had turned loose of the water, Curtiss accepted his invitation.

A stiff tide was running that morning. Spuds Ellyson and Charley Witmer, one of the civilian students at North Island, rode out to the battleship in a launch. Curtiss took off from Spanish Bight, landed near the ship and was made fast to the launch. He was then towed alongside. A wire sling was hooked onto a hoisting crane. As there had been no opportunity to test the strength of the wire sling, Curtiss slipped one leg over the crane hook as a precautionary measure, while the machine was being lifted to the deck.

After a brief visit with Captain Pond the hydro-aeroplane was swung back over the side. It skimmed the surface and was off the water again, without delay, while the sailors and laymen aboard the ship cheered loudly.

The *San Diego Union's* account gives an idea of the general editorial reaction to the landing and take-off alongside a battleship:

> It was just like any other day's work for Curtiss. He set about it with the same assurance with which he flew the now famous *June Bug*

at Hammondsport, N. Y., and put a crimp in the plans of the Wright brothers for cornering the aviation business in the United States.

The entire program required less than half an hour to carry out. There was no hitch and not the least difficulty was experienced in hoisting the plane on board or lowering it over the side. The officers were enthusiastic over the ease with which the landing was accomplished.

"We know now," Captain Pond said, "that a machine can rise from the water, fly alongside and be picked up, then go over the side and sail away. Or the process may be reversed as necessity requires."

Secretary of the Navy Meyer has been shown. Another page in aerial history has been written full by the hand that already has penned so many chapters. But that is nothing to the unassuming, almost bashful king of the birdmen. He had set about doing an ordinary day's work and inwardly hoped the boss of the Navy Department would be satisfied.

This time the journalistic hymns of praise did not fall on deaf ears. Captain Chambers, staunch champion of flying for sailors, said:

"Rising from and alighting on the water is the most important development of the flying machine, from the standpoint of the Navy Department, yet made. The Navy has decided to purchase one of the Curtiss machines."

There it was . . . the Navy buying a flying machine.

Further, in the 1911-1912 Naval Appropriation Act there was an item of $25,000 for aeronautics, and Captain W. I. Chambers, in March, 1911, was detailed to the Bureau of Navigation and directed to devote his entire time toward the establishment of an aviation service. That made the United States the first country in the world to adopt naval aviation.

The United States Army also had a representative at the first and subsequent flights of the hydro-aeroplane. He was Lieut. John C. Walker of the 8th Infantry, who had been detailed for instruction to North Island. Lieut. Paul W. Beck of the Signal Corps, Lieut. G. E. M. Kelly * of the 30th Infantry were the next Army detail to the Curtiss aviation camp. Their names had been selected from a list of thirty applicants. In February Ensign Charles Pousland of the destroyer *Preble* was also detailed to North Island from the Navy.

Within a week after the flight to the cruiser another new type machine took off on pontoons from the inlet which formed North Island, and came down at Coronado Beach on wheels. They called this earliest ancester of the modern amphibian the Triad because of its three spheres— water, air and land—and the first U. S. Naval aircraft was of this type. Then Lieut. Ellyson was taken up by Curtiss in the amphibian as the original naval "observer."

Professor H. La V. Twining of California, who had made a special study of the water-flying experiments up to that time, pointed out that an aeroplane could be carried aboard ship, and knocked down. It could be re-assembled in a short time and launched. It could then take off, lower its wheels and land on the shore, take off again, raise its wheels and settle down alongside the battleship. "Under these circumstances," he said, "it can at least become the eye of the fleet, and what other possibilities are in store for it yet remain to be developed."

So that the aeroplane might be more than merely the eye of the fleet or the land forces, it was essential to increase carrying capacity, in order that explosives as well as an additional man to drop them might be taken into the

---

*Kelly Field, San Antonio, Texas, is named after this flyer, who in May, 1911, became the second Army flight casualty.

air. The wing-area of the biplanes at North Island was therefore increased. Carrying capacity was also increased by 200 pounds through the addition of a smaller third wing. This experimental triplane could accommodate the load of two passengers and a pilot.

More power was of course an essential factor in developing carrying capacity, and the factory at Hammondsport developed first the 80 horse-power Model O, and then the 100 horse-power OX engine. Several sham bombing attacks were made in connection with the experiments to increase carrying capacity. Lieut. Paul W. Beck, who was the champion marksman among them, afterwards had a hand in the development of instruments for the exact determination of altitude, forward speed and wind velocity, and of machinery by which projectiles might be launched from the air with relative certainty that they would hit the target.

In May, 1911, Curtiss perfected a system of dual controls for aircraft which revolutionized the whole problem of military flight training. Flying Headquarters had been transferred to Hammondsport that spring, and further experiments carried on there.

On the way to Chicago to watch some of his exhibition planes fly at Grant Park, Curtiss was preoccupied trying to figure out a method for launching hydro-aeroplanes other than lowering them over the side. Suddenly the problem resolved itself: they might try launching one from a powerful cable, similar to the forestay of a ship. The rest of the summer, Ellyson and Curtiss, whenever they were together, discussed the device from various angles. Then they carefully went about setting it up.

Two heavy posts were sunk into the ground near the lake shore to form an inverted vee, the apex of which was sixteen feet above the ground. A 250-foot length of ¾ inch steel cable secured at the top of the vee, extended downward at a ten percent incline to a submerged piling. A metal-lined groove was cut in the keel of the pontoon to fit the cable. The vee was braced and a small platform built around it near the top. After the hydro-aeroplane had been placed on the cable and backed up to the highest point, the pilot would, if all went well, take off from the cable after the plane had gathered sufficient momentum. Two lighter cables running parallel, on which the wingtips rested, were intended to keep the machine from rolling over sideways before flying speed had been attained. As it began to move, two men, each holding a wingline, would run alongside to help balance the plane as long as they could keep up with it.

After numerous preliminary trial trips of the plane down the cable, they were ready, on September seventh, to test the device under power. Two men stood by grasping the winglines, another was on the platform ready to spin the propeller. Ellyson climbed in and tested the motor.

The thing still looked more than a little risky to Curtiss. He fingered his camera nervously and hesitated about giving the signal to cast off. The pilot spoke up:

"I have a feeling in my bones that it's going to work."

"Well, if you feel that way about it, go ahead."

And the plane began the perilous slide.

It worked, and so much better than they had hoped that, to the undying amazement of the bystanders who had learned to expect a grunt or at most a smile in a moment of triumph, Glenn H. Curtiss waved his arms and jumped up and down like a youngster when school is out.

In the two shipboard flights by Eugene Ely, Curtiss's landing alongside and the cable launching, the groundwork was laid for flying to and from ships as it is practiced today. The modern catapult was designed at the Naval Gun Factory in Washington, by Naval Constructor H. C. Richardson and Lieut. Ellyson. The first successful catapult launching was made with Lieut. Ellyson at the controls of a Curtiss plane on October 12, 1912, just thirteen months after the wire cable launching at Hammondsport. Shortly thereafter, catapults were erected over the after decks of two United States cruisers. The first turntable catapult was built and installed on the *USS Maryland* in 1921, and today each battleship and light cruiser in the Navy carries its complement of aircraft, with fighting and observation planes always ready for action.

In 1922, the collier *Jupiter,* first electrically-driven ship in the Navy, was rechristened the *Langley* and commissioned as the first aeroplane carrier. Since then two ships, originally laid down as battle cruisers, were converted into carriers, and in 1936, the *USS Ranger,* built from keel up as an aircraft carrier, was commissioned. Another carrier is in process of construction. Some seventy-five aircraft designed for scouting, fighting, torpedo and bombing are attached to each of these self-contained, completely equipped floating aviation bases.

The first "war flight" was made early in 1911 when Charles Hamilton and Roland Garros, of the Moisant International Flyers, flew across the Rio Grande at Juarez, which was in a state of siege. Pascual Orozsco, the insurrecto leader, had granted permission for the aviators to reconnoiter over his camp, subject only to the danger that his own men might think the aeroplanes were sent by the Mexican government. Hamilton flew his Curtiss plane, while Garros flew an American Bleriot, built for John B. Moisant.

In April, 1914, a United States military aircraft for the first time flew in the face of hostile fire. During the occupation of Vera Cruz, a plane attached to the *USS Mississippi*, piloted by Lieut. P. N. L. Bellinger made scouting flights on three consecutive days. The plane was struck by Mexican bullets. These scouting missions proved extremely helpful in coordinating ship and shore operations.

But the awakening of military interest in this country was a long and very gradual process. Congress had appropriated $125,000 for U. S. Army aeronautics in February, 1911, and decided to establish aviation training stations at San Diego, College Park, Maryland, and Omaha, Nebraska. In March, of that year, the first Curtiss military aeroplane was accepted by the Army and sent to the Texas-Mexican border for use by the U. S. Army encamped there. It was the second plane purchased for use in the Army flying school, and was officially designated Number Two.

After the first spurt, Governmental interest in aeronautics again tapered off. The Navy could not see any way in which so large a sum as $25,000 could be expended to advantage during 1911-1912, and a surplus was reported as returned to the Treasury. As a result of the efforts of Captain W. I. Chambers, a board was appointed in October, 1913, to make a careful study for an aeronautical organization within the Navy. In accordance with one of their most important recommendations, the first U. S. Naval Air Station was established on the site of the abandoned Navy Yard at Pensacola, Florida, in January, 1914, and equipped with marine aircraft.

Chambers was constantly urging increased appropriations, on the grounds that we would soon be at a disadvantage unless we kept step with other countries. "In hydro-aviation," he said, "the United States has maintained her lead from the beginning. France, Russia, Germany, Italy and Japan have purchased our hydro-aeroplanes and they will probably continue to improve them as we continue to do so. Unless we give substanial encouragement to our manufacturers, we will soon find ourselves our-stripped in this line of endeavor also."

The lack of concern about aviation was confined to this country. Other governments were spending comparatively fabulous sums. The United States stood fourteenth in a list of appropriations for the year 1912, below not only Spain but Greece and hostile little Bulgaria. An estimate, as of March, 1913, on the total governmental expenditures for aeronautical work during the preceding five years approximated a hundred million dollars. The itemized report credits Germany with 400 aeroplanes and 30 dirigibles, acquired and maintained at an expense of $28,000,-000; France had the same number of aeroplanes and 25 dirigibles, with expenditures at $22,000,000. England with 100 aeroplanes and six dirigibles had spent $3,000,-000 for equipment and operation of governmental air services, whereas the United States had spent, during the five-year period, $435,000. Its flight equipment consisted of 28 aeroplanes and one dirigible.

Because they had so little money to spend, U. S. Army officials were forced to demand an unusually high return on their investment, and specifications for military aeroplanes were stiff. They called for such qualities as greatly increased speed, increased range and expensive equipment features. In one instance, their requirements were so far in advance of current developments that Lyman J. Seely said, in an article in *Aircraft* for May, 1913: "Robert Fulton might almost as well have been asked to build the *Mauretania*."

The fact that Curtiss in every case was able to produce an aircraft to meet the requirements was chiefly due to the experience gained as well as the income derived from building military aircraft for foreign powers. The exorbitant demands made by his own country served as a constant prod and led to the development of many features of military significance which, during the war years, netted substantial gains for the Curtiss Company.

No specific impetus to war flying was given in America, however, until May, 1917, when Congress appropriated $10,800,000 for aircraft, with a subsequent appropriation of $43,500,000 and of $640,000,000 in June and July of that year. But through the years 1912 and 1913, Curtiss was able to continue in aircraft production only because over-water flying caught on with the public as a sport, especially after he developed the flying boat. He perfected the first one of this type at Hammondsport in July, 1912, and in May, 1913, an amphibian flying boat was developed and flown by Lieut. B. L. Smith of the Marine Corps at Hammondsport. The flying boat type, because it was able to combat waves and hold its own in rough water, was of tremendous military value, and was rapidly adopted by governments all over the world, especially after a twin-engined cabin flying boat was designed at Hammondsport in 1914.

The Naval officers detailed worked closely with Curtiss in his over-water flying experiments. In the spring of 1911, Lieut. John Rodgers, Lieut. John Towers, and Ensign V. D. Herbster were detailed to aviation duty. Rodgers and Herbster were sent to the Wright flying camp and Towers to Hammondsport. Theodore Ellyson was later designated Naval Aviator No. 1, while Rodgers was No. 2, Towers No. 3 and Herbster No. 4. Towers was left as No. 1 of living Naval Aviators after both Ellyson and Rodgers were killed in crashes. Paul Beck, of the North Island camp, was designated the first Military Aviator after that title came into use.

In the summer of 1911, the Navy purchased one Wright

and two Curtiss planes and set up a camp at Greenbury Point, near Annapolis.

The first naval flying organization in the world began operations, with Ellyson and Towers as instructor and assistant instructor of flying. Naval Constructor Richardson, Lieuts. Bellinger, Billingsley, and Ensign G. deC Chevalier, of the Navy; and Lieuts. Cunningham and B. L. Smith of the Marine Corps, were all detailed to aviation duty in 1912.

At Hammondsport, the Navy had a tent hangar and a group of Naval officers and Navy mechanics was about most of the time. The mechanics looked after the Navy planes, and with the run of the Curtiss factory, they had an excellent opportunity to learn about aircraft and motor assembly. The officers, at the same time, learned about aircraft design from Curtiss, while he had the benefit of their assistance in thrashing out knotty problems. They were invaluable to him with their consistent demonstrations of the speed, climbing ability and endurance of his machines. Most of them later came to hold important positions in the Naval service.

The young Naval officers, who were in and out of Hammondsport on special details from the spring of 1911 until the fall of 1914, were without exception, thrilled at the opportunity to be associated with Curtiss. To them he was not only a famous aviator, but the fabricator of so much that was vital to their flying careers.

News of large European appropriations for aeronautics gave rise to the rumor that Curtiss would be welcome as a manufacturer in three different countries and that the problem of financing would be simple. The Naval flyers who had studied and worked with him were deeply concerned, knowing from personal observation how hard pressed he was financially and also how harassed by legal controversy. They earnestly hoped he would not be forced to transfer his operations to Europe.

Then the formation of an aeronautical department for both Navy and Army activities was officially proposed. And because of Curtiss's ability as a designer and flyer, as well as his instinct in selecting men who would make good aviators, it was suggested that the Army should brevet him as a Colonel and put him in charge of the joint aerial corps.

After some thought, he rejected the idea. It would not leave him enough time to work out new ideas in aircraft, and he could not see himself in such a position. Nor could the men who were apprenticed to him by the Navy, or anyone who had ever known him, picture Curtiss as a gold-braided Colonel.

Pontoons and Hulls

THE scheme of starting a flying machine from and landing on the water has been on my mind for some time. It has many advantages and I believe can be worked out . . . An arrangement of floats to support the flyer when at rest would be necessary. Then small hydroplanes to carry it up out of the water and to catch the shock of landing."

This, from a letter written in August 19, 1908, indicates that even before that date Curtiss had thrown in his lot with the cause of off-the-water flying. Bell's preachments about the softer, safer landing had ploughed a deep furrow in his mind which could be smoothed out only by discovering how to fly from the water.

It was not a new idea. Hugo Matullath of New York had suggested it in patent applications in 1899. The United States Navy had considered the need for an aircraft which was able to rise from and alight on the water, and extensive experiments had been made abroad. The first A. E. A. water-flying experiments were made at Hammondsport in December, 1908.

At Baddeck, Dr. Bell and Casey Baldwin had retackled the old problem of speed over the water. The findings of their hydro-planing experiments were applied in the design of the floats for the re-christened *June Bug*. A canoe-shaped wooden framework was decked over tightly with rubberized cloth to form each of the two pontoons; then the *Loon* was hauled down to the lake on a pair of cart wheels, and launched in the water. McCurdy and Curtiss alternately took the controls.

While they could glide over the water at a high rate of speed, they could not leave its surface, as the suction which held down the machine was much greater than they had anticipated. They concluded that the quickly heated air-cooled *June Bug* engine was not equal to the task of lifting the *Loon* which now had a total weight of a thousand pounds. They decided to repeat the experiment with the newly designed water-cooled engine.

But though the pontoons were raised slightly out of the water in the second trial, they still found too much drag. The best speed they could make was 25 miles an hour, which was not fast enough to get into the air without the help of a strong headwind. Naturally they could not risk flying in a strong wind and they were forced to postpone experimenting until after dark because the wind blew all day.

Then one of the pontoons caught in the dock and a hole was torn in the fabric covering. Curtiss reported:

"McCurdy, who was riding the machine, did not know of the accident. He made a circle of the lake and returned to the starting point. Then it sank."

That same night, which was the second of January, 1909, this dejected message went forward to Dr. Bell in Nova Scotia,

GAVE VAUDEVILLE PERFORMANCE TONIGHT BY MOONLIGHT WITH LOON FIRST HYDRO TEST SUCCESSFUL SECOND AERODROME TEST FAIRLY SUCCESSFUL THIRD SUBMARINE TEST MOST SUCCESSFUL OF ALL EXPERIMENTS ENDED.

CURTISS AND McCURDY

After the Experiment Association was dissolved in March, Curtiss continued experimenting. The *World* prize offer for a flight down the Hudson gave new impetus to his efforts. During the next year, his mind was constantly fumbling with the problem. He was sure that he could never make a pontoon tear loose by force, no matter how powerful the motor. The hydro-surfaces must be given a definite sense of lift.

The Frenchman, Henri Fabre, had done it in March, 1910, on the Seine River. He had risen from the water and flown five or six kilometers, but he had crashed in landing. Whether his airmanship lagged behind his engineering ability, or whether the design of his machine was not adequate to the double problem of take-off and landing was not determined. Unquestionably, skill as an operator has often lent priceless aid to creators of automotive patterns.

In preparing for the journey from Albany to New York, Curtiss temporarily abandoned the idea of taking off from the water and devoted himself to devising emergency water-landing equipment. The ungainly flotation gear for the *Albany Flyer* had no slight gift for doing anything but keeping a plane afloat, although it enabled him to make the first recorded landing on water. But he wanted to go on with the development of a bona fide water flying machine.

Fabre had used three floats, but Curtiss, recalling his experience with two on the *Loon,* decided that a single main supporting surface would offer more chance for getaway. Some sort of device at the ends of the wings would keep the machine from tipping when it was at rest.

Had Curtiss known more about the action of the hydroplane type of hull in and on the water, his task of shaping a pontoon would have been much simpler. But while a few hydroplanes had been built and proven, the type was not generally adopted. Under American Power Boat Association rules, all championship motor boat contests were still run with displacement hulls, the theory being that the longer, narrower and more sharply pointed they were, the faster they could be driven through water.

Curtiss had been planning a type of float with a shovel nose, and he sent sketches to the factory. All the summer and fall he was in touch with them by mail and wire on the subject of the new flotation gear. Damon Merrill brought it to North Island in January, but when it arrived it proved useless. The main pontoon, which was two feet wide by eight feet long, gave not nearly enough supporting surface for the load of the biplane, the motor and the pilot.

Curtiss and Ellyson and Damon Merrill, chief mechanician of the little shop on the island, worked together throughout the month of January, 1911, trying this scheme and that. They even tried to get more lift by adding a third wing. Nothing would serve so long as the main pontoon clung to the water. It was essentially a question of finding the right curvature so that the water would not wrap itself around the pontoon and create a suction. That meant trying out pontoons until they got the right one.

At least fifty changes in size, position and angle of incidence were made. They worked for ten days and the better part of ten nights in high-topped boots and bathing suits. Many times Curtiss said:

"Now I have it, I think we can do it this way."

They did it that way. Still it did not work. When they did hit upon the right combination, neither Curtiss nor the other men knew just why that particular float chose to get off the water.

Ellyson spun the propeller and Curtiss sent the machine across San Diego Bay on its newest float. The machine felt increasingly lighter and was fairly skipping along. With the controls, he tilted the machine up in front just as he had a hundred times before. This time it rose from the surface of the water, flew for a minute and a half and landed, took off again and flew a half mile. It was the most fun Curtiss had ever had in all his life, this water flying. He took off a third time, flew two miles out over the bay and back to a landing a hundred feet from the shore of North Island.

The younger men were turning handsprings on the beach, while Merrill gave one long yelp of joy. Ellyson and Walker splashed into the shallow water when he landed again, pulled him out of his seat and galloped down the beach with him on their shoulders. Curtiss was dazed. The A. E. A. members had been less demonstrative than the men from the Army and the Navy.

Some part of the people of San Diego had witnessed his flight. Within an hour, the whole town was celebrating, as special editions told how Glenn Curtiss had made the first successful flight ever made off water.

Whereas the *Albany Flyer* had three varieties of flotation gear, the first hydro-aeroplane had a main float, a forward float, a canvas spray-shield, two wing skids partly encased in rubberized cloth to help balance the machine, and a small hydro-vane in the extreme front.

It would seem that any self-respecting flying machine would be compelled to take off in self-defense against additional hydro-gadgets. At the moment they were tremendously concerned not with streamlining, but with getting the machine to stay right side up while it was riding across the surface of the water, and with keeping it afloat long enough to give it every chance to rise if it should be so minded. And having risen, they proceeded to remove everything unnecessary and re-vamp what was left.

They knew that the scow shape of the main pontoon in the rear was basically right. But it was much too wide and too much surface was in contact with the water, so they made it longer, narrower and deeper. The old float had tapered off, toward the front, the new one had a uniform depth throughout, with a definite curve upward away from the surface in the front and a downward curve in the rear. The pontoon was attached to the aeroplane so that the center of gravity was slightly to the rear of the middle of the pontoon.

The new pontoon was 12 feet long by 2 feet wide by 12 inches deep; while the old one was 7 feet 1 inch long by 6 feet 1 inch wide by 10 inches deep at its deepest part. Cylindrical pontoons were attached to the ends of the lower wing in place of the wing-skids. It was this trimmer and more efficient flotation gear which Curtiss used in his flight out to the battleship *Pennsylvania*.

The second hydro-aeroplane had one further change. The original water-machine was, like all Curtiss planes, a pusher. In the second hydro-aeroplane, the engine was reversed with the single propeller in front, making it a tractor. But Curtiss found that the propeller blast interfered with his vision, and immediately returned to the pusher idea.

While the second hydro-aeroplane was emerging, Curtiss and Ellyson were busy with still another type. Why not put wheels on a water machine, they reasoned, wheels that could be dropped with a lever down below the bottom of the pontoon for landing on the ground, or raised again if the pilot desired to make a water landing? And so the first amphibian was born and flown by Curtiss on February 23rd. Four days later, Curtiss made the first recorded flight from the water with a passenger in the new amphibian.

Adding wheels to a hydro-aeroplane was no great feat for Curtiss who had already combined flotation gear and wheels to good advantage in the *Albany Flyer*. It was just one more manifestation of the indefatigable curiosity that would not let him stop experimenting, edging his way around another crag that barred the way to wider paths through the air by way of the water. He was doing things with land planes at the same time, but actually they did not matter tremendously. It was the water stuff, the expanding of its possibilities that became a beautiful game which he had been a long time learning to play.

Since 1909 Curtiss had battled for the right to build aeroplanes legally. In August, 1911, he filed basic patent applications, covering every form of hydro-aeroplane and flying boat. In this field he wanted protection against infringement suits; as for infringers, of which there were many, he never bothered to prosecute.

On the other hand, he was accused of pirating the ideas of others, even here. But these accusers had no legal recourse, because of his patent protection. Nevertheless, there were some who honestly regarded him as a patent thief. And because of his own tribulations in this respect, he was very tolerant with these men, even when they denounced him publicly at great length. And nothing any of his friends could do or say ever made him adopt a sterner attitude toward them.

Once an inventor came to him in a rage because he thought the Curtiss hydro infringed on his patents. Investigation disclosed no infringement, but the man confided that he was in difficult circumstances and could not pay his rent. Curtiss promptly mailed him a check. Within a short time the inventor distributed a slanderous circular about Curtiss and his work. When the plant manager called his attention to it, he looked it over carefully and shrugged his shoulders.

A week later, Curtiss' secretary reported: "Mr. Curtiss has sent that fellow more money!"

"But how can it be possible?" the manager asked.

"Well, he figured if the man spent his money putting out that circular he would need some more to live on."

It was the way Curtiss' mind worked and there was nothing anybody could do about it.

His method of coping with infringers was, as it had always been, to keep bounding so far ahead of them that by the time they had caught up to one type he was two or three types beyond. Within a year's time, he produced ten new types of flying boat, each one an advance, in one way or another.

The hydro-aeroplane had come along at a moment when flying was very unpopular. The winter of 1910 - 1911 was a black one. Not only dare-devil circus performers, but well known pilots like Ralph Johnstone, John Moisant, one of the pioneers, and Arch Hoxsey crashed to their death. The public lost all the confidence which had been built up through flying exhibitions, distance flights, and records. While America was writing letters to its Congressmen asking them to pass a law to make people stay on the ground, and generally giving aeronautics a piece of its mind, an aeroplane mounted on an assorted collection of contrivances designed to lend buoyancy, decided to take off from the surface of San Diego Bay, and gave the public pause in its recriminations. Within a year there was a gradual reawakening of interest in flying. People were again disposed to look kindly at young aeronautics.

But there was no immediate rush of orders; Curtiss had plenty of time to develop his original product, and very little wherewithal for the costly trial and error stages.

Curtiss did most of the initial off-the-water flying himself, partly because he knew what he could do with a machine, and partly because he had something of the same sense of fear, which Dr. Bell had in such large measure, of seeing somebody get hurt. And there was so much guesswork in these water fledglings that he preferred to assume most of the risk.

In developing the "hydro," there was only one serious mishap. While he was skimming over the lake, the pontoon sprang a leak and took in a quantity of water before he took off. During the flight, the added weight made no great difference, but when he nosed down for a landing, the water rushed into the bow of the pontoon, causing the machine to somersault in landing. Curtiss was thrown clear, and the motor boat which started to his rescue met him calmly swimming ashore. He told them to go on and see to the plane while he swam in. He shook himself like a dog when he landed to make sure he wasn't hurt. Then he growled:

"I have to get up to the shop and tell Kleckler to change the pontoon specifications. By dividing all floats into several compartments, we can keep this fool trick from happening again." Dripping wet, he climbed into his car and drove to the factory.

By November, 1911, the hydro-aeroplane had become standardized and Curtiss was ready to dip into another phase. A true boat hull with wings would be more at home in the water than the hydro. He therefore tackled the job of getting a boat to fly off the water. The first boat hull, with a pair of wings attached, was modelled somewhat after the shape of the hydro pontoon. From the front it resembled an ordinary flat-bottom boat. The motor was in the hull in front of the pilot's seat. It had two chain-driven tractor propellers. It was shipped to North Island where winter quarters had again been established and Curtiss motor-boated patiently all over San Diego Bay in it, with never a take off of any kind.

Henry Kleckler and the flying instructors and students at the camp struggled along with him trying to make the boat fly. Every fine morning it was mounted on beer kegs, rolled over the beach and launched on the water. Then the fun would begin.

"Mac, how about sitting in here back of me?" or "Lanny, will you climb on the tail and hold it down in the water?"

Once Curtiss forgot about his human ballast, started up the motor and began racing madly over the inlet, with Lanny Callan clinging to the tail and fervently hoping there would be no take-off right then.

Carrying out afterthoughts on the hydro project had been much less arduous than on the boat with wings. They planned and built and destroyed and rebuilt nevertheless.

"No, that's wrong," Curtiss said over and over, "We've got to change it."

Presently one of the students would say, "That doesn't seem to work, G. H. How would this do?"

Very likely Curtiss's face would light up. "Y'know, I never thought of that. Maybe it'll work."

And always they tried it, and it never worked. In December, 1911, he was called East to receive both the Robert Collier Trophy and the Aero Club's gold medal for advancing aviation during 1911 through the development of the hydro-aeroplane. After he returned to San Diego, Curtiss managed, on January 10, 1912, one brief departure from the water in the boat. But he was not able to follow it up as he had with the hydro. Obviously the one take-off had been an accident, and the flat-bottom hydro-pontoon shape was not the answer. There was a hitch somewhere that had to be figured out when he returned to the factory at Hammondsport that spring.

For the second time Curtiss was dissatisfied with the tractor idea. The motor was accordingly put back between the wings of the flying boat. Still other structural changes were made without, however, inducing the boat to rise. After an exhausting session on Lake Keuka, trying to make the experiment work, Curtiss suggested to Naval Constructor Richardson, "Why not attach wedge-shaped blocks to the bottom of the hull, forming a step so that it can be rocked and the suction broken up on the after part of the hull?"

He took out a pad and make a sketch.

"Henny, will you go up to the factory and saw it out yourself?"

In twenty minutes, Kleckler was back. The wedges were screwed on the bottom of the hull, the motor started, and without further debate, the first flying boat in the world took off. The little step on the bottom had done the trick and is still getting flying boats off oceans, rivers and lakes in the same way it did at Hammondsport in the summer of 1912.

The rest of the process, most of which was a matter of streamlining, was clear sailing. And the bullet shape, similar to that of a flying fish, evolved for the hull that year, as well as the general structural principles of flying boats, have survived through to the present and are still inherent in the big boats that today carry mail and passengers across assorted oceans.

Having perfected the flying boat, Curtiss announced the new sport of aerial yachting. Here, according to the sales patter, was a "flying machine as nearly absolutely safe as any fast vehicle can be. It rides the water at fifty miles per hour and flies at more than sixty."

There was no immediate rush of orders for flying boats, although orders for hydro-aeroplanes had begun to come in from abroad. Louis Paulhan became the first Curtiss Company foreign agent; an order for a two seated hydro and a request for a demonstrator came in from the Russian Aerial League. In February, 1912, Hugh Robinson made the first water flights in Europe while demonstrating the hydro at Nice before official representatives of various governments. That August Curtiss went abroad to close contracts for hydros to be delivered to England, Germany, Italy, France, Russia and Japan. Twenty hydros had been previously shipped to foreign naval bases. Private business did not begin until early in 1913.

Curtiss had gone to San Diego in January, intending to stay until May. When he heard that Harold F. McCormick of the International Harvester Corporation, was interested in the flying boat and might come to Hammondsport for a demonstration. Knowing that the sporting career of the boat was launched if one well known sportsman started using it, Curtiss turned back East, called on McCormick in Chicago and proceeded to Hammondsport. McCormick followed him there, liked the flying boat and ordered a new type tractor boat for commuting between his home at Lake Forrest and his office in Chicago. Charley Witmer, a former Curtiss student, was engaged as his pilot.

However, after the tractor boat was finished, they were unable to get it into the air. Again, regretfully, Curtiss had failed in applying the tractor principle whose advantages over the pusher were manifest. In the pusher type, for instance, everything that got loose around the engine or passenger compartment found its way into the propeller. Propellers had been broken when goggles, gloves, radiator caps or small parts which had vibrated loose were sucked into the slipstream.

When the new boat was remodeled into a pusher type, it flew right enough and presently Witmer was flying McCormick daily along the Lake Front and dropping him at the Chicago Yacht Club basin, only a few yards from Michigan Avenue. The newspapers exclaimed at this modern phenomenon, and it occurred to other sportsmen that here was something which had the flavor of a water sport with the added zest of flying thrown in.

Logan A. (Jack) Vilas of Chicago led the procession of would be sportsman-pilots to Hammondsport in the spring of 1913. Marshall E. Reid of Philadelphia was the second customer, and then William Thaw III of Pittsburgh and W. Stevenson MacGordon of New York drove gaily up to the Curtiss factory looking for a brace of water aircraft. G. M. Heckscher of New York ordered a flying boat and sent "Buzz" King to Hammondsport to learn to fly it for him. There were orders for boats from William B. Scripps, Detroit publisher; from George L. Peck, vice-president of the Pennsylvania Railroad, and from George U. von Utassy and Harry Harkness of New York.

With customers like these buying hydro-aeroplanes at $5,000 and the standard two-passenger flying boats at $7,000, Curtiss began to see a little easing of the financial strain. He could afford to widen the scope of his experiments.

Within one year he produced ten distinct types of over-water machines, ranging from a single-passenger monoplane racing boat built for Raymond V. Morris of New Haven, Connecticut, through several styles of two and three passenger machines to pleasure cruisers for four and five passengers. The most important development among them was the amphibian flying boat built for the Navy and first demonstrated by Lieut. B. L. Smith of the Marine Corps in May, 1913, at Hammondsport. A cabin flying boat built for the Italian Navy, was demonstrated by Raymond Morris on January 31, 1914. He was accompanied on the test flights by an official observer. This first cabin boat with its handsome hull of crotch mahogany showing the grain of the wood had a higher bow than previous Curtiss boats. It was built for operation from large battleships, and its two seats were in tandem rather than side by side.

Bill Pickens, ballyhoo artist for flying circuses, approached Curtiss with a suggestion that a thousand mile overwater race from Chicago to Detroit would give his new machines a good deal of publicity. Curtiss was noncommittal; he knew the dangers of flying over that unexplored region, but he finally agreed to enter a boat if the event was scheduled. Pickens persuaded E. Percy Noel of *Aero and Hydro* magazine to sponsor the race and sent out advance notices.

The entries were Tony Jannus and Hugh Robinson, flying for Tom Benoist of St. Louis; DeLloyd Thomsen flying for Walco; Glenn H. Martin in a Martin hydro; Roy M. Francis in a Patterson machine; Weldon Cooke, Becky Havens, J. B. R. Verplanck, and Jack Vilas, in Curtiss boats. All the entries but Robinson, who had wrecked his machine before reaching Chicago, reported in time for the start. Most of the machines gave a good accounting, although only Havens and Verplanck arrived at Detroit, chiefly because they had not received word that the race had been called on account of bad weather.

The thousand mile trip in the boat piloted by Becky Havens and owned by J. B. R. Verplanck of Fishkill-on-Hudson, had demonstrated the efficacy of the flying boat as a long distance cruiser. Other features were exhibited to the public by private owners who did much to build up public confidence in flying by means of the flying boat.

Harold McCormick demonstrated its convenience as an aerial ferry, and Marshall Reid gave numerous exhibitions of aerial gymnastics, popularly known as "fancy flying." Steve MacGordon and Bill Thaw demonstrated its ocean-going ability and they all combined to give frequent proof of its possibilities as a pleasure craft for the business man. But it remained for Jack Vilas to offer the most convincing proof that aircraft was a practical convenience rather than an expensive luxury.

Vilas was the first man to win a pilot's license in a flying boat as well as the first amateur to get any real fun out of aviation and still save money. He made practical use of his boats at his summer home in the Thousand Islands by hauling food and other supplies, calling on friends, visiting the clubhouse or going over to the polo field in them. He even did his courting via the flying boat, and thus became the first Romeo of the air.

In aviation magazines, there were tales of a thousand men buying boats the following year. Curtiss knew the number was exaggerated, since he had sold only 44 machines to sportsmen in 1913. But boom days for private over-water business had definitely arrived and he had more reason than ever before to be optimistic.

Not only was the flying boat, as Curtiss saw it, a safer proposition for sportsmen, but he offered other points in its favor. He is quoted in an article in *Popular Science Monthly*:

> I look forward to steady development and increased use of the flying boat for crossing the Great Lakes, wide bays and gulfs, and flight along river courses.
> The reason I believe that marine flying will be developed quicker than land is because there are no new landing fields needed. In other words, terminal facilities are already provided. Quiet

harbors, rivers and small lakes are ideal landing places for seaplanes and flying boats.

Furthermore there is no limitation in the width of a plane because there is ample room for even the largest boats to maneuver.

Boats are slow as compared to trains. The flying boat will therefore capture seacoast travel. And we know more about weather conditions on the sea, more about tides and more about general directions of the wind than we do on land. Mariners have been studying meteorological conditions of the sea for years and the Government already issues wind charts and has a well-organized service covering weather conditions.

Another thing, the relative speed of boats is slow as compared with the speed of railroad trains, so that aerial transportation with a speed of some 75 to 100 miles per hour is bound to cut down materially the time required to go from one seaport to another.

The flying boat was his personal pride and joy, and his relentless imagination explored its future interminably. He had always known that aircraft would some day travel as far as other carriers of passengers and freight, and much faster. But only a seaworthy craft like the flying boat was fit to cope with long stretches over water.

His most exciting project for 1914 was a large cabin flying boat ordered by Rodman Wanamaker for the avowed purpose of flying across the Atlantic Ocean.

North Island

THERE were few communities in the country which did not yearn to see some flying after Glenn Curtiss flew down the Hudson on May 29, 1910. And civic leaders everywhere stepped on each other's heels offering cash inducements to airmen. Two hundred thousand dollars in prize money was posted within a week.

The ten thousand dollars offered by the *New York Times* and the *Philadelphia Public Ledger* was claimed almost immediately by Charley Hamilton, who had planned to compete for the Albany flight prize. He made the first round trip flight between large cities on June thirteenth, at an average speed of 49 miles an hour.

But covering 175 miles by air was one thing; flying the 980 miles that lay between Chicago and New York was quite another. Curtiss believed that such a race "would have the effect of nearly deafening an aeroplane driver."

"When going at high speed," he explained, "the air rushes past one's ears so that it is difficult to hear even after the airship reaches the ground again. I experienced that in coming down the Hudson." Fuel capacity would be the greatest problem, with endurance second. "There are," he said, "many other hard features in a trip of that kind. There is the vibration of the wires, for instance, the possibility of nuts and bolts wearing through and of surfaces tearing off."

Still, he hastened to reassure interviewers, it was "a good idea."

Although the motives behind the prizes were excellent, the time limits expired on several of the offers before aircraft could catch up with the advanced ideas of their donors. The tempting prizes did inspire aviators all over the country to groom themselves for competitive and exhibition flying. Curtiss spent most of the ten thousand dollar *World* prize in preparing equipment for himself and others to take advantage of the consuming public curiosity about aeronautics.

Atlantic City offered five thousand dollars for a flight over the water, and Glenn Curtiss claimed it on the Fourth of July, by making ten laps over a five-mile course before a boardwalk crowd of 35,000. Since no one had flown fifty miles over water, it was an American record, which he bettered by flying 64 miles across Lake Erie from Cleveland to Cedar Point on August 30th. John McCurdy, A. E. A. member, who had joined Curtiss in exhibition work, broke this over-water record on January 30, 1911. He flew 90 miles off Key West, Florida, in an attempt to fly to Cuba, which, incidentally, was the first time any flyer had ever gotten "out of sight of land on a clear day."

Curtiss next gave some exhibitions at Pittsburgh, and then proceeded to Sheepshead Bay, Long Island, where he staged a five-airplane meet together with McCurdy, Willard, Ely, Mars and Post. They worked out a show which had to run a second week in order to accommodate the crowds.

Merely getting off the ground was no longer enough of a novelty. What the public wanted was something that looked spectacular. They got it. Some of it was pure hokum, as, for example, blowing off hats with the propeller slip stream. As they clutched their headgear or galloped after it, the members of the audience felt they were personally involved in the flying. The ladies loved it when their plumes stood on end, and were oh so thankful for their hatpins.

Quick starts, accurate landings, and quick climbs were dramatized to the utmost. The flyers usually managed to slip in a few really significant demonstrations, though other features were merely designed to amuse the crowd. Post, who had learned to fly that summer at Hammondsport, put on a broncho-busting act over a succession of hurdles; Ely flew over to Brighton Beach for a bowl of oysters. Anything to please the customers.

At Squantum Field, near Boston, a meet was staged by the Harvard Aeronautical Society. Curtiss did not fare so well in competition with Ralph Johnstone, Walter Brookins and Arch Hoxsey, all flying Wright planes. Johnstone established new American distance and nonstop records, and Brookins made an altitude record of 4,732 feet. Claude Grahame-White of England captured the ten thousand dollar *Boston Globe* prize in the speed race, with Curtiss second.

The gate receipts at the Long Island and Squantum meets were enormous and there were many distinguished guests in the audiences, among them President Taft who earnestly assured Curtiss that only his weight prevented him from accepting an invitation to fly.

New York had been selected as the site of the international aviation meet for October, although there had been furious bidding by Oakland, St. Louis, Washington, Des Moines, Portland, Oregon, and other cities. Americans who had expected him to again compete for the Gordon Bennett Cup were amazed when Curtiss announced that he would give up competitive flying. Even before this, he had grown weary of exhibition flying, which was really an alien conception to a sober young married man who was brought up by a severely Methodist grandmother. Curtiss never learned to smoke, and was frankly afraid of alcoholic stimulants. It was difficult for him to adopt the genial, easy-going attitude of more seasoned troupers. He felt like a glorified circus performer and did not pretend to enjoy it. Thanks to efficient advance promotion, he found his picture plastered on the billboards everywhere he went. He was always in the limelight and hard pressed to fulfill the fantastic promises of press agents.

Some of his companions had been acrobats and tightrope walkers, most of them were professional showmen whose ego had come to demand publicity and applause. They were hardworking and honest fellows and capable flyers, but men like Hamilton, who consumed quantities of rye whiskey; and Jack Frisbie, with his rumpled cap, flushed face and enormous laughter, had no interest in aeroplane design or the future possibilities of flying which so engrossed Curtiss.

Since Curtiss was enjoined from selling aeroplanes, it was necessary for him to retain ownership of the machines. If he employed aviators to fly them, he would have to carry expensive liability for their safety. He therefore leased the machines to others and they flew them on their own responsibility.

But it was impossible to satisfy the thrill-loving public without constant, costly breakage. Because the show had to go on, spare parts of every kind and extra mechanics for repair work were required. And sometimes, when they were forced to land outside the grounds, there were damaged fences and corn patches to be settled for. His transportation bills were tremendous, as he had to use express cars at prohibitive rates, rather than freight cars, in order to keep engagements on time. All in all, trouping

THE LIFE OF GLENN CURTISS

was a thankless chore and Curtiss could not see his way clear to going on with it.

The Curtiss Exhibition Company "for the purpose of training aviators and giving flight exhibitions" had been organized September 1, 1910. Jerome Fanciulli, the general manager, with booking offices in New York, took care of promotion work. He arranged dates, engaged flyers and handled all the machinery of the flight exhibitions. Occasionally he persuaded people they might like to be exhibition pilots, and sent them up to Hammondsport for flight training.

Fanciulli was always on the lookout for new material. When Blanche Stuart Scott became newsworthy because she had driven an automobile across the continent, he suggested a flying career as a logical step, and sent her up to Hammondsport to learn to fly. The factory staff did not think women should fly aeroplanes, but since Fanciulli had regarded it as a good idea, Curtiss proceeded to give her lessons. And she later became the first woman professional pilot in America.

As a student, she was eager to start actual flying and hard to hold down on the ground. Once Curtiss read her a mild lecture on the need of more care. But Damon Merrill was less tolerant. When she called him over to her hobbled machine one day, declared she was ready to leave the ground, and ordered him to remove the solder that prevented her from pulling the throttle open, his reply was:

"Miss Scott, Mr. Curtiss will be back from Rochester in the morning and I'll go just as far as he'll let me. If he's willing for you to break your neck, it's all right with me."

Curtiss would supply aeroplanes and train aviators for the exhibition company, but henceforth he would leave

284

show-flying to those who liked it, and confine himself to testing and demonstrations. First, however, there was the Belmont Park meet to be disposed of. Curtiss had prepared a little pusher monoplane which offered much less head resistance than his biplanes. He shipped it to New York with the other four machines which Ely, Willard, McCurdy and Mars would fly in the meet. Possibly the new racing plane would be entered for the Gordon Bennett event, with Hamilton as the pilot.

The weather between October 22nd and 30th was generally unsettled so that flying was hazardous. It played unaccountable tricks with the foreign planes which took pot luck with the wind. Hubert Latham, flying an Antoinette, was blown nearly upside down at 3000 feet and fell off into a dive from which he barely recovered a few feet off the ground. C. Audemars and Roland Garros in Damoiselle monoplanes made a circuit of the course for a special prize in a small tempest that tossed them about like hapless butterflies. A number of machines were wrecked, and there was never a dull moment for the audience, but it was hard on the contestants, particularly the Americans among them.

The Wright company had a number of capable flyers at the meet, but refused to allow them to take part in the cross-country events, though they were permitted to make altitude attempts, which looked very spectacular in the high winds. Curtiss, too, said thumbs down on practically all flying in his ships, although Ely, Willard, McCurdy and Mars did enter some events and win a small share of the $55,650 offered in prize money.

The Curtiss monoplane never started. It was very fast according to tests; faster than any of the ships entered, Curtiss estimated. But it had one serious defect: a tricky response to the controls which at high speed made it definitely unsafe. So the evening before the Gordon Bennett race, he withdrew it. The Aero Club members the newspapermen and Curtiss's friends were frantic and begged him to reconsider. But he remained firm because he knew the odds were against him.

Walter Brookins, in the speedy little Wright biplane, crashed in a preliminary trial at an estimated speed of 80 miles an hour, and John B. Moisant, the only American flyer who started, was forced down before the end of the race. The prize went to Claude Grahame-White of England, in a Bleriot, at an average speed of 63 miles an hour.

Curtiss scrapped the little monoplane he had hoped to enter for the Bennett Cup and prepared to wind up business in the East so he might set up winter quarters for experimental work on the West Coast. He was determined the ice on Lake Keuka would not again deprive him of three months' experimental work on the water.

He arrived in Los Angeles on December ninth together with a carload of experimental equipment and began looking around for proving grounds. When North Island, near San Diego, was offered to him by the Spreckels Company, he accepted gladly. This isolated spot four miles long and two miles wide, flat as a pancake and covered with sagebrush was uninhabited save for jackrabbits, quail and other small game. Spanish Bight, a strip of sheltered water, lay on one side of the island. At low tide, a stretch of narrow sand connected it with Coronado Island, but it was completely cut off by water from the mainland.

It was an ideal location for a flying camp, as it was practically inaccessible to the curious. The work of clearing the field of weeds and sage brush was started immediately. To Curtiss, accustomed to anything from a rough meadow, to a class C baseball park, this landing field with space for two courses (or "runways," in our terminology) was unparalleled luxury.

Colonization of the island went forward rapidly. A machine shop was installed and tools brought from Hammondsport, together with Curtiss' newest idea for a pontoon, by Damon Merrill, who was to be the shop foreman. The work shop and two hangars were erected by the San Diego Aero Club. They were wooden frames with canvass and tar paper covers, which blew off with maddening regularity. Several machines were especially prepared for training purposes. A tent hangar for the hydro-aero equipment was set up on the beach.

The only structures already on the island were a little cottage and an abandoned boxing pavilion. The cottage served as living quarters for a few men, though most of them roomed in San Diego and shuttled back and forth daily by motor boat. Those who lived at the island did their own cooking and washing. There was plenty of edible game there, but it was so tame that the students preferred to make pets of the rabbits and quail and have their meat brought over from San Diego.

Spuds Ellyson, first man detailed in response to Curtiss's offer to give flight instruction to officers of the Army and Navy, arrived on January second. Others followed him and flight work at North Island went briskly forward.

For the first time in two years, Curtiss found himself in an isolated spot away from the drudgery of barnstorming. He was in the company of well educated officers enthusiastic about the aeroplane as a new military weapon. They were technically trained; he was not. But they recognized his genius for breaking new trails, and eagerly served under him. In their friendly company he lost the moodiness which had settled down upon him within the past year, and some of his natural reticence.

If he had something on his mind, some experimental idea or other, he liked to talk about it, and Ellyson and Walker and Beck and Kelly were good listeners. They found G. H. companionable. And they had a great respect for his workmanlike capacity for original aircraft design.

A few civilians drifted into the camp. Uncle Tom Baldwin was a frequent visitor, and Charles Witmer and Robert St. Henry, from Chicago came seeking flight instruction. Then Lincoln Beachey, who had made a reputation for himself as a balloonist, turned up. He had had his first aeroplane flight with Curtiss at Atlantic City in July, 1910, and decided he wanted Curtiss to teach him how to fly.

With Hugh Robinson as assistant instructor, a rigid system of throttled-down motors was worked out. The instruction process was begun by seating the student in the plane and letting him study the movement of the controls. Then he was headed down the short runway, with the throttle on the motor stopped at a certain point by means of a wedge-shaped stick. He attempted to steer a straight course to the end of the runway where another student was waiting to turn him around. Power was so limited that he could not take off or travel much faster than five miles an hour on the ground.

After several days and innumerable runs up and down the field, "grass-cutting" for all he was worth, the power was gradually increased until the student could keep the plane in a straight line under almost full throttle and he was ready for the first hop. Starting from the far end of the short, quarter-mile course, and heading towards the instructor, the tyro was told to give it all of the limited throttle, and as the plane reached top ground speed, to gently pull back on the control and the plane would take the air. As soon as he was off the ground, he was instructed to push the wheel forward to a neutral position and watch his course, while he kept the ship balanced by means of the shoulder yokes. After a few yards, the machine would gradually begin to settle, and the steering wheel was then to be brought back in order to accomplish a landing on the two rear wheels.

If the student failed to pull the wheel back or pushed forward so that the machine first touched on the front wheel, a "bucking broncho" effect was produced, much to the annoyance of the entire student body, for even slight breakage meant delays.

When many straightaway hops had been made, the power was increased to full throttle and the student was permitted to make flights for the length of the long course, generally at an altitude of only a few feet. The machine at this stage was always landed and turned on the ground preparatory to the return trip. Gradually the altitude was increased and half turns were made to right and left. Finally, full turns, and the student was ready to advance from the famous Lizzie to the 60-horsepower exhibition type planes.

The flight course often gave rise to exciting incidents. Once the mechanic forgot to readjust the screw on the throttle when a lightweight student followed a heavy man, and the machine rose off schedule. And men like Beck, Ellyson and Beachey were hard to hold down. Occasionally Curtiss glanced out of the shop door and chuckled to see them at the far end of the field frightening the jackrabbits in their desperate efforts to make a throttled-down grass-cutter fly.

As in the A.E.A. days, flying was still done at dawn and just before sundown when the air was almost still. The students spent all day at "lab-work," studying the mechanical side of the aeroplane and the engine, and patching up damages to machines. Curtiss was busy keeping in touch with the Hammondsport factory, as well as the exhibition company. Whenever possible he worked at his experiments, day and night, until it was almost time to go out for sunrise practice with the students.

Next to the hydro experiments he was making with Ellyson, Curtiss was most concerned with devising a means of making the instruction process less speculative. But it was not until that May, back at Hammondsport, that he succeeded in perfecting the system of dual controls which enabled a flying schoolmaster to show a student how to manipulate the controls of a machine while it was in flight. He could teach by act rather than by word of mouth.

Curtiss now actively pushed his plans for a flying school, which he had announced when he retired from exhibition flying. Business had called him East early in the spring, but he returned to San Diego. In the middle of April, he came East again, with Ellyson and Tom Baldwin, stopping off long enough to give demonstrations with the hydro-aeroplane enroute. They stopped at Salt Lake City and flew off Winona Lake, where Billy Sunday and a genial Methodist bishop entertained them with amusing stories and Curtiss's favorite beverage, buttermilk.

Mapping out a plan for a school was easy enough but providing equipment, finding instructors, and financing it was quite a problem. That dismally dead thing, the Herring-Curtiss Company, had been officially wound up through bankruptcy and the Curtiss Aeroplane Company formed, and now Curtiss started organizing the flying school.

The first enrolled student was waiting for Curtiss when he arrived in Hammondsport. Beckwith Havens of Red Hook, New York, had been a dirt track automobile racer, had sold automobiles in Los Angeles, and returned

East when he was bitten with a consuming desire to learn to fly. He was introduced to Augustus Post of the Aero Club, who promptly sent him over to the Exhibition Company office at 1737 Broadway. Fanciulli decided they could use an aeroplane salesman and engaged Becky to attend two aeronautical expositions in that capacity. Though he sold no planes, Havens had earned for himself the proud title of first aeroplane salesman in America.

Curtiss informed him that the tuition fee would be $500, but Becky replied that he was an employee of the company and ought to get flight instruction for nothing. He did, but in a desultory fashion. Curtiss was busy completing his dual control method, and often away demonstrating hydro-aeroplanes, sometimes with Ellyson, sometimes alone. Becky could find nothing but an abandoned balloon hangar at the Kingsley pasture on the lake. He was beginning to get discouraged when Naval Lieutenant John H. Towers turned up for aviation duty, and Ellyson made up his mind he would teach both of them to fly.

With the help of the shop, they rehabilitated an old exhibition plane, installed a four-cylinder motor and began grass-cutting. When they were not charging up and down the field they were hanging around the plant talking about aircraft with Curtiss and Kleckler, or observing the hydro experiments on the lake. Becky Havens was flying nicely at the end of a few weeks, and in June, he was asked to join the exhibition flyers.

Presently Cromwell Dixon, the boy balloonist, W. Elwood (Gink) Doherty of Buffalo, and Lieut. J. B. McClaskey, U. S. M. C., retired, signed up for the course. Charley Witmer and Bob St. Henry reported for advanced training. Jack Towers had soon completed the flight lessons as well as his ground course at the factory, and a representative of the Aero Club of America came to Hammondsport to observe his pilot's license test. He passed it easily and was awarded license No. 62.

The F.A.I.* license test required the flyer to take off and make five consecutive figure eight's around two pylons set a thousand feet apart, and to make an accurate landing, stopping the machine within fifty feet of a given mark. This test was made twice and, either during the flying of the figure eight's or during a separate flight, the plane had to reach an altitude of five hundred feet.

Curtiss found little time to do instruction work that summer. He was engrossed with improving the hydro-aeroplane and the problems of trying further to popularize flying. He had always maintained: "When we've got the aeroplane perfected, we won't have to press its claims on the Post Office. It will become the long distance postman automatically."

Paul Beck, one of his Army students, who was by now a Captain, liked the idea and together with Curtiss, arranged for a mail-carrying test on September 23, 1911, during the second Nassau Boulevard air meet on Long Island. As a result, Postmaster General Hitchcock, who accompanied Beck on the flight with the first bag of air mail, included in his budget for 1912 an item of $50,000 for experiments in carrying mail by aeroplane. Earle L. Ovington made the first authorized demonstration over a regular route, and Becky Havens and others also carried mail by air at an early date.

Curtiss felt the experiment was incomplete unless mail was carried far; and on October 9th of that year, Hugh Robinson, in a Curtiss hydro-aeroplane, carried a load of first class mail a distance of 375 miles, from Winona, Minnesota, to Rock Island, Illinois, with stops at Prairie du Chien, Wisconsin, and Clinton, Iowa. Though this

* Federation Aeronautique Internationale.

flight made an excellent impression, Congress failed to approve the recommendation by the Post Office Department of an appropriation for air mail experiments.

Another demonstration designed to arouse interest in flying was the first recorded doctor-to-patient flight. Dr. Philias Alden was flown by Hugh Robinson to the home of an injured child. The boy's condition in this case was not desperate and the physician could have reached his bedside by automobile in less time than it took to get to the field, make the flight and reach the house. Nevertheless it was a breath-taking item as it reached the public, and won enthusiastic applause.

Arrangements for again moving the school equipment to San Diego for the winter were practically completed when another prospective civilian student appeared at Hammondsport. His family had refused to give him money to spend on learning to fly, but J. Lansing Callan had two hundred and fifty dollars of his own.

"It's all the money I can get," he announced.

"Well, maybe you can work out the other half of the tuition some way," Curtiss agreed, although he had learned to turn a deaf ear toward candidates who tried to get flying instruction without paying for it.

Letters came in frequently from people who had achieved fame of one kind or another, offering to learn to fly for nothing. They would be celebrated aviators some day and the publicity value of having taught them would more than repay him for his trouble, they declared. Comers to Hammondsport included men who boasted loudly of their plans to purchase aeroplanes. In the meantime, they would pass the time learning to fly. Curtiss' answer to them was always: "Why not deposit the five hundred dollars for the flying course now? Then if you buy a machine, I'll credit you in that amount toward the price of it." The company could not afford to run the risk of possible damage to planes with no reserve fund to pay for repairs.

But young Callan was in such deadly earnest that Curtiss agreed to extend him part credit and took him along to San Diego, where a goodly number of students were enrolled that winter. Among them were Mr. and Mrs. William B. Atwater of New York state; S. C. Lewis of New York City; Rutherford Page, recent Yale graduate; Captain George Capitsini, of the Greek Army; J. B. McCalley of Pennsylvania; John Kaminski of Milwaukee; Kono Takeshi and Motohisa Kondo, from Japan; and Julia Clark, early woman flyer; as well as a number of others who later became well known as exhibition pilots. Lieut. MacClaskey was appointed instructor of that winter's group, and since he was brought up in the stern tradition of the Marine Corps, he became a gruff taskmaster who never minced words with an over-ambitious student. When Lanny Callan had mastered the art, under Mac's tutelage, he was employed as assistant to him and in that way worked out his tuition.

That winter there was another recruit from the Far East. Mohan Singh, had come from far off India to enroll in the school. This tall gaunt young oriental, who seldom smiled, never ate meat and never drank anything but water, was still one of the most agreeable souls that could be encountered. He passed his F. A. I. test at North Island, but wanted to know more about the flying boat type which Curtiss was developing that spring and announced that as soon as he had perfected his flying he would buy a machine and take it to India.

A few members of the San Diego group entered the air meet at Los Angeles that winter, and Bill Atwater established an American speed record of 73.08 miles per hour in a Curtiss machine. He and his wife bought a pair of Curtiss hydro-aeroplanes and took them to China and Japan for demonstration and exhibition.

The hydro had already been demonstrated in Europe by Hugh Robinson and, as foreign orders came in, Curtiss was compelled to send mechanics abroad to assemble the machines, and pilots who could teach their new owners how to fly them. More frequently he economized by sending a man who was a pilot-mechanic and could do double duty. These travelers returning to Hammondsport gave it a cosmopolitan air not often found in small villages.

Those graduate flyers who were not demonstrating Curtiss planes abroad were mostly flying them in exhibitions in this country that summer. The Curtiss Exhibition Company had made 541 flights in 210 cities and towns during 1911, and from December, 1910, to December, 1912, its gross receipts were close to a million dollars. The overhead expenses were so heavy there was little net profit, but the main purpose of keeping Curtiss planes and motors before the public was amply fulfilled.

Cromwell Dixon, Jimmy Ward, Charley Walsh and Lincoln Beachey had all become popular exhibition flyers, particularly Beachey after he dazzled the country on June 28, 1911, by flying over Niagara Falls, down the gorge and under the suspension bridge.

Beachey had a curious background as a pilot. Despite his skill as a balloonist, he was a complete failure at first with aeroplanes. He seemed to have no sense of direction or altitude and crashed several planes trying to learn to land during the second Los Angeles air meet. Nobody could understand why anyone let him wreck so much equipment, but somehow Curtiss was sure he would eventually conquer whatever was holding him back.

After Beachey came to North Island, he improved.

"Flying didn't come to me at first; then all of a sudden it came big," was his way of explaining it.

Beachey won prizes, records, praise. Seemingly he had no fear and the rhythmic beauty of his flying has never been equalled. This reticent, red-headed little chap with a nasal voice and a weakness for feminine worship was a born showman. He would climb into the nearest group of clouds, if there were any, and then could be seen skipping from cloud to cloud, visible only at times. When he was through with this, back to earth he would come in a steep dive that seemed to guarantee extinction. With his motor cut off, down he came like a plummet, three, four, five thousand feet, making no move to straighten out. Then he would pull back on the controls, make a couple of steeply banked turns, and land wherever he chose, as lightly as a feather.

His famous "ocean roll" was a series of wicked-looking left and right swings, which made his craft wallow through the air as if it were riding a procession of giant breakers.

But luck kept pace with Beachey. Once at a race track, because the crowd liked to see him moving close to the ground at full speed so that they could compare his speed with that of a horse or auto, he undertook to fly over the race course at a height of only fifteen feet. Down the home stretch he swept at sixty miles an hour and nobody had thought to remove the finish wire that crossed the track in the air at the judges' stand. It was good stout copper wire, and Beachey was headed straight for it. If it struck him, he would be cut in two. He saw the wire and tried to clear it but struck it with the center of his small front landing wheel. An inch or so lower or higher would have turned him upwards or downwards to disaster. Instead the wire was cut in two and snapped.

A favorite stunt of the time was to announce the appearance of an eccentric woman flyer from France. Dressed in the most elaborate and inappropriate fashion, seated on the exposed little seat in front of the lower wing, the "lady" would do all sorts of tricks in front of the grandstand, while making an heroic effort to keep down skirts and avoid an exhibition of lacy lingerie.

Many flyers tried to imitate him, and "The flyer met his death while imitating Beachey" came to be a stock line in crash stories. Beachey himself was so irritated at its recurrence that he sent word to the papers that he would give an exhibition to prove how mistaken they were. Accordingly he went to a height of four thousand feet, made a long dive just as most of the flyers who had been killed had done, and levelled off easily while still a safe distance from the ground. He landed and explained that most of the others had met death not because they were copying his perfectly safe tactics, but because of lack of experience and, in some cases, because of faulty machines.

It is certain no flyer has ever won so much sincere admiration from his fellow pilots. They worshipped Beachey's genius for flying aeroplanes.

Beachey and the other Curtiss exhibition pilots were frequently in and out of Hammondsport with glowing tales of the road. Becky Havens, for example, who had flown in New York, Maine, Iowa, Illinois, Ohio, Wisconsin, Kansas, Oklahoma, Texas, Arkansas, Georgia Florida and Cuba, returned with the verdict: "It's a dandy game, once you've learned how to get out of baseball parks and race tracks without breaking your neck." At the beginning he had worked on a basis of twenty-five percent of the gross contract price, later for fifty percent. As the contracts ranged from a minimum of five hundred dollars a day to a maximum of two thousand, Becky soon amassed a nice bank account.

To the adventurous youngsters the "big money" talk
was very alluring. Then Bill Pickens appeared on the
Hammondsport scene and found a veritable congress of nations. He could not resist proposing that they organize
a flying circus. Pickens, formerly Barney Oldfield's manager, was an excellent press-agent who had early in life
made up his mind that most people would believe anything they were told, and who devoted his literary talents,
which were of first- rate calibre, to telling them anything.
The advertised motto of the International Flying Circus
thus became:

ONE MILE WIDE AND THREE MILES HIGH
FLIES RAIN, SHINE OR CYCLONE

The fact that, among other things, no plane existed
in the world at the time which could fly so high disturbed
neither Bill nor the public.

Among the featured acts of their program was that of
Horace Kearney, who was billed as the Peck's Bad Boy
of the Air. His favorite stunt was placing an egg on a sheet
in the middle of the field and breaking it with his front
wheel. Another was going fishing by air, except that he
shattered the illusion for the audience on one occasion
when he landed safely with his catch in his hands *and*
a large piece of brown butcher's paper clinging to the running gear. Kearney conscientiously lived up to his program
title by becoming the pride of the hospital accident wards
all along the route.

Mohan Singh, the first Flying Hindu, in his high turban,
was the center of attraction, with Kondo, the Flying Jap,
a close second. Lanny Callan, who had grown a black
mustache and was billed as Monsieur Jean Callon of Paris,
played his part very well until a delegation of loyal Frenchmen in Milwaukee announced they wished to interview
him and present a medal. M. Callon, who could speak no

French, made an abrupt disappearance over a high fence surrounding the flying field, while Pickens informed the visitors that their countryman was suffering from bronchitis. Julia Clark, the Bird Girl, Farnum Fish, the Schoolboy Aviator and Kaminsky, the Pole, were other leading attractions.

The Circus played in several towns. Then Julia Clark crashed to her death at Springfield, Illinois, and the group disintegrated. Most of the flyers returned to Hammondsport where the summer school session was in full swing.

Aviators' Home

THE 1912 school at Hammondsport was entirely different from the school of the previous year, when an occasional student turned up for such casual instruction as he could promote.

The students enrolled during 1912 came from all over the world. The first entries for the spring class were Louis Gertson of Toronto, Lieut. Augustine Parla of Cuba, Rafael Marti of Porto Rico, and Frank Seidel and Glenn Tate of Alexander, Indiana. Mohan Singh came on from North Island for advanced training. David McCullough arrived from Pennsylvania to visit the Hildreth family, became fascinated with flying and enrolled for a course.

Harry Higgins, son of the former governor of New York state, also joined the class, and Gink Doherty, back on a visit, began flying again. Others who visited at Hammondsport that year were Henry Ford, automobile manufacturer, who wanted to see the new flying boats, and pilots Hugh Robinson, John McCurdy, F. J. Terrill, William Hemstrought, Nick Berlin, and Charley Witmer. The Army sent Lieut. Harold Geiger and Lieut. Frank Kennedy, and they were later joined by Lieuts. Brereton, Goodier, Parks and McCreary. Several Naval officers were there on aviation duty.

Curtiss made Francis Wildman, a local boy, an instructor at the school. He was a young mechanic from the factory who was generally known as Doc, because he was a good hand at doctoring up motors. Wildman, one of the steadiest flyers on record, was in charge of hydro instruction, with Callan in charge of the land plane classes.

As a result of the tour of the Orient by the Atwaters, the Japanese government sent Lieut. Kono, Lieut. Yamada and Naval Engineer Nakashima for flight training. During that summer session and the following one, there were also pupils from England, France, Germany, Italy, Russia, Holland, Scotland, Ireland, Spain, Poland, China, Mexico and Greece.

The juxtaposition of various racial temperaments gave rise to some tense and some comic moments. The three Japanese officers were fatalists and wanted to imitate Beachey's dives after a few lessons, except that they did not see the necessity of levelling off as they neared the water. Fortunately, the instructors were strong enough to wrest the controls from them. Wildman, ordinarily a peaceable fellow, lost his temper completely one day and shouted:

"You gosh-danged idiot, we'd have been killed if I hadn't grabbed the controls."

The answer was a shrug and, "We must all die some time, what matter when?"

"The Hell you say! Well I don't intend to die just yet, in the first place, and in the second place, it takes time and money to fix up these machines."

Not only the instructors but the students had to learn to be careful not so much for the sake of their own bones, as because of execrations heaped upon them if one of the machines had to go to the shop.

Lieut. Nakashima, of the Japanese contingent, was a little short on patience. One day his instructor carefully told him not to attempt a half-turn around a certain barn. Nakashima disobeyed. He side-slipped, fell twenty feet and smashed the wing of the machine. The plump little man was dreadfully hurt, not in body, but in pride. He sat in a corner of the hangar for several hours like a whipped child.

Kondo, of the circus flyers, had come to Hammondsport with the ambition to buy a hydro and take it back to Japan for exhibition purposes. He struck up a friendship with the Japanese officers and through his superior knowledge of English materially aided in their instruction. While he was waiting for his machine, Charles Kirkham asked Kondo to test a plane which he had built at Savona. Kirkham, who was an expert on motors, had seen a good deal of flying and thought he had some valuable design ideas. Instead of the old shoulder brace for the ailerons, all three controls were combined into one control stick or steering column. Although this method was radically different from the one in the Curtiss planes, Kondo believed he could operate it.

The machine was set up in a field near Savona and he made a few short hops without any trouble Then he attempted a circle in the air. Evidently confused by the new control, he was instantly killed as the machine dived into a steel-framed windmill. All the school students, even Kondo's philosophic countrymen, were upset by the accident.

The hydro and boat courses were especially popular. To speed water training, a turntable was built in the ramp on which the machines came out of the lake. When one student stepped out of a machine, it was immediately turned about without stopping the motor; another student took his place and went roaring down to the water.

In the beginning both pupils and teachers were trussed

up in cumbersome cork life preservers which impeded free muscular movement. Later Curtiss worked out an ingenious bib stuffed with kapok, which was strapped around the flyer's neck and hung down on his chest. In case he fell in the lake, even though he was unconscious, this extraordinarily buoyant device would keep his head floating above water until he was picked up by a boat. The instructors, who had to splash around in the water all day, or make flight after flight with the students, wore heavy kapoklined jackets especially made for them at the plant.

Landings, of course, caused the most mishaps. Often students who misjudged their distance or their ability to maneuver, ran into the marshes at the edge of the lake. Or failing to shut off the engine as they crossed the white lines marked on the field to tell them when to do so, they crashed into the stone wall at the opposite end of the course.

When J. D. Van Vliet, a Dutch engineer, made his first free flight he shut off his motor too late and crashed into the wall. He was pitched forward and draped over the stones. One of the Japanese students gently lifted the limp form off the wall, folded his arms across his breast and tucked a flower into the peaceful hands. When the instructor arrived to go sadly about the business of untangling the machine from the stone wall, Van Vliet, who had only had his wind knocked out, blinked and sat up. Seeing the flower he stuck it gratefully into his buttonhole arose and helped untwist the wreckage of the machine. Thereafter the self-contained Hollander was known as Stonewall Jackson.

Even with dual controls on all the school hydros and boats, flying was never too safe. Curtiss constantly stressed the need for caution, the instructors preached it, and consequently accidents were as a rule not critical. The single student fatality was not due to inability or carelessness on the part of its victim.

Fred F. Gardiner was a likable young fellow who was rated highest of all the prospective pilots scheduled to take license tests in June, 1913. He finished his first figure eight and was flying at about 400 feet altitude when something went wrong. The machine came darting and swooping down. It stalled and dove straight into the lake. When Buzz King and Charley Witmer reached the flying boat two minutes later, they at first found no trace of the pilot. The coroner's inquest later revealed no water in his lungs and no bones broken. The verdict was that he had died of a stroke due to excitement.

Each year's training group differed from the last. The 1911 group was entirely professional, most of them men accustomed to hazards. The 1912 group was half professional and half sporting, while there was a large influx of wealthy sportsmen in 1913. Time was when a student spoke of owning a plane his classmates knew he was only bragging; while these sportsman-pilots had every intention of buying one or more machines.

In spite of the more substantial financial rating of the sportsmen, the run-of-the-mill students were on very friendly terms with them. Jack Vilas, who had whiskers like a Castilian grandee, won a host of friends, as did Marshall Reid.

The old grads and new fledglings came wandering back year after year, too, because human beings like to foregather in a spot where the very air reeks of the subject they are most interested in. And having been there once, they could not stay away.

For most of them it was a wonderful holiday, although each man was absorbed in his own work and in the new jobs Curtiss wisely enough had always in store for them.

The classes were so crowded that no new enrollments could-be accepted in the summer of 1914, when there were two school hydros and two flying boats, instead of only one each, as in 1913. Besides the Navy and Army machines, there were apt to be private owner planes about. Often as many as seven planes at a time were flying above Lake Keuka, including several training machines.

There were no instruments to guide the fledgling or the aviators. The pilots flew the plane in those days, not the plane the pilot, as it would seem to the oldtimers. Today an accurate rate of climb indicator tells a flyer whether or not he is climbing too steeply; then he rocked the ship to test for a stall. If the ailerons responded sluggishly, he nosed the plane down a little.

"When in difficulty, nose down," was a cardinal rule of the school. Difficulty usually meant that the student was climbing too steeply or banking at the wrong angle, and the machine was consequently getting out of control. By nosing down sharply, he increased his speed and made the controls normally effective again.

Nose down! If you are losing speed, nose down! If in a stall, nose down! They were constantly reminded to maintain altitude and be prepared to glide down in case the motor or propeller failed.

The Curtiss flyer relied upon the rush of air against his face or the flutter of his coatsleeve to assure him that he was going ahead at the speed he expected from his machine. He could estimate his revolutions per minute by listening to the motor. Wright pilots used a piece of yarn on a stick in front of the pilot as a speed and drift indicator.

In 1912 a primitive tachometer to measure revolutions per minute was introduced, and the Warner aero-meter was devised by A. P. Warner for measuring speed. The

Elliott Instrument Company of London had developed a very elaborate instrument panel which had devices for measuring speed, altitude, r. p. m's., and an oil pressure gauge. But they were not, in the beginning, very dependable.

Lawrence Sperry, one of the Curtiss students, was working on an interesting idea for a gyroscopic stabilizer, which held out promise for the future. Sperry, first appeared at Hammondsport in 1912. His father, who was Dr. Elmer Sperry inventor of the gyroscopic compass, had become acquainted with Curtiss and both were convinced that a gyroscope might be harnessed to the controls of an aeroplane. Since 1908 Curtiss had anticipated the obvious advantages of an automatic means to keep a machine on an even keel, and he eagerly agreed to cooperate with Dr. Sperry and his son on such a project.

Young Lawrence, known as Gyro Sperry, was a tall, rangy youth who had lost his heart to flying when he saw Farman make a flight on Long Island in 1908. He enrolled in 1913 for a flying boat course and qualified as a pilot in October. Gyro was a friendly boy, but for all his easy-going nature, he had tremendous courage and preseverance.

The Curtiss shop was at his disposal and he worked for months trying to perfect the strange-looking gyroscopic stabilizer. He found helpful allies in Naval officers Richardson and Bellinger. During the summer, Gyro made an almost entirely automatically controlled flight of 20 miles or more in a flying boat with Pat Bellinger.

The device had defects and needed patient adjustment Its two most trying peculiarities were sudden failure to function and the tendency to over-control. When the latter occurred, the plane was apt to be thrown into a dangerous bank from which it could only be righted by releasing the gyro and reverting to manual control.

The experiments were continued during the winter at North Island. And during the following summer the aeroplane stabilizer won a prize of 50,000 francs offered by the French War Department for a "stable aeroplane." The judges were amazed to see young Sperry walk calmly out on the wing of the Curtiss flying boat, while the automatic pilot flew the plane "without human aid."

It was typical of the practical optimism of Curtiss and the men working with him at aviation that they appreciated the value of such a device in 1912, although it did not come into general recognition until years later.

"On good days we learn to fly; on rainy days we learn why," was the order of events at Kingsley Field. On stormy days, every man put on his overalls and went into the shops and hangars to learn the mechanical answers. They cleaned out carbon, ground valves and took machines apart. Curtiss had a theory that a flyer must know the inside of his motor as well as he knew the controls, so that he could tell exactly what was wrong with it by listening to it purr.

The flight routine was strenuous enough, especially for the instructors, who seldom put in less than 400 miles' flying a day. They were up at 3:45, doing alarm clock duty with those socialites still asleep. In small groups, the students trekked over to the lake shore, where the sun was peeping over Urbana Hill, and the flying day began.

"Who's first? You, Horsepower?"

Student H. P. Harris climbed into the seat of the hydro just under the leading edge of the lower wing beside Instructor Callan. The mechanics stationed at the wing-tips helped guide the hydro through the hangar doors and down the runway.

Once afloat, the throttle was opened, and with a roar from the exhaust and a swirl of spray, the machine skimmed the surface, and then they were off. In the air the instructor climbed the ship to about four hundred feet and signaled the student to take the controls. For a mile or so they flew along on a level, while the instructor sat with his arms folded and his eyes alert for errors. Just off Willow Point he ordered the student to head for a landing. If he put the ship down too fast, there would be a restraining hand on the controls; otherwise every student was given his head until they were close to the water. Then came the signal to reduce speed and level off gradually.

The instructor put his hands on the controls and guided the student to an easy landing. Then the throttle was opened again and they went up for another mile and a half turn before landing. One or two more landings completed the daily ritual.

After two hours of lessons it was time for breakfast. If Bill Thaw with his Fiat roadster was at the field, a dozen or more men mounted his running boards and fenders for the ride to breakfast at Mrs. Mott's boarding house, otherwise known as Aviators' Home. After breakfast they sat on the bench built around the big butternut tree in the front yard. At eight o'clock, they were mostly back at the field and if it was calm, there was flying throughout the day. At five o'clock they returned in a body for the sort of dinner to set up a tired man.

Mrs. Lulu Mott, whose squat two-story house on Sheather Street housed many of the students, supplied meals to most of them. Her terms were "Pay five dollars a week and eat all you can." And the meals were ample and delicious.

As the students were a mixed lot, they occasionally became a little unruly and Aviators' Home was the worse for wear. If matters grew serious, Mrs. Mott called on the instructors to restore order. Once a wild Russian student and an equally wild fledgling from Buffalo challenged each other to a pistol duel at a distance of nine feet. One of the principals was stationed in the parlor bedroom, the other in the room directly above. At a given signal they began firing enthusiastically through floor and ceiling. Mrs. Mott hastily summoned Professor Callan and he threatened the ringleaders with two days' suspension from flying. That settled it.

Evenings the students went dancing at Mrs. Young's pavilion down the lake, or to the movies over the firehouse and they visited the bowling alley installed by James H. Smellie next door to his drug store. He got along fine with the boys, until one day when the telephone rang and he answered it:

"Smellie, Hammondsport."

Whereupon they shouted: "Say! Aren't you ashamed to run down a nice clean town like this," and brought his wrath down upon their heads.

The socially inclined Army and Navy officers and civilians spent their evenings calling at village homes, several of which had an excellent idea of what entertainment should be. The Chaplain, Hildreth, Drake or Seely homes were particularly hospitable. The Seelys had lost the key to their house the week they moved in. Lyman J. (Lad) Seely was an ardent stamp collector and made philatelists out of many students.

Curtiss could never understand why Seely, who was his sales and advertising manager, should keep open house continuously. He often shook his head and said: "I don't see how you can stand all that crowd around your house. I should go crazy."

He had his own Aerohut up the lake and the flyers were always welcome there or at his home, but in installments. He was too preoccupied to pay much attention to them. Nevertheless, although nobody could ever discover why, he was considered a good host. He liked to provide entertainment for others on his trips to New York and frequently bought theatre tickets, though his own enjoyment of the drama was very slight and he habitually left before the performance was half through. The only play which he ever really enjoyed was "The Easiest Way," by Eugene Walter, in which Frances Starr played. His sympathies were so aroused by the misfortunes of the heroine that he forgot to sketch engines all over his program, and stayed to the end of the show to see the villain properly punished.

Jim Bauder who often went to the city with him, told about attending a musical comedy performance with him.

"Pick out the best-looking woman," Curtiss said suddenly, to his companion's astonishment.

Bauder selected one he thought was very pretty, but Curtiss shook his head. He pointed out another member of the chorus and said decisively:

"Now there's a girl who looks like she had some sense."

It was an excellent indication of his guarded attitude on the subject of women. Once he had received an invitation to be the guest of Anna Held, who had been photographed with him during the Rheims meet, at the Ziegfield Theatre. Curtiss decided:

"I don't see any reason to go, I saw her in France."

However much they might disagree with him about the importance of hearing Anna Held warble entrancingly, "Won't you come and play wiss me?" There was no question about how the students at the school felt toward Glenn Curtiss. They never doubted for a moment that flying was the greatest game in the world or that they were learning it under the man who could teach them most.

Even if they did not get firsthand instruction from him, they were in the thick of a new industry and were privileged to stand at his side, watching and helping it grow. New and vital structural principles were constantly being evolved. Curtiss had a theory that all aircraft improvements depended on discarding the old and starting in with the new, as soon as its efficiency could be established. He had an amazing knack of making the students feel that they were on his own level, the reason being that he never stood in awe of himself. There was no condescension in him.

In 1912 they were using the flying boat as an outdoor wind tunnel. Wing sections were balanced on braces a few feet above the top wing, and, through a system of springs, levels and indicators, they endeavored to obtain performance curves. Observations were made while the ship was moving over the water and in flight. A man was obliged to stand on a light scaffolding erected over the pilot's head and hang on precariously while he took the readings. Dr. Alfred Zahm, of the Smithsonian Institution, who built the first aerodynamic laboratory in the world, supervised these experiments. Later on, the findings of the Navy's wind tunnel were at their disposal.

They tried out new wing curves, new fabrics, and performed a series of experiments to determine the best mixture for doping wings. More power was another problem, which was first dealt with in the 80 horsepower Model O engine.

Then John H. McNamara (Johnny Mac), superintendent of the motor factory, spent time while Curtiss was in Europe testing the new valve action for the Model O. The first trials on the test block were perplexing. Instead of developing 80 horsepower, the motor was producing at normal speeds some 90 to 95. Placid, rotund Johnny Mac was certain he must be deceiving himself. He kept his own counsel until Curtiss returned, when he announced with considerable hesitation that the new Model O was showing, on a brake test, a maximum of more than 105 horsepower.

Curtiss was too surprised to do more than suggest there must be some mistake in the figures. They checked in every possible way and found them accurate. The new model was triumphantly renamed the O+ until somebody made on X out of a plus sign by mistake and made it read OX.

In a plane built for Eugene Ely to fly at the San Francisco air meet, Curtiss had reduced head resistance by double-covering the wings, and had cut down the front elevator to a single surface. These features were adopted as standard, but he was slow to admit that the front elevator could be dispensed with altogether because he considered it a safety factor. Eventually, he yielded on that score. In the interest of further reducing head resistance, fuel tanks were slung flush alongside the motor. Wing pontoons developed backwards in a sense, since the pontoons used in 1914 were almost identical with some he tried out on the 1911 experimental hydro-triplane, and not at all like the cylindrical pontoons he had been using in the meantime.

The 1913 classes had an opportunity to observe the development of a new type scout plane to specifications more drastic than any issued up to that time.

Colonel Samuel Reber of the Signal Corps had said: "We should have a tractor plane."

And Curtiss had replied, "Yes, I think you're right, I guess we should."

Having repeatedly tried out the tractor idea, he was not too optimistic. But this time he made it work and produced the two-seated J tractor. For the first time, a complete set of stress analyses were demanded. Intricate mathematical calculations had to be made to determine whether the material which went into the plane could stand the probable maximum strain to which it might be subjected. According to modern standards, it seems rather important to have definite assurance that the wings of a plane won't come off in flight. But in those credulous days, they had been in the habit of gambling on it.

The reason why no structural failures of any kind had occurred on any of the Curtiss machines was due to the tendency toward over-strength rather than the reverse, at the expense of lightness and maneuverability. At the instance of Colonel Reber, it now became possible to determine beforehand exactly how light all the parts could be and still be strong enough. Construction was accordingly lighter and more efficient.

With very little experience to guide them the Curtiss plant undertook to furnish exhaustive engineering data, as well as drawings of every detail of the machine. The struts, strut sockets, wiring, turnbuckles, must be shown in cross-section and in perspective. It was, considering the engineering equipment of the day, a stupendous assignment.

But with Dr. Zahm to supervise the mathematical calculations and the assistance of B. Douglas Thomas, English engineer, and Alfred Verville, a promising young American engineer employed at the plant, Curtiss produced a volume of drawings which the European government engineers afterwards pronounced the most complete and satisfactory set ever prepared.

Thomas applied what he learned about the principles of streamlining from Thomas Sopwith, enterprising British designer and flyer. And for the first time, the radiator, motor, and cockpit were set in line in an enclosed fusilage, in this new tractor. Thus the parasite resistance caused by rough uncovered surfaces, as well as the head resistance, was cut down. The struts, braces and landing gear were redesigned to further reduce head resistance.

After the birth of his son, Glenn, Jr., in June, 1912, Curtiss had promised his wife he would do no more land plane flying. John Cooper, instructor-pilot, therefore put the machine through the very severe performance tests which it had to meet. Then he took it to North Island to teach Army officers to fly it.

Later that year, Beachey returned from retirement. The French flyer, Pegoud, had successfully looped the loop, and this was too much for Beachey, who thought he was to be forever the world's greatest stunt flyer.

"Damn it," he swore, "I knew those things could be done if only someone would build me the right machine," and started off for Hammondsport. Curtiss was just leaving for Europe, but Beachey persuaded him to stay long enough to design a little plane for him which was relatively twice as strong and maneuverable as the standard biplane.

It was completed while Curtiss was in Russia and taken out for a trial. Beachey made several flights and was coming in for a landing, when the unfamiliar, sensitive machine skidded. He struck the ridge of the Navy hangar, where part of his audience was perched, killing Ruth Hildreth and injuring her sister. The only reason he was not killed himself was because for the first time in his career, thinking he might try to loop, he was securely strapped into his seat. The next year, Beachey crashed to his death in California in a machine, of his own design.

Curtiss hurried back from Sevastopool when the news of the fantastic tragedy at Hammondsport was cabled to him. The group was badly shaken, but his presence helped to restore their morale.

The year 1913, which wound up on such a tragic note, had gotten off to a bad start. In January, the fortunes of the schools were down. Judge Monroe Wheeler, general counsel of the Curtiss companies, had a serious disagreement with Fanciulli, of the Curtiss Exhibition Company, and Fanciulli resigned. The New York office was closed and the company was left without a sales or promotion manager. Then Judge John R. Hazel of the United States District Court in Buffalo on February 21st, granted the Wright Company an injunction permanently restraining Curtiss from using machines equipped with allegedly infringing ailerons. Although notice of appeal was filed immediately, the decision had an adverse effect on enrollments for the class of the spring of 1913.

Early in March, it appeared as though Wildman would be able to handle the classes alone. But before long, more students drifted in. Among them was W. B. (Old Bill) Luckey aged 50, of Chicago, who later attracted attention by winning the race around Manhattan in competition with master-flyers like Charley "Do-Anything" Niles. Callan was summoned for hydro-instruction work, and Van Vliet was employed as land plane instructor. Havens dropped in and helped out on the flying boats. Dave McCullough who, together with Charley Champlin, had been demonstrating the hydro in Brazil was back in town. Presently Aviators' Home was again filled to the rafters.

John Cooper, having just returned from San Diego, announced that he intended to take a much needed rest. The next day he was requisitioned to take the place of Callan who had been sent to Lake George to give a series of demonstrations with the flying boat. Two days later Cooper was asked to drop the school job and start for

Russia where a new consignment of hydros was to be delivered. A cable ordered him to report to Curtiss in London as soon as he was finished and start demonstrations on the new flying boat.

Life for the Curtiss school alumni was like that. They never knew where they would be a month or a day hence, but whatever the assignment, it was sure to be stimulating. But until the War brought prosperity to Hammondsport, there was apt to be more pleasure and glory in these jobs than financial reward. The years 1911 and 1912 had been financially difficult for Curtiss, and more than once he persuaded students to stay on at Hammondsport for little or no pay and work for the school. It was not the force of his argument so much as his need of their services which made them stay. Or he may have won them over to his gospel of helping to build up flying. Whatever the reason, they stayed and he profited.

Frequently they were shorthanded at the plant or the school. Instructor Callan and some of his students, working one day near a blow torch, were complaining about how badly an additional mechanic was needed to work on the school ships. A little later, Curtiss told Callan quietly: "Better be careful when you talk around a blow torch, Lanny. It carries your voice a long way." Then he realized Curtiss had overheard every word of their conversation.

They got the extra mechanic, though Curtiss was forced to take him away from another part of the plant where he would be missed. Practically every instance of apparent niggardliness was due to one cause: Curtiss did not have the money to spend. His overhead was large, as always when production is on a limited basis, and his profits were eaten up to a terrific extent by court actions.

Summer of 1914

ON HIS return to America in February, 1914, Curtiss faced an old problem. Judges Lacombe, Cox and Ward of the United States Circuit Court of Appeals on January 13th had confirmed the opinion of Judge Hazel, who ruled that the aileron constituted an infringement because it was used in conjunction with the rudder "sometimes," and "a machine that infringes part of the time is an infringement, although it may at other times be so operated as not to infringe."

The higher court had granted a permanent injunction restraining Curtiss from the manufacture and sale of planes equipped with ailerons.

Curtiss' own associates were greatly distressed when they received word of the ruling. Unless more reasonable royalty terms than those previously discussed by the Wright Company could be agreed upon, there was no way to go on manufacturing without incurring heavy losses. Although the injunction applied only to Curtiss planes and by implication to Farmans in this country, it actually signified an impasse for the manufacture of all aileron-equipped aircraft.

The opinion of the press, the trade magazines and practically every builder of aircraft coincided with that of officials at the Curtiss plant and with counsel for Curtiss. This time the sole hope was to make a peaceable settlement with the embattled Wright forces. Everybody was beaten, ready to bow to the Wright claims and thereby tacitly admit that the aileron was an infringement.

Everybody except Curtiss. He could not give up as long as there was a higher court left. He had cabled on January sixteenth from Nice that he would carry the case to the Supreme Court of the United States and bade his associates announce that none of the activities of the Curtiss companies "would be affected by the decision."

As he saw it, there could be no question about continuing to manufacture aeroplanes. He had obtained orders for thirty machines during his visit abroad and had received offers to move his factory to Europe. If necessary, he could drop his American business altogether. Or, since the injunction applied only to machines using the aileron or similar allegedly infringing balancing devices, he could manufacture the planes and motors at Hammondsport and form a subsidiary company to produce the ailerons in Canada or any other foreign country that had not acted on the Wright patent claims. Purchasers of planes would buy their own ailerons and attach them though the manufacturer might still be adjudged a contributory infringer.

But such action did not suit his mood. He sincerely believed his aileron method of lateral control—on which the United States Patent Office had issued a patent to the Aerial Experiment Association in December, 1911, with Curtiss as one-fifth owner, differed from the Wright wing-warping method. He felt his cause was just and was determined not to be driven out of the country. At this trying juncture, he recalled an incident of the previous year.

While lunching with Lyman Seely at the Brevoort in New York, a tall, thin, graying man had walked over to their table and addressed him:

"You're Glenn Curtiss, aren't you?"

Curtiss bowed.

"Well, I see they have you with your back nearly to the wall. When they get you right up against it, come to see me."

He walked away as abruptly as he had come.

Curtiss, still blinking with surprise, inquired: "Who was that man?"

"You're joking, aren't you?" said his companion. "Surely you recognized Henry Ford."

Now that Curtiss really was up against a wall, Ford was reminded of the incident. He replied that during his own most difficult period of the Selden patent litigation, when it appeared he was never to be allowed to build another automobile, there was just one man who had been able to see a way out. He advised Curtiss to get in touch with W. Benton Crisp of New York, patent attorney and former judge.

Curtiss followed this advice, and with Judge Crisp as his counsel, evidence unknown or unavailable when the patent suit first started, was exhumed and extensive preparation for the defense of a new suit brought by the Wright company in the Western District of New York was engaged upon.

Instead of appealing the case to the Supreme Court, Curtiss had, following the decision of the Appellate Court, changed his aileron system. Instead of moving one aileron up and the other down, as he had theretofore been doing, and instead of moving the aileron on the lower side down in acordance with the specific teaching of the Wright patent, he moved the aileron on the high side up and provided an interlock which prevented simultaneous movement of the aileron on the low side. The Wright company promptly brought suit against this new combination and an answer was duly filed.

Due to the late filing date of the new suit, and to a considerable number of extended postponements at the time America entered into the World War the case had not yet come to trial before Judge Hazel, when the litigation was dismissed by mutual agreement in August 1917.

During nine years of litigation, Curtiss and the Wright brothers had only one personal contest in the press. After the decision of the Court was announced, the metropolitan newspapers published a long interview with Orville Wright. This time Curtiss was stung to open retort, and he issued a statement to the press:

In some New York daily papers there have been published during the past weeks certain statements attributed to Mr. Orville Wright, regarding his attitude in the aeroplane patent suit. Mixed in with these direct quotations were interpolated insinuations impugning my good faith in the patent litigation and carrying suggestions easily interpreted as such untruths as I cannot see how Mr. Wright or any other sane man ever made.

The idea that any single line or part of any machine was either copied from the Wright machine, suggested by the Wrights or by their machines is absurd if not malicious. My first public flights, as a member of the Aerial Experiment Association, are a matter of record, and were made mostly before the Wrights exhibited their machine or made their first public flights.

I have never had an item of information from either of the Wrights that helped me in designing or constructing my machines or that I ever consciously used. I believe today, as I always have believed, that the Curtiss control differs fundamentally from that employed by the Wrights, and that its superiority to that of the Wright system is demonstrated by the records of the two machines during the past five years.

That I was unable to satisfactorily demonstrate this intricate technical point to the court I consider a misfortune largely due to the fact that our knowledge of aviation was vastly less when this case went into court several years ago than it is today.

My feeling with regard to Mr. Wright's declarations of his attitude in the matter of royalties is well reflected by the attached reprint from the editorial columns of the *Boston Transcript*.

The editors of the *Transcript* had strongly favored the Wright side of the question; but after the interview with Orville Wright appeared, they vigorously criticized the Wright company and its royalty demand of twenty percent of the retail price on each aeroplane produced.

Curtiss resolved to go on with the most ambitious project he had ever tackled, the building of a boat to fly across the ocean. This too, however, gave new reason for dissention when the Wright company insisted that Curtiss would either have to take out a license or stop manufacturing, and added that his choice of Canada as a starting point of the trans-Atlantic flight was a wise one, since Canada was the only civilized country in which Wright patents were not recognized.

"I have not enough expectation," Orville Wright said to an interviewer, "that the craft will ever land near enough to any country where our patents are validated—that is anywhere in Europe—to make it worthwhile to tell you what I would do in that case."

When the Englishman who was selected as pilot of the flying boat was asked to comment, he threw up his hands and said:

"O Lord, let me out of this. It's going to be a nasty mess."

Another of that summer's projects proved to be the most controversial issue of all.

Since 1908, the Smithsonian Institution had considered the possibility of making trial tests of the Langley machine. When in January, 1914, Beachey suggested that it would be interesting to determine whether the essential features of Professor Langley's aerodynamic theory, as aplied in the 1903 model, were correct, Dr. Charles D. Walcott, Secretary of the Smithsonian Institution, wrote to the Curtiss Aeroplane Company:

> "In connection with the reopening and development of work under the Langley Aerodynamical Laboratory, it seems desirable to make a thorough test of the principles involved in the construction of the Langley heavier-than-air, mancarrying, flying machine, especially the question as to tandem arrangement of the planes, and the general stability, especially longitudinal stability."

When, in response to their request, a bid of $2,000 was submitted for refitting and making tests, machine and engine were shipped to Hammondsport in April, 1914.

Curtiss naturally was glad of the opportunity to study the Langley aerodrome which had a method of control that could not possibly be considered an infringement of the Wright wing-warping method. He was eager to secure data for the design of a large tandem plane as well as to vindicate Samuel Pierpont Langley. Before the machine was ready for trial, Curtiss said in an interview:

"Since we have had the machine here and have studied it carefully, certain features of it have attracted our attention which seem to have been overlooked during the last ten years. It may be that the rebuilding of it may mean more than the establishment of Professor Langley's rightness. I mean that we may find something that will affect the form and structure of aeroplanes."

The aerodrome was refitted in a little courtyard at the factory between the office building and the aeroplane assembly room. The space had been walled in and roofed over so that only those connected with the work knew anything about it.

The engineers wished, as nearly as humanly possible, to restore the machine to its exact condition at the time the attempts to launch it were made in 1903. As they overhauled the engine, the Curtiss staff was impressed with the superb piece of work Charles Manly had done in its design. But immersion in salt water and eleven years of rust had harmed it to such an extent that it was impossible to bring it back to its original condition. It was developing only three-quarters of the horsepower it had originally shown. This was unfortunate, since in these new trials they did not want to catapult the plane as originally planned, but to take off with pontoons from the surface of the lake. And the additional weight of the pontoons, as well as the necessary inter-bracing would increase the horsepower load as well as the wing load.

The exquisite accuracy with which the parts of the aerodrome itself had been fashioned also impressed the workmen who fitted them together.

The framework, controls and wings were repaired, although more than half of the original ribs of the wings which had suffered most in the launching accident were still intact. These ribs, it was found, has been carefully hollowed out for the sake of lightness, but expense prohibited the Curtiss workmen from hollowing out the new ones. They successfully duplicated their curves however, in solid spruce. The original wing covering of oiled silk, which was torn and rotted, was replaced with doped cotton fabric and the original propellers were also re-covered. Meticulous care was taken during the re-assembly process that none of the aerodynamic principles might be in any way altered.

Manly, who was at that time manufacturing hydraulic trucks, had supervised the reconditioning of the engine and its installation, and Dr. Zahm, recorder of the Langley Aerodynamical Laboratory, was the official observer. They announced that the machine would be ready for trial on the second of June. While Dr. Walcott, Manly, Dr. Zahm, as well as the newspaper men then stationed at Hammondsport, the Army and Navy officers, the flying students, and local citizens looked on, the Langley aerodrome was launched, with Glenn Curtiss at the controls.

According to the report submitted by Dr. Zahm and seven other persons designated as witnesses, the venerable aerodrome moved along with the engine running evenly, and as it gained speed, the pontoons broke loose from the water. It rose a few feet above the surface of the lake, flew on a level for a short distance, and landed evenly on the water.

Because it was greatly underpowered, since it now weighed 350 pounds more than the original model, and the motor was delivering about 40 horsepower rather than the 52 Langley had reckoned on, Curtiss installed an 80 horsepower motor and made a number of short flights with pontoons. The following March, he removed them and attached skids, with which he made short flights from the ice with the original engine.

It now occurred to the Curtiss counsel, Judge Crisp, that valuable data might be obtained for use in the patent suit and he, together with John P. Tarbox, Curtiss patent attorney who was also an engineer, therefore directed subsequent experiments conducted for this purpose. The machine was modified somewhat in keeping with modern experience and many officially observed flights made, during 1915, by Walter Johnson and Gink Doherty. The longest of these was a ten mile flight of nearly thirty minutes' duration, in the face of a stiff head wind.

Doherty, who made most of these flights, was enthusiastic about the performance of the aerodrome. He reported that its inherent stability was so perfect that there was nothing for him to do but guide the machine from left to right and give it more or less power according to whether he wished to ascend or descend. But the effort of the Smithsonian Institution to demonstrate once and for all the scientific value of the aeronautical experiments of its former secretary gave rise to a situation which Professor Joseph S. Ames of Johns Hopkins University rightly characterized as "involving temptation for one side to exaggerate and distort favorably Langley's work, and for the other side to belittle and deny it."

The exhaustive reports prepared on the Langley flights were filed away when the Government in July, 1917, arranged a patent truce and the Wright suit was discontinued. Nothing, save the accumulation of certain technical data, was accomplished by the flights. Whereas out of them a very boring and distasteful controversy was born.

It was Gilbert Brewer, an Englishman, who first made a public issue of the Langley trials. He had begun by trying to discredit the first flight and had been promptly refuted by the evidence of the official witnesses. Whether he was motivated by sincere loyalty to the Wright brothers, with whom he had been closely associated, or whether, patriotically enough, he felt that by generating antagonisms he might be able to have the first heavier-than-air plane deposited in one of his own country's museums, has never been determined.

Dr. Bell was not fully in accord with the idea of the aerodrome trials. Perhaps he recalled what a firm believer his friend Langley had always been in the wisdom of letting sleeping dogs lie. Or perhaps he divined with extraordinary accuracy that it was going to be what Lieut. Porte would have called a "nasty mess."

The feud still continues, and Orville Wright has shown no signs of a willingness to discard his feeling that the Smithsonian Institution did a great wrong to him and his brother. But for the most part, the stormy patent war has been forgotten. Only recently, an official of the present day Curtiss-Wright Corporation referred to Hammondsport as "the town where the Curtiss brothers came from."

But many people who have heard of the patent suit are convinced that Curtiss lost his fight and stands convicted of patent piracy. They do not realize that at the instance of the Government an aircraft patent truce was arranged so that the war production program might proceed unhampered.

A cross-licensing agreement was adopted by the aircraft manufacturers similar to the one under which the automobile industry had been operating for many years. Under this a nominal blanket royalty fee was collected for each airplane and apportioned among the patent owners as stipulated. The agreement was administered by an impartial group, formed for the purpose and known as the Manufacturers' Aircraft Association. The inventors and owners thereof always felt that the broad Wright control patent covered every practical modern plane, just as the Curtiss hydro-aeroplane and flying boat patent owners felt that theirs covered every water plane. The Government's patent committee appraised the Wright and Curtiss patents as separate groups of equal value.

The wing-warping patent of the Wright brothers expired in 1923, while the aileron patent owned by the A. E. A. members expired in 1928. But the aileron has been consistently used in modern construction, while the wing-warping method of lateral control upon which it allegedly infringed has long since fallen into disuse. There was never a final adjudication on the question of whether the aileron did or did not infringe upon the method patented by the Wright brothers.

Of all the aircraft designs patented by Curtiss, none was more significant from the point of view of passenger flying than the twin-engined cabin boat built for Rodman Wanamaker.

On June 7, 1910, just a week after the Albany flight, Edwin H. Gould offered a prize of $15,000 to the man who should produce the first aeroplane successfully employing two motors and two propellers. Three years later the *London Daily Mail* offer of $50,000 for the first trans-Atlantic flight brought the need for such additional power to the forefront. Once more the inveterate Lord Northcliffe had cued aviation achievement.

It was in England in the fall of 1913 that the idea for an American attempt at the prize was first generated.

Captain Ernest Bass, who was the son of a prominent manufacturer of paper currency, postage stamps and bonds, had traveled extensively throughout North and South America in behalf of his father's firm. Finding his own business dull, he tried bull fighting with some degree of success. Then, bitten with a desire for another form of excitement, he returned home to take up aviation. Lieutenant J. C. Porte, invalided from the British Naval Service, who was regarded as one of the best pilots in England, became associated with him in this field. Porte had been the English representative of the Deperdussin monoplane but had joined forces with Bass when that company went into liquidation.

When John Cooper demonstrated the flying boat at Shoreham, near Brighton, Curtiss allowed Porte to take the machine up. After making two flights, he was so delighted that he persuaded Bass to buy a boat. Then Porte approached Curtiss with a scheme which the efficient little flying boat had put into his mind. Why, he suggested, would it not be feasible to build a large flying boat and enter it for the *Daily Mail* prize contest, which called for either a hydro-aeroplane or a flying boat? Bass knew Rodman Wanamaker's English representative very well, and had good reason to believe Wanamaker would finance a project if someone would produce a machine.

And Porte himself would gladly volunteer to serve as its pilot. He was suffering from tuberculosis, in such an advanced stage, that the doctors had advised he could not hope to live much longer at best. If he had to die, why not die in trans-Atlantic glory?

The idea of building a machine which could fly the ocean naturally appealed to Curtiss. He had unbounded faith in Porte's ability as a flyer, knew of his extensive experience as a navigator and appreciated the logic of his disregard of possible consequences. Nevertheless, Curtiss saw no point in the attempt unless there was reasonable hope of making the trip with a considerable margin of safety. He was therefore noncommittal about Porte's idea, but promised to talk it over with his associates as soon as he returned to America.

Back at the plant, fairly definite plans for a machine were formulated. Then Curtiss staggered the members of the company's board of directors by asking:

"What do you think of building a machine to fly the Atlantic?"

They frankly thought very little of it and told him so. But Curtiss was by now convinced that the idea was feasible, and, with the assistance of his engineers, prepared the essential data. All the figures regarding fuel consumption, oil, and the necessary rate of speed, were computed and some fairly complete sketches prepared. In December, he contracted to build a large flying boat for Rodman Wanamaker at a cost of $25,000.

The world opened its ears when the project was announced in February, 1914, with June named as the probable time of departure. There was fascination in the idea of attempting what Walter Wellman had tried to do in a dirigible in 1910 from Atlantic City, and what John Wise of Philadelphia had proposed doing in 1843 in a free balloon. The newspapers at home and abroad were, on the whole, kind to the project, though they doubted a machine for a flight of nearly two thousand miles could be constructed in a few months' time.

"Perhaps we had better send a man to Hammondsport, New York. It looks like they really mean to try to fly the Atlantic." Some thirty news editors were saying that in the spring of 1914. For the second time in history, reporters were glued to the scene of a trans-Atlantic venture. Papers as far north as Boston and south as Washington sent special representatives. The town swarmed with correspondents during various stages of the preparations. And when three London news writers arrived, Hammondsport was promoted to an international news center.

Most steadily about the premises were Gordon (Azra) Stiles of the New York *Tribune*, Frederick Eppelsheimer of the *Herald*, Jack Binns of the *American*, Herbert Bayard Swope and C. M. Lincoln of the *World*, J. C. Clarke

THE LIFE OF GLENN CURTISS

of the *Sun* and Joey Toy of the *Boston American*, Norman
G. Thwaites of the *London Daily Mail*, sponsor of the
contest, Frank Hillier of the *London Times*, and George
Bateman of the *London Daily Chronicle*.

Construction went forward rapidly behind closed doors,
and details were revealed gradually. Porte, who had been
named the chief pilot by Wanamaker, was a typical service man, accustomed to keeping his mouth shut and mind-
ing his own business. The reporters nearly drove the tall,
gaunt, rather hollow-eyed "Grapenuts" (or "Cereal")—
as they insisted on calling him—wild with their questions.
Porte was, of course, keeping faith, according to his lights,
with the *World*, which had contracted for his exclusive
story. He was not popular with the men whose job it was
to get news because his conception of tactful treatment
of the press was so exasperating. Once, for example, he
said very seriously:

"I gave that to the *World* today, but I can tell you all
about it tomorrow."

The thwarted journalists, however, found ample material to occupy the time spent waiting on the trans-Atlantic
flight preparations. Startling new aircraft for foreign governments were built and tested almost daily. The factory
was a constant source of stories about new types, radical
new design features. Further it was actually equipped to
construct 250 planes a year. Aviation appeared to be easing into the big industry category, and that, of course, was
news.

The little champagne town, which was a hot-bed of
aeronautics, was filled to the bursting point with sportsmen and professional pilots, Army and Navy officers, gen-
erals and admirals from abroad shopping for fighting
craft; many of them picturesque personalities. Distinguished scientists or other dignitaries were arriving by

every train. Moreover there was Curtiss, directing all this frenzied activity. Somehow he was much easier to interview in his own environment, where he could back up against a factory wall while he answered their questions, and tell them about the various experiments going on out in the plant and down on the lake.

It was one of Curtiss' greatest charms and, from a business standpoint, one of his most serious failings, that he was always ready to waste time listening to the suggestions of others, young or old, obscured or celebrated. Even a newspaper man's aerodynamic brainstorms received his attention though his interest was often more perfunctory than his callers imagined. After listening to a lengthy discourse, he was very apt to appeal to Genung or Kleckler;

"What in the world was that fellow talking about?"

His boyhood love of a good wager was as strong as ever, and he made innumerable "little bets" with visitors to the factory. Once, having installed an aeroplane motor in his big six cylinder Keaton automobile, it worked so well, he announced he would lay a bet that he could travel to Bath and back on one gallon of gasoline. The distance was sixteen miles and ten miles to a gallon was good average mileage at the time.

"Sound old J. B. R." Verplanck, sportsman-pilot, led off by putting up a suit of clothes and a hat, so certain was he of the preposterousness of Curtiss' wager. The correspondents, students, and others followed his example. The tank was drained, two gallons put into it, and Curtiss and an observer started.

When they returned from the trip to Bath, there was great excitement. While the crowd looked on, four quarts were drained out of the tank. Curtiss glanced up to ask whether anybody wanted to bet him he wouldn't get another quart, and found more takers.

One more quart was drawn out. "All right," said Curtiss, "how about another pint?" The few diehards who responded: "Sure, I'll see you," whistled in amazement when another pint, with a few drops over, was extracted from the tank. According to exact calculation he would have made, at that rate, twenty-four and a half miles to the gallon. And Curtiss spent the next several years trying to wear out all the shirts, collars, ties and other clothes he had won.

Life was very social in Hammondsport that summer, with the lake swarming with sleek flying boats, boat races, dancing parties and christening ceremonies for each new over-water craft. The *Logan A. Vilas III,* Victor Vernon's *Betty V,* and other machines were launched with accompanying festivities.

At last the big flying boat was taken to the lake shore, and the public had a chance to examine it. The physical dimensions outstripped anything ever attempted. The hull, was 35 feet long with a 6 foot beam, having a fully enclosed cabin in which were the dual controls, the instruments, the gas tank and the spare oil supply. The upper wing had a spread of 72 feet with a chord of 10 feet. Two 100-horsepower pusher type OX motors were mounted between the wings. And because it might have to stand up for a long time in rough seas in case of a forced landing, the wooden hull was covered with cotton fabric which had received several coats of bright red deck paint. The overhang of the upper wing was so much greater than in the standard boat type, that the lower wing looked stubby.

The name *America,* the same one Wellman had given to his dirigible, had been chosen for the twin-engined colossus, and hundreds of motorists from all over western New York drove to Hammondsport for the christening, on June 22d.

Curtiss was concerned about the possibility of injury to
members of the audience or sixteen-year-old Katherine
Masson, who was elected to christen the ship. Wine fer-
mented in the bottle may develop a pressure of more than
a hundred pounds to the square inch, and bottle testers
wore fencing masks at work in the cellars. The banging of
a bottle against the *America's* prow might be risky and
Curtiss advised a dress rehearsal, but Porte laughed down
his American caution.

A bamboo scaffolding was erected in front of the bow,
and a bottle of champagne was attached by a chord. Then
to make reasonably sure of its breaking, horseshoes were
tied to each side of the bottle's neck.

The speeches over, Katherine Masson, christener, in a
white ruffled gown and picture hat, and carrying a bunch
of red roses presented to her by Glenn Curtiss, stepped
forward and spoke the verses written by Dr. Zahm for
the occasion:

> *Majestic courser of the sea and air,*
> *Within this ample hold,*
> *Two navigators bold,*
> *The Atlantic main abridging, are to bear*
> *Glad greetings from the new world to the old,*
> *Peace herald of the century,*
> America, *I christen thee.*

Then she lifted the bottle of local champagne and let
it swing once, twice. Lieutenant Porte looked glum; not a
very auspicious christening, this, he thought, as he went
to her rescue. He struck the nose of the ship with such
force that he bruised it, with no effect on the glass.

The crowd grew hilarious as Porte in desperation picked
up a sledge hammer and struck the bottle. Still it resisted.

He gritted his teeth and struck it blow after blow until it finally crashed, spouting champagne over the *America* and the Englishman, from his hair to his shoes.

Several pilots had volunteered to accompany Porte on the trip. Lieutenant Towers, who was Wanamaker's choice, could not go because official etiquette forbade his serving in a subordinate capacity to a retired British officer under the American flag. A mechanic who could also fly would be the best possible assistant on the trip and George Hallett, because he weighed less than the other mechanics at the plant and had exceptional knowledge of motors, was chosen from among several volunteers.

Since Wanamaker's announcement, three French flyers, Garros, Pourpe and les Moulinais, had declared their intention of attempting the flight that summer; and Enea Bossi of Italy, was preparing a machine at a camp on Long Island. Visitors flocked to Hammondsport to reassure themselves that the *America* would get away first.

Curtiss of course intended that, but he also meant to leave nothing undone to insure the success of the venture. From the beginning he realized that the crucial moment would come when the ship attempted to rise from the water at Newfoundland. She would be carrying the heaviest load of the voyage and conditions in Trepassey Bay were such that the boat might easily suffer damage in the attempt to take off. The sponsor, who was also eager to guard against any possible failure, agreed to the building of a duplicate machine.

An elaborate series of test flights continued through June and well into July. When the *America* was first launched, on June 23d, it was decided that the hull was too narrow to allow it to take off with the maximum load. Curtiss, Porte, and Towers and Bellinger, who had been detailed by the Navy to assist with the project, went into conference. To increase the planing surface they decided to attach auxiliary fins, or sponson, at the bottom of the fore part of the hull, following an idea previously developed by Richardson.

The first set of fins made it possible for the boat to get off with a moderate load, but it could not be induced to rise with the load required for the long flight. Larger fins were designed. A third engine with a tractor propeller was installed above the upper wing, but the performance tests did not justify the added weight and head resistance and it was removed. Porte's friend, Captain Creagh-Osborne came over to adjust the compasses and check the instruments.

Only after many changes, was it possible for Porte to get the *America* off with the quantity of fuel necessary for the long flight to the Azores. But he had worked and worried himself sick. And when he had a severe hemorrhage, his managers insisted he would either have to take a rest or abandon the flight. They took him to the Adirondacks, where he regained a fair degree of strength.

By August, two *Americas* were completed, and parts were ready for a third. The sight of the great flying boat in the air was so impressive that one pop-eyed correspondent wired his paper: "There seems to be no reasonable limit to what may be expected of flying and this man Curtiss."

Everything was at last in readiness for the courageous trip. Callan had mapped the course, which was to be from St. Johns, Newfoundland, to Horta in the Azores, with a possible additional stop at Ponta Delgada. Thence to Vigo, Spain, and its final destination, a port in England. The impression was given that the flight would be direct from St. Johns to Europe in order to discourage foreign builders, as it was considered practically impossible to construct a ship capable of such a long flight. By breaking the journey into three jumps, Curtiss felt confident the flight could be made. Callan sailed from Boston for the Azores under an assumed name to throw the newshawks off the scent. He established bases on the islands for fuel and spare parts and was to join the *America* as relief pilot from Horta on.

When the actual flight plans became public, a camp was set up at St. Johns. The *Americas* were boxed for shipment, and accommodations to Newfoundland booked for Porte and Hallett. Everybody was on tiptoe for news of the take-off.

Just then war broke out in Europe, and the chief pilot immediately offered himself for duty in the Royal Air Force and was accepted. The "peace herald of the century" was sold to the British Admiralty for war duty, and crossed the Atlantic ignominiously hidden under tarpaulins on the deck of a liner.

Five years went by before the Atlantic was crossed by air. And not until 1927 did another *America*, captained by Commander Richard E. Byrd, realize Rodman Wanamaker's ideal, which was crowded out by pressure of events in August, 1914.

V

GLORY BE TO WINGS

A Keel a Day

AVIATION went to war in 1914, along with the other industries. Germany immediately made use of the new fighting implement which had already demonstrated promise in the Balkan War and other minor disturbances. The Allies found it imperative to follow suit.

Europe needed aeroplanes.

"Why don't we build them?" was the question which was asked around the Curtiss plant. Many of the embattled countries were already familiar with the Curtiss hydros or flying boats. Great Britain had two of the twin-engined boats and had ordered two more. It should be an easy matter to sell substantial consignments of aircraft abroad.

While business firms on both sides of the Atlantic were breathlessly grooming themselves to supply the war markets, Curtiss was quietly at work at North Island, developing a new tractor plane for the United States Army, which was to be a definite improvement upon the rather clumsy Model J.

337

They had crossed it with the N hydro, which had a very excellent wing curve, put it on pontoons and tried it out on the lake at Hammondsport before Curtiss took it to the Pacific Coast for further experiments. He was much too wrapped up in the task of designing a two-wheeled undercarriage for the new tractor, which had been designated the JN, to give much attention to the glib war-business talk.

But the sales department at Hammondsport felt that it could not afford to sit back and ignore these foreign prospects. Most of September and October was spent following up clues around New York City, where all sorts of fantastic rumors were rife. The financial district was infested with go-betweens who had inside information, and no authority to close deals, but hopes of fat commissions.

One firm, whose members were obviously of German extraction offered to buy the whole Curtiss output on a basis of that year's production. They wanted the planes, they claimed, for France. Later, they admitted they were for Germany, and demanded the privilege of burning the machines in the field behind the Curtiss factory if they were not able to ship them to Central Europe. The offer was promptly rejected.

There were many curious inquiries, and preposterous offers. It was an exciting time of great secrets, with big money in the offing. Seely wrote to Curtiss urging him to come East and take charge, but he used his own judgment and stayed at San Diego. A number of fairly good foreign orders were picked up through New York representatives. Enea Bossi, Curtiss agent in Italy, ordered three flying boats, and was advised that it must be a strictly cash transaction as the world exchange system had been disrupted. Bossi arrived with the initial payment, nearly a trunkful of soiled and worn one dollar bills: nine thousand of them.

The government had scoured every small town bank in Italy to obtain the necessary sum.

Russia spoke early for a consignment of flying boats, and Spain ordered several hydro-aeroplanes with retractable wheels. But when the order was ready, she permitted the planes to be turned over to one of the warring countries.

This was still not big business. Lyman Seely felt that men should be sent over to secure contracts. He told a directors' meeting so. The directors decided he would no doubt get some orders but so far aircraft manufacturing had shown little profit. Suppose he did get an order for ten airplanes, the net returns would not be very large, and they had not the facilities for quantity production, nor the capital necessary to secure them. They finally agreed that Seely's idea was worth trying and started by sending a man to Italy.

Then an export house convinced Seely that if he would go to London and call on the head of their firm, he would be put in touch with a Russian general, said to have some fifty million pounds to his credit in London banks, who was making extensive purchases for the Russian Government. They urged him to start the following day.

Since Curtiss was beyond reach, Seely called Genung from New York and asked advice. He was directed to use his own judgment. When Seely asked for funds with which to make the trip, Genung replied sadly that business was so poor that he did not have enough money on hand, but could get it soon. On the strength of this assurance, Seely borrowed five hundred dollars from Henry Woodhouse, then secretary of the Aero Club, and sailed the next day.

In England, the Curtiss representative found difficult going, fraught with intrigue, plots and counter plots. For a time he was occupied trying to adjust the various claims of alleged Curtiss agents in England. Curtiss had left a trail of agreements and semi-agreements behind him on his last trip abroad, the details of which he had neglected to give his colleagues.

The Russian general, it developed, could not speak English and knew nothing of aviation. Neither did Gaston, of Gaston, Williams and Wigmore, who had induced him to come abroad. He had been turned down by both the Army and the Navy. At last, he maneuvered a meeting with Squadron Commander Spencer Grey, who was a protege of Winston Churchill, First Lord of the Admiralty, and had taught Churchill to fly. Grey had previously condemned the Curtiss boats as badly made, but was very enthusiastic over the book of drawings of the new Model JN. He arranged for orders amounting to about $750,000, and accompanied Seely back home to see what the Curtiss plant could produce and how fast.

Seely's expense account had been protested by the company treasurer in the meanwhile, and the sales manager appealed to Curtiss who was still in San Diego. Curtiss promptly backed him up and told him to go back to England and try to get more orders.

It was a good move, although it at first appeared the second trip would be profitless. The pet formula for the departmental clerks and petty officers, who blocked his way to the men of authority, was that American planes, like Ford cars, were "cheap, but nasty." Seely's answer was that they were perfectly right in saying that they were cheap, since his firm was asking about half as much for a finished JN, complete with motor, as the British manufacturers were getting for some of their planes of about equal efficiency, without power plants.

London, cold, foggy, and unfriendly to his product, was beginning to get on the Curtiss representative's nerves. He was almost ready to pack up and go home, when he received a message from Commodore Seuter asking him to call at the Admiralty.

Seuter said: "Mr. Seely, we want more of your planes."

"That's nice."

"In fact, we want a great many of your planes."

"Still better," said Seely, with as much composure as he could muster.

"To tell you the truth, we want everything you can produce; either in your own plant, or by subletting to other manufacturers capable of meeting your specifications. Will you cable for them at once?"

"Certainly, if you will give me an idea of what you require."

He suggested that they would like to have about ten planes a day.

Up to then, Seely had simply accepted word of mouth, even telephone orders for anything required. A large part of the business with the British Admiralty was being transacted on that basis at the time, and no reason to question it had arisen. He felt, however, that with an order so extensive he perhaps should have some sort of a chit or memo. Commodore Seuter therefore gave him a brief note which stated that the British Admiralty would accept everything the Curtiss plant could produce during the next six months, with the added provision that if the war continued, the order would be renewed.

The report of Commander Grey had obviously been favorable, for Churchill's instructions, in effect, stated: "Buy everything America can produce to these specifications."

The order was cabled and Seely was startled to receive a reply stating that the firm already had plenty of business and could not accept the order for lack of capital. He cabled back, asking if Curtiss had seen the message. Curtiss had not, it developed, and when word of the British order was relayed to him it woke him up to the fact that the time for profits in aircraft manufacturing had arrived. He cabled his sales manager direct:

"Congratulations. Starting for Hammondsport immediately."

But when he realized the extent of the order, Curtiss cabled again saying that in order to meet the British requirement, they must have money for increased facilities for both motors and planes. The amount needed, in his estimation, was seventy-five thousand.

Seely relayed the cable verbatim to the Admiralty Board, and two days later, he was summoned before a meeting of its contract department. He was greatly embarrassed when the chairman of the board said:

"Mr. Seely, we are inclined to grant your request for an advance upon the proposed aeroplane contract. Before we do so, we ask your personal assurance that all such monies will be used exclusively for His Majesty's service."

He assured them that he believed they would be used in good faith for the purpose designated. Then, to his great surprise, the chairman advised him that they had decided to advance more than the 75,000 pounds requested. Curtiss had, for reasons of economy, omitted the word dollars after his cabled figure, and the Admiralty Board had taken it for granted that he meant pounds.

The gross amount of that first large order was something like $14,000,000.

No single man among the original executives of the Curtiss plant had suspected the volume possibilities of aeroplane orders which now came in from Great Britain, Russia and Italy. The whole routine of life was adjusted to meet the changed conditions.

There were not enough men in Hammondsport to carry

on the work and additional men were drafted from nearby towns and from all over the country. It was impossible to feed and house all of them. Curtiss therefore took a trip to Buffalo with Genung to look around for a factory building. At dinner that night at a hotel in Buffalo, William Chadeayne glanced over to an adjoining table and recognized them.

"I'd like to have a talk with you," Curtiss told him as he was leaving the dining room. They arranged to meet in the hotel lobby later in the evening. Chadeayne found him resting comfortably with long legs draped over the arm of a red plush chair. He always had a way of "relaxing in a bunch," as Chadeayne expressed it.

"Well, Billy," Curtiss said casually, "it looks like we've outgrown Hammondsport. We have a rush order for planes from England and can't handle it. Do you think we could build them here in Buffalo?"

They worked all night over a plan for housing the booming industry. They calculated what wood-working, what metal-working, what pattern-making facilities they would need. Before morning, Chadeayne had turned over his entire motorcycle plant to the Curtiss Aeroplane Company. His superintendent and his employees became theirs, and he himself agreed to take charge of all woodwork construction on the planes in the Cutler Desk Company, which was to be transformed into an aeronautical woodworking plant. One building proved inadequate, and another was erected on Churchill Street in Buffalo. It was a hundred feet wide and five hundred feet long and was composed entirely of sheet iron bolted together in sections with the thrifty idea that it might some day be taken apart and shifted to Hammondsport. This unique structure proved to be a radiator in the summer and had to be stuccoed.

Curtiss felt that his organization needed a man of wide experience in manufacturing and financing, and selected K. B. McDonald, one of the Thomas Motor Car Company executives and a well known engineer. McDonald agreed to join the enterprise, and proved invaluable to the Curtiss organization, which was not accustomed to conducting an undertaking of such vast scope. John P. Tarbox, an attorney for the company, and C. W. Webster, former newspaper man, also figured prominently in effecting the necessary reorganization for large scale production. W. L. Gilmore and Charles M. Manly were among the engineers who assisted in working out the program.

The Curtiss Aeroplane and Motor Corporation was organized in 1915 to take over the Curtiss Aeroplane Company and Curtiss Motor Company, with $6,000,000 worth of preferred stock and $750,000 worth of common stock. Those employees who owned stock in the old companies became wealthy immediately. Curtiss had at last led them into prosperity.

Once, when the company in 1911 was unable to pay pilot Witmer for an exhibition flight, they gave him five hundred dollars worth of stock. He knew the Curtiss companies never paid any dividends and tried his best to sell the stock for a hundred dollars. But he found no takers and carried it with him to Russia. Now he received a cable advising him he had better rush back home because he was a rich man. The value of his $500 in stock had increased to well over a hundred thousand.

Financial expansion was only one of the major problems of putting aircraft production on a wartime basis. Another was expansion of methods. Standardization of parts, for example, was something which aviation had to learn from the ground up. While machines were built on a one-at-a-time basis, the parts were made especially, or anything that happened to be lying around was adapted to the purpose. It now became essential to design all the necessary parts and have them machined in quantity.

Technically trained engineers were gradually brought into the scheme to supervise the men who had grown up with the company. These engineers were conversant with the technical jargon which was necessary in dealing with men from various countries who came to the factories and camped there while they checked up on every item of material ordered.

A single employee's story is indicative of the expansion of the engineering department. Paul J. Zimmermann a graduate engineer with a strong interest in aeronautics, first came to Hammondsport in November, 1914. George Toms, who had just been given the power to hire and fire, was besieged with applications from young engineers just then. He told Zimmermann he could go to work as an office boy, as there was no engineering work for him to do at the moment. The applicant gladly accepted the job, at a salary of fifteen dollars a week. A few weeks later, he was called in and asked to do some motor design work. They could not find the clearance volume for a cylinder and having figured it out for them, he qualified for the position of chief draftsman.

When he came into the department, there were some 800 tracings on hand. A few drawings were still filed on the wall and had to be copied off. Three years later, there were 14,000 drawings. In the same way, there were six young men in the engineering department in 1914 and a hundred and fifty in 1917.

For the first time, beginning with 1915, there was a need for organized work. It was no longer possible when a necessary detail was required, to have Kleckler go and find it somewhere on the wall, or to have G. H. sketch it up from memory. Not that Kleckler's work was inadequate, but he could not do the work of several persons. He had a vast respect for technically trained men, and when Zimmermann acknowledged him as his chief, Kleckler insisted:

"Oh no, I don't want to be the boss. You have a college education."

For all their book learning, the trained engineers respected his ability. He seemed to know instinctively how much a strut could support without stopping to calculate. And sometimes when their calculations were off, his instincts were correct. In the same way, they always got Curtiss' opinions on a new model before it went into production.

One spring night in 1916, a special train moved the aeroplane section of the engineering department bodily, including their families and household goods, to Buffalo. The next morning the men were ready for work in their new quarters. That was no time for dawdling methods.

There was more than enough scope for creative energy. They were constantly developing new flying boats to meet new demands, fitting a new type ship into the production program, or building an entirely new departure in aircraft. Curtiss was an inventor first and last. If he had a notion he wanted to try out a new idea, he tried it out even if it meant slowing up a large order. He was more interested in getting out new types than in the mass production of something he had created a year or more earlier.

But he never seriously impeded production. By 1916, three large factories and two auxiliary plants were operating full blast in Buffalo. This expansion process of course entailed considerable frenzied finance. And at least once, even as in the old pedestrian days of the business, income lagged far behind outgo. That time, with huge payrolls, staggering bills to meet, everybody gave up. Nothing short of a miracle could save the whole impressive structure from toppling around their ears. Highly geared executives sat grimly with heads in their hands, or paced the floor, waiting for the blow to fall, while others tried to figure out last minute expedients.

Lanny Callan dropped in at the Churchill Street plant that day and learned of the crisis on his way in to call on Curtiss. He knew that Curtiss usually kept his head in a tight place, but this time he really expected to find him disturbed. He wasn't though, not in the least.

"But, G. H., aren't you worried? What are you going to do about it?"

"Well, I'll tell you, Lanny. When you don't know what to do, do nothing."

A few hours later, a check for a million dollars arrived to pay for a British consignment, and saved the situation.

Dramatic crises in design occurred frequently. Once they built a ship for the Army on a single order at Hammondsport. It was no great success and they had a hard time delivering it. Then word came through from the sales manager, John Scott, that the Navy wanted ten ships of the same model. Since they had no drawings or specifications on it, they were forced to borrow it back from the Army, duplicate it and mount it on pontoons. There was no accounting for tastes, they decided.

Once, after America entered the war, Josephus Daniels rang up on long distance and demanded thirty planes on pontoons right away, kind not specified. Congress had called upon him to report what planes he had on order, so he decided to order some. The engineering department went into conference and decided to evolve the JN4C for the Secretary of the Navy.

Many versions of the JN were developed, including the well-known JN4D or Jenny. It was the training plane on which most of the ten thousand American aviators were trained during the World War. And although it looks like an unwieldy mother hen today, it was once the last word in training ship efficiency. It could stand up under the terrible punishment of rookie air soldiers. The British used them in great numbers for this purpose also, and more than five thousand Jennies were produced.

Production facilities had been further expanded when the United States entered the war. A new factory on Elmwood Avenue in Buffalo became the largest aircraft factory in the world, just as that city, with six aircraft plants, was the largest center of aircraft production. Buffalo now also overflowed into Elmira and Tonawanda, with a huge engineering laboratory at Garden City, Long Island, and a plant at Toronto, headed by John McCurdy. All told, there were seven large plants and three auxiliary plants under active operation. They worked at such high speed that they were for the most part fifty percent ahead of schedule on their American and British contracts. In one week they delivered 115 ships to the United States Army. They were turning out ships faster than the Army could absorb them.

Personnel departments to supervise employment and recreation of the employees were installed. There was a publicity department and a house organ called *The Curtiss Fusilage,* edited by Fay Faurote. Company pine, uniforms, and all the rigamarole of war time industrial standardization was introduced into the various plants. Patriotism was strong among them and the slogan of the flying boat factory at Buffalo was: "A Keel a Day to Put the Kaiser Away."

Eventually all the aeroplane work was transferred to Buffalo, then an additional motor plant was installed there. But the Hammondsport plant produced fifty-five percent of all the motors used on the JN4D's and twenty-five test blocks were running day and night, making a noise like a thundering squadron of fighting planes. Shop No. 1 and Shop No. 2, where the main assembly and sub-assembly aeroplane work had been done, now built motors. One building was set aside as a test laboratory for materials. The progressive steps, until the finished motor came off the test block, were uphill as always.

Hammondsport was a two-fisted, motor building center where two thousand men worked continuously. They were only a fifth of the total number of employees who punched Curtiss Aeroplane and Motor Company time clocks daily. Charles Kirkham, who machined Curtiss' first successful motor, was chief engineer in charge of motor construction. He developed several important types, including the OX-5.

They produced more motors in a week than were formerly produced in a year. Between two and three thousand men tried to find lodgings in Hammondsport and Bath. Many of them slept in the same bed in three relays of eight hours each. Many of the men had families, and, to meet the acute housing problem, a hundred new houses were erected. A substantial addition to the public school building was insufficient to accommodate all the pupils, and the school was run on a double shift, morning and evening plan.

Just to complete the metamorphosis, somebody dropped a hint, long before America entered the war, that German spies were watching the plant. Out of this grew wild rumors of sabotage, and National Guardsmen from Hornell policed the entire hill. Every person who went up the hill had to present an official pass, and powerful searchlights played on the factory buildings all night long.

With the various plants going full swing in straight manufacturing, Curtiss established the engineering laboratory at Garden City, and built a home near it. There, from the time the United States entered the war, he, as chairman of the engineering committee, devoted himself to research, both with motors and machines.

One day in 1916 Curtiss announced that he wanted to follow through the additional load capacity experiments made with triplanes in San Diego back in 1911. Out of that experiment, four types of triplanes, including a training plane, two scout planes and a flying boat for sportsmen, were later developed. Among the more important types evolved in 1917 were four types of tractor flying boats, one of which was the forerunner of the twin-motored model F5L for Channel defense, and of the H-16 and the R2A, the first mail ship.

Curtiss now had no part in the administration of any of the plants. Some of the men who had formerly worked directly under him occasionally came to him with their personal problems. Once a man resigned when the executive of one of the plants tried to shift him from engineering to production work. "I'm sorry," Curtiss told him as they said goodbye. "You see, I'm convinced the directors have decided that they want you back in the engineering department, but it will take them a year to admit it."

Frank H. Russell, who was in charge of the Garden City plant, reported that Curtiss was always unhappy to see any old Hammondsport man go. But sometimes it was necessary because they could not fit into the modern production patterns. Once when Russell suggested that they make up a purse to buy a little gift for one or two of the men, Curtiss objected. He opened a desk drawer which contained a quantity of gold watches.

Whenever you fire a man, I give him a watch, if he's an old Hammondsport man. Let me have their names in advance so that they may be engraved and ready."

He did not stop there, but followed their movements and sent them money when they needed it—always as a loan. If he knew about it, none of his men went uncared for.

Curtiss had little contact with mass production during 1917 and 1918. He kept occupied at the Garden City plant, with its fine wind tunnel and other experimental facilities, working closely with Army and Navy engineers to develop military types of aircraft; though he also designed a fast marine tender, a marine ambulance, and was hard at work on a gyroscopically controlled aerial torpedo, when the Armistice was signed.

Navy work claimed most of Curtiss' personal attention. Europe was chockful of yarns about what America could do with planes when we entered the war. People over there were led to believe this country would fly them across in large squadrons, supplying both machines and men by air. Curtiss thought something might be done in this direction.

In the summer of 1917, he went to Washington for a conference with Admiral D. W. Taylor, Chief Naval Constructor, who had definite ideas on the best way to combat the submarine peril.

"We can curb or wholly destroy this menace from the air," said the Admiral, "if our work in developing the proper aircraft is well done. Let's fight the U-boats with big flying boats and let's make our flying boats powerful enough to cross the Atlantic on their own wings if necessary, and so avoid the dangers and difficulties of transporting them as cargo."

Working closely with Commander Richardson and Commander J. C. Hunsaker, Curtiss designed the Navy-Curtiss or NC boat with four Liberty engines. When the Armistice was signed, a monster flying boat was in its trial maneuvers along the Atlantic Coast.

In May, 1919, the N-C1, 3 and 4 started from Tres-passey, Newfoundland, across the Atlantic, via the same route charted for the *America* in 1914, with Commander Towers in command of the flight. Each ship had a complement of five men. They encountered very stormy weather, and the NC-1, with Lieut. Commander Bellinger in command, was forced down. Unable to take off again, the crew was picked up and carried to the Azores by a freight steamer. The flagship landed in the fog to determine its position and then unable to take off again, steered a perilous course for 52 hours over rough seas into Ponta Delgada. But the NC-4, with Lieut. Commander Albert C. Read in command, landed at Horta, and later flew on to England, having completed the first aerial trans-Atlantic crossing. It was successful enough to indicate that if these ships had been built before the war ended, the plan to fly ships and supplies to our troops in Europe might have been made effective.

After the war, Curtiss was still a director of the Curtiss Aeroplane and Motor Company, but he served only as technical adviser on design. Clement M. Keys, a Canadian with considerable experience in American financing, bought the company from the Willys-Overland interests who had controlled it since 1917, when the war slump came. And under his direction, it eventually became the nucleus of a large group of aviation companies.

After 1914, flying school activities were transferred from Hammondsport to Newport News, Virginia, and huge classes of pilots were trained there. In 1915, Curtiss had donated a trophy to be awarded to the winner of an annual race in a plane "capable of starting from and alighting on water." The Curtiss Marine Trophy race remains one of the featured seaplane events of the year.

Within a short time after war was declared in Europe,

a number of former Curtiss students distinguished themselves in the British Royal Flying Corps and the Lafayette Escadrille. After this country entered the war, most of them signed up under their own colors.

One day, the whistles and bells and drums announced the Armistice in Hammondsport. The roar of motor production was shut down. Most of the workmen moved away and the population shrank to fewer than a thousand persons. The coming of prohibition had also paralyzed the wine industry. Old Lazarus Hammond's town slept.

To keep it from becoming a deserted village, Curtiss joined with McDonald and Seely in the formation of Keuka Industries, Inc. They bought up the Curtiss plant and planned to rent the buildings to a number of cooperative enterprises, which were to include the manufacture of balloons by Witmer, Callan and Havens; the manufacture of airplane parts by a group headed by Kleckler, and the manufacture of high speed motors and motor parts by the central organization.

The plan was never entirely effected as the various units could not be brought into coordination, nor could any demand for aeronautical equipment be detected at the time. For the time being men were satiated with flying, as well as with other methods of destroying each other. The project was abandoned.

Callan went on building balloons and rubber boats for several years; otherwise the hill was deserted. Recently all the buildings were torn down to make way for the Curtiss Memorial High School. The Curtiss home was moved to another location on the hill and now is back on active duty again, as a practice cottage for students of Home Economics.

Just Before Sundown

ALTHOUGH there was nothing of the local booster about Curtiss, he was a Hammondsport native to the core. It was home to him, and he signed hotel registers all over the world "G. H. Curtiss, Hammondsport, N. Y.," long after he had ceased to live or work there.

However, Curtiss intensely disliked the bitter upstate winters, and after 1910 he spent most of the winter months in California. In 1917 he went to Miami during the cold weather, and liked it so well that he decided soon after the war to settle there.

On his first trip South, he visited the Curtiss Flying School headquarters near Miami. Adjoining their flying field was Bright Ranch, where Curtiss met James H. Bright, a former cattleman from the West. They formed a friendship from which sprang an ambitious real estate venture. Their first major project was a town designed as a playground for visitors from the North, to which they gave the Seminole Indian name, Hialeah. A large tract was set aside for the Miami Jockey Club, and a luxurious clubhouse as well as the finest race track in the country, was built. The Miami Kennel Club was organized and quartered. And *jai alai*, Cuba's national game said to be the fastest in the world, was introduced into this country, at a handsome, marble-walled court, or *fronton*. Next the

Miami Studios, for the production of motion pictures, and the *Hialeah Press,* made their debut.

With Hialeah prospering, the Curtiss-Bright Industries moved across Miami Canal and began to develop a second town, which they called Country Club Estates, although it was later renamed Miami Springs. There Curtiss erected a home for his own family, and another for his mother and sister and his half-brother. A bank and administration building were built.

In 1925, Opalocka, north of Hialeah was started. Several buildings, including a pretentious Arabian administration building, were erected, and a large tract set aside as a flying field. Hangars were constructed and a canal was dug and designs prepared for a concrete ramp for overwater flying.

All that was needed now to complete their pink and white adobe empire was a sense of permanence, and the two partners decided that they should encourage a steady orange-growing, chicken-raising class of settlers. They set aside tracts for small, half-acre to five-acre ranches and sold them at low cost. Large mango swamps were transformed into flat farming land. No feat of engineering or architecture seemed too vast or too costly. They were acquiring supposedly worthless territory in million-acre parcels, spending fantastic sums to develop and market it, and realizing fantastic sums from its sale. Within a few years, they multiplied their original investment several times.

Curtiss was much pleased with the new enterprise and spent much time drawing up plans to widen its scope, or fretting over some landscaping detail. He wanted a spring effect in front of his house and had water piped into it, but when it was completed, he decided the arrangement of rocks in the bottom of the spring was not right, and shoved them around so they looked prettier. The aesthetic side of his nature, which he had inherited from his mother, had been stifled most of his life. At forty, it seemed to come actively into play. Making things look pleasing became a passion with him, but it worried him that his mother, who had lost her sight, could not see the artificial spring, or the colorful houses or the towns and streets, bridges and swimming pools they were building.

His engineering ability was useful in visualizing town-building projects which architects and engineers carried out. And when the city of Miami was faced with the problem of providing water free from alkaline substances, he conceived a plan by which an unlimited supply of pure artesian water was obtained, and at a saving of several million dollars over the outlay originally anticipated.

Curtiss was as contented as it is possible for a man of his restless temperament to be. He was healthier, and looked younger than he did in his early thirties. As soon as the real estate developments began to yield returns, he sent for his old Hammondsport associates. Among the first to join him was Tank Waters, whose knowledge of shrubs and flower culture led him to landscape gardening. There was work of various kinds for other old friends, and more money than Curtiss knew offhand what to do with.

He had no great difficulty however in finding ways to spend it. Now that he had large surpluses, he entertained his friends, and made life easier for them in ingenious little ways. He was a thoughtful rather than a prodigal spender.

In one instance a former friend and business associate did him a service which he valued very highly, but since it had been done out of friendship, the other man insisted that Curtiss was in no way in his debt. He was then invited to Florida for a visit, but could not get away at the time, and forgot all about the incident until he received a note saying that Curtiss had bought an option on a plot of land in his name and had just sold it. The check enclosed in the letter represented the profit realized in the transaction. The recipient never was able to discover whether such an option really had been taken out or not.

In tribute to his grandfather's memory, Curtiss gave a new pipe organ to the Methodist Church at Hammondsport. And on certain rare occasions, he was subject to bursts of unaccountable generosity.

Over the telephone he said one day to Lad Seely, "How would you like to buy that roadster I got last week? Sell her to you for half price—$1,750."

"Sorry, G. H., it's a nice car, but I can't afford it," was Seely's answer.

The same day, Curtiss met young Bill Seely on the street and asked him, "Want to buy that new roadster of ours?"

It sounded like a joke to Bill, then a senior in high school, so he laughed and said, "Sure, I'd like to Mr. Curtiss, but I'm afraid it's a little out of my reach."

"Can you pay a dollar for it?"

"Yes, sir, I think I could do that all right."

"Well, come over this afternoon and we'll close the deal."

Vast wealth changed Curtiss' mode of life, of course. He traveled some, but always simply. Ostentation bothered him. And when going by train, he always took an upper berth because "the air is better up there." A roast beef sandwich in a hole in the wall always appealed to him much more than dinner in an expensive restaurant. Instead of a yacht, he used a little fishing cruiser. He was always well groomed, though never dressy, in his opulent days and came to look the part of a man of the world.

Presently Curtiss leased a grouse moor in Scotland and

found pleasure in having friends of his earlier flying days join him there, although he did not greatly enjoy hunting. His favorite sport was archery and he achieved amazing skill with a bow and arrow. Once, having read that a tribe of Bush Negroes held their arrows poised in their toes instead of their fingers, he was discovered on his back in the garden endeavoring to the best of his ability to emulate their peculiar technique.

The post-war jazz age irritated Curtiss beyond measure. It bothered him to see his friends drinking, and he could not reconcile himself to prohibition standards. Only on very rare occasions would he accept a single cocktail. Strangers sometimes thought him anti-social. He never learned to care for parties, but often accepted invitations rather than give offense. Sooner or later, he grew abstracted, detached himself from a group which was discussing something he was not interested in and left abruptly.

"Whatever have I done to offend, Mr. Curtiss?" the agitated hostess would inquire.

In his own home, he had a little staircase built especially for unobtrusive disappearances. Usually it was a brand new issue of some technical magazine which lured him away from his own parties as well as those of others.

After he had listened to a radio for ten minutes, he was apt to say almost prayerfully: "Do you think anybody is listening to that? Can't we turn it off now?"

There was one phase of modern life which he found fascinating: Speed, and its future possibilities. The whole imposing Florida development was merely a diverting interlude. He had never let business worry him, and it was too late to begin at forty. His offices in the administration building at Country Club Estates and at Opalocka were merely elegant dust-catchers; he seldom entered them.

Most often he was to be found in the garage at the back of his home.

It might be just a new type of arrow for archery practice, or a streamlined golf club he was working on, but motor cars were his special prey. Once he bought a costly highpowered car and drove it a few weeks. Then it disappeared. When next seen, the two rear wheels had been replaced by four with springs mounted between them. He had achieved smoother riding. A favorite trick was to buy two new cars, tear them apart and build one which had unique features not found previously in either.

As a motorist he was a terror to the uninitiated. If a passenger suddenly noticed a tree directly in their path, and shrieked: "Look out!" he smiled and shrugged his shoulders. He knew the exact adjustments of cramping and speeding that would get around the obstacle safely. Or if a five-ton truck came crashing into their path, Curtiss would grin and say: "I thought we could squeeze by all right", and he was never mistaken. This sort of thing was a game with him.

When the Florida bubble burst in 1926, he stayed on through the rehabilitation period, because he had a fortune invested there and he was convinced recovery would inevitably come. Meanwhile he devoted himself more actively to speed problems. For years Curtiss had maintained that other phases of automotivation should lean on aviation experience. As early as 1912, he tried to persuade Henry Ford that he should try out a light aviation motor in a Model T. Ford was interested but his chief idea at that time was quantity production of low cost cars.

Curtiss built a single step, flat-bottomed hull on which, a few feet above the rear deck, a 400-horsepower Liberty motor was mounted. The motor was cooled by fresh water from a radiator mounted in a well of salt water in the hull. The thrust of its aerial propeller was so strong that the boat could travel up an inclined runway into the boat-house under its own power. Its top speed was 50 miles an hour.

His first important manufacturing venture in the South was a streamlined, two-wheeled trailer for luxurious cross-country traveling, produced in 1929. He tested it on a smooth stretch built through the Everglades, known as Tamiami Trail. With the trailer, which weighed 1,500 pounds and had 75 square feet of floor space, the roadster made 83 miles per hour, which was six miles faster than it did without the trailer. The streamlined effect of the trailer actually obliterated the powerful suction or vacuum which otherwise followed in the wake of the roadster. It was a successor to the cruder "home away from home" which Curtiss had put into production in 1920, and which was the great grandfather of all the American touring trailers.

When Hamilton Wright, Jr., of the *Miami Herald*, hunted him up in his backyard workshop, in March 1929, Curtiss gave out, the longest interview of his entire life, on the subject in which he was at that moment most deeply absorbed.

Curtiss began by citing the automobile as a "horrible example of inefficiency." After he had issued his diatribe, he outlined with clear foresight not only today's motor car trends, but tomorrow's:

> The motor car has double the amount of machinery, a hundred more working parts, has double its necessary weight and has put itself in a ridiculous position when compared to the meteoric rise and capabilities of the airplane.
>
> Man can move on the ground in almost any-thing. It is the easiest thing to do. Even the cavemen enjoyed log-wheeled transportation.

But when it comes to staying in the air, man has had to plan for one thing only—efficiency.

There is no more useful reason for some things in the modern style of automobile than there is for the style of a man's neckties or a woman's hat. The modern car is sadly lacking in comfort and efficiency. The automobile today in some respects is not far advanced from the horse and buggy stage. All it has gained in twenty years is power and reliability. It has gone backward in economy. With all its power, machinery and conglomeration of accessories, it can carry but four people in comfort and at a cost that is extravagant.

The design of the motor car lends nothing to cut down wind resistance. At 60 miles per hour practically half the motor's power is used to overcome this element. Paradoxical to the airplane, overcoming of wind resistance is the last improvement considered in the automobile. As a result, a minimum head resistance, minimum gas consumption, far superior engine performance and less weight and horsepower are in favor of the airplane. But it, too, has much room for improvement. We have done little to economize in motor car design. With a 56 inch tread, a cumbersome motor, over a ton of steel and a kaleidoscopic array of nickel trimmings, wheels, oversize fenders, lights, and fittings, all taking up enough space to house a Nairobi family, it still costs more to travel per mile than it did with a four horse team and coach a century ago.

I believe there will be a complete revolution in automobile design very shortly. It will be based on a study of present-day aeronautics. According to recent experiments, we learn that a body designed to cut down wind resistance will give the average car five miles per hour more speed at 25 miles per hour as compared to present day design.

The modern radiator, is a fallacy. The cooling effect on the motor when the car goes with the wind and against the wind varies considerably, constantly changing the temperature of the motor. For instance, a car going up hill with the wind gets overheated quicker than a car going up against the wind. No fan can control the whims of nature or serve to keep the motor at a constant temperature. The flow of air should be kept constant and the pressure should be the same. Proper heating and proper temperature have as much to do in maintaining the efficiency of the gasoline engine as do many of its integral parts.

Automobile style should be based on utility. As soon as we begin to follow the trend set by our most efficient form of transportation today, the airplane, the style of the American automobile is going to be such that it will speed up travel 100 per cent. There are only two things that prevent a motor car from going 1,000 miles per hour.* They are friction and head resistance. At high speeds 80 per cent of the power is used to overcome head resistance and the other 20 per cent is taken up by friction.

Railroads have done more for comfort, reliability and safety of passengers on long and short trips than automobiles.

The automobile will never supplant the airplane and the airplane will never supplant the automobile. The function of the airplane is to make long, fast journeys.

Curtiss anticipation of unrealized speed possibilities in aeronautics was expressed in October, 1922, when he made this prophecy: "It was in 1910, if I remember, that someone asked my opinion on future speed; and I predicted that two hundred miles an hour should be possible. In the light of present knowledge and based on past performances, it is not improbable that 500 ** miles per hour will be made in the future."

When Paul Zimmermann, who encountered Curtiss in New York in the spring of 1929, asked him: "How is Florida?"

Curtiss replied sadly: "Well, there's not much doing now, it's about like aviation after the war." He finished: "But, Paul, y'know, I've got a good idea for a new boat."

In this frame of mind he went on to Hammondsport, called Kleckler and Merrill out of partial retirement, and established an engineering organization to work on several half-conceived but steadily rotating ideas. On the original factory building behind the deserted house, they hung a sign which read simply:

AUTOMOTIVE RESEARCH—INC.

A year later, in 1930, Curtiss was designing and experimenting with a new type of automobile. The body was shaped into as nearly perfect an example of automobile streamline as possible. The motor was so small and light it could be stowed under the driver's seat and, at first glance, appeared to have vanished. It weighed pounds less per horse power than the average automobile power-plant of that date. By closely adhering to airplane design practice, all unnecessary chassis and body weight was eliminated.

Yours of the 16th at hand. I will be glad to join with you in the proposed organization. I

---

* The unlimited racing car record is 301.473 miles per hour, made by Sir Malcolm Campbell at Bonneville. The record for American stock cars is 105.0533 miles per hour.

** Today's top speed record is 440 miles per hour, by Francesco Agello of Italy in a seaplane. The land plane record is 352.388 miles per hour, set by Howard Hughes.

THE LIFE OF GLENN CURTISS

will soon be old enough to reminisce. Go ahead.
Let me know what I can do.

G. H. Curtiss

The Early Birds, a group of pioneer flyers, was in
process of formation, and this was how Curtiss, at the age
of fifty, felt about the plan.

There was more thinking back to the early days that
some year, 1928, with the anniversary of the trophy-
winning *June Bug* flight. Twenty years before, the Aerial
Experiment Association had announced that one of their
members would fly an aerodrome a certain distance on a
certain day if the weather was right. And just before sundown, the weather had been right.

Hammondsport was inordinately proud of its flying
past, and of its citizen who had built aircraft on the side
of a hill and flown them between the aisles of other hills.
And there was a monster celebration of the July Fourth
event.

Early in May, 1930, Representative Ruth Bryan Owen,
of Florida, introduced a bill to award Curtiss the Con-
gressional Medal of Honor. And on May 30th (rather
than May 29th) the Aeronautical Chamber of Commerce
arranged an anniversary flight down the Hudson.

Among the early associates who joined in the celebration
were Jacob Ten Eyck, starter of the flight from Albany
in 1910, and Augustus Post, official timer: Alan Hawley,
Ernest Jones, and Stanley Beach, all judges at the *June
Bug* flight; Jerome Fanciulli, Commander Callan and
Frank Russell.

Don Seitz, business manager of the *World* in 1910, who
was there also, reported that Curtiss on this occasion was
"about as communicative as a cigar store wooden Indian."
And added, "He was always that way, too shy to let any-

one know how he really felt about anything." But though neither Seitz or nine-tenths of the assembled company suspected it, Curtiss had a good time. Only his wife and his closest friends realized it. Perhaps the years had brought him poise. At any rate, he enjoyed every minute of the day except his time at the microphone.

He spoke; but barely three and a half minutes, to the embarrassment of the program committee which had allotted ten whole minutes of radio time to the guest of honor. And although no record of the speech exists, he was quite miserable and almost as laconic as he had been at a dinner given by the Los Angeles Press Club during the 1910 International Air Meet, when he arose, and said in all sincerity:

"I can't talk. I can't even tell a funny story. When I get up to speak I feel as uneasy as if my motor had stopped and there was nothing below to alight on but church steeples. So, if you'll excuse me, I'll sit down and let somebody else, who can, talk."

After the dinner at the old Hotel Ten Eyck, the entire anniversary group drove out to the airport and piled into transport planes for a flight to New York. Captain Frank Courtney, the pilot in charge of the big Condor which carried Curtiss and his party, had accepted on their face value the newspaper guarantees that Curtiss would fly the ship himself. The Englishman was ignorant on two points. He did not know that Curtiss had not flown a plane in sixteen years, or that he had never used the standard modern controls.

Courtney accordingly took the ship off, and after climbing to two thousand feet, shifted the controls over to Curtiss, while he turned his immediate attention to snapping pictures of Albany and Hudson River. Afterwards, co-pilot Curtiss said:

"Y'know, I didn't know just what to do. The plane seemed to be going all right, so I pulled back on the wheel very gently and saw the nose come up. That was like my old control. I pushed forward a bit and the nose went down. Fine. Knowing that the wheel also operated the ailerons, I turned it first to the right and then to the left and felt the plane bank as I expected.

"The real trouble I had was with my feet. They were on the rudder bar, which I had never used, and I just did not know what to do with them. By experimenting, I soon found out what happened, and it was not long before I began to feel much more comfortable than I did when I saw Courtney lean out of that window, leaving me practically alone to pilot the largest ship I had ever flown."

Over Storm King Mountain, the big Condor encountered the same unstable air conditions; an anniversary touch which Curtiss relished far more than his load of distinguished passengers. After circling Governor's Island, he turned the ship back to Captain Courtney for landing at Curtiss Airport at Valley Stream, Long Island.

The trip had been made in the twenty-place ship in less than half of the time it took Curtiss in the *Albany Flyer*, at a speed of 110 miles an hour rather than 52.

Shortly thereafter, Curtiss returned to Miami to receive an acknowledgment which pleased and embarrassed him. The University of Miami at commencement time conferred upon him the degree of Doctor of Science.

"A lot of nice things I don't deserve," he said when the academics paid him their conventionally lavish tributes.

Less than a month after the Albany flight anniversary, Merrill was injured at the Automotive Research plant, when a board kicked back from a buzz saw and struck him in the stomach. He sat down to rest for a few minutes and then decided to go on working.

"Better take it easy, Dame," Kleckler told him. "Something might be hurt that you don't know about. Come on I'll drive you home." Three days later Merrill was dead.

Curtiss' friends had difficulty trying to keep his mind off the subject. If certain things had been done, he argued interminably, the accident needn't have happened. He was busy figuring out how Dame's death could have been mechanically avoided.

In the early part of July it was publicly charged that Curtiss was not really ill, but only wished to escape further appearance at hearings of the Herring suit. There followed a searching examination of physicians sent to check up on his truthfulness. And a *New York Times* story was headlined:

Curtiss Excused in Suit

Doctors at Rochester Clear Plane Maker of Feigning Illness

This sort of thing was disagreeable, naturally, but no one guessed at the time just how intense his humiliation had been. All his life he had been particularly cowardly about wounding anyone. The newspaper columns were always open to him, but he rarely issued a statement in his own defense and never used the papers to attack another man. His opponents used them to belittle him. When derogatory statements or deliberate distortions of evidence were published, his press presentative raged time and again:

"But we've got to answer; make them retract."

Curtiss' customary retort was: "No, I'm afraid it wouldn't sound so nice."

It was because of his innate friendliness that he had sat down one day and dictated a letter to Orville Wright proposing that they meet sometime for a friendly chat.

The remaining Wright brother was not ready yet to loosen his clutch on the resentment of years. He could not forget that it was Curtiss who endeavored to prove the Langley plane capable of flight. It was Middlewestern pride against rural-Eastern, and the Ohio variety was more impervious.

There was a persistent kinship between Langley and the man who endeavored to show the world how wrong it had been to call him an imposter because he built an aircraft which did not fly. Both men were inevitably concerned with the public's estimate, though both were shy of publicity; Langley much more so even than Curtiss.

"What has posterity ever done for us that we should care so much for the opinion of posterity?" had been one of Langley's favorite sayings. Yet when a copy of a resolution from the Aero Club of America, expressing appreciation of his high contribution to the science of aerial navigation, was read to him a few hours before he died, he pleaded hungrily:

"Publish it!"

Curtiss' final surrender was even more abject.

He looked worn and tired during the period following Merrill's death because he was suffering with chronic appendicitis. But not until he could no longer avoid it did he consent to an operation, which he dreaded very much. He recovered rapidly and easily, and was up and about ten days later in his room at a Buffalo hospital, dictating letters and attending to his affairs by long distance telephone. He called Hammondsport regularly.

On the night of July the 21st he was feeling very fit. When he got Kleckler on the wire, he said:

"Well, Henny, let's get this car out of the way so we can start building boats. I'll be down at the end of the week."

"Don't get too foxy, G. H.! You'd better be sure you are all right before you do any traveling," cautioned his assistant.

The next night, after one of his almost infallible premonitions, Curtiss summoned his secretary, Florence Illig, and dictated a long statement * * * "in case anything happens to me."

In an open letter to all his opponents he denounced the methods they had employed against him and defended himself. "If I die, "he dictated," they are responsible."

When he finished dictating, he instructed Mrs. Illig to come back the next day with the transcription and a notary public, so that it might be sent out for publication immediately. But his statement was never sworn to. Early the next morning the little blood clot, traveling unnoticed through his veins, found a choke point. Death came along with a padlock. The statement sometimes almost incoherent in its vehemence, was never made public.

Curtiss' last conscious act was strangely uncharacteristic of a man whose reticences were in striking contrast to the sensational nature of his accomplishment. His taking-off so quietly, at the age of only fifty-two, after a lifetime of swift daring on the ground and above it was equally inconsistent.

The streamlined car experiment he had been working on was never fully completed. And there was essential tragedy in fact that he never got into metal, wood and fabric the new idea for a boat, which he discussed in glowing terms with friends who came to visit him at the hospital.

When they buried Glenn Curtiss at Pleasant Valley cemetery, not two hundred yards away from the half-mile track at Stony Brook Farm, beside his grandmother, his grandfather, his father and his little son, Hammondsport became again, for one day, the aviation center of the world. Flyers, engineers, mechanics, scientists, lawyers; former students who were now high-ranking officers of the Army and Navy, or aviation executives; and representatives of foreign governments, came back to town—many of them by airplane. They flew singly and in formation above Lake Keuka, Kingsley Field and Stony Brook Farm.

From all over the world came messages, all saying in their individual way: "He held my affectionate regard."

C. G. Grey, English aviation editor, who first met Curtiss at the Rheims meet in 1909, made one estimate of him which was quite unlike the cut and dried stuff of most obituaries. It ended:

"His outstanding characteristic was kindness. And perhaps his next most outstanding characteristic was his humor. Beyond that he had immense courage, great physical strength, a good sound business head, and withal that simplicity which only great men have. Nobody has done more for the progress of flying than G. H. Curtiss, and few have done as much. He was a good man and a kindly man, and the world is very much poorer for his loss."

An Album
of
American Aeronautics

Because she thought this ravine in Hammondsport, New York, was so pretty, with its sparkling waterfalls, Lua Andrews Curtiss named her son after it. It was known as the Glen, and she added an "n" to make it look more like a name.

The bicycle shop in Hammondsport which Glenn Curtiss opened, backed by James H. Smellie. Young Curtiss stands before the shop with his friends and a customer who offered a dollar bill in payment. There wasn't enough cash in the place to make change and the photograph was taken to commemorate the event.

Below, Glenn Curtiss being pushed off by one of the younger local boys in a bicycle race. Curtiss and his team-mate, "Tank" Waters, won most of the cinder track events within a radius of a hundred miles.

Curtiss in his racing costume, streamlined, and in his "hairpin" position in the saddle. At Ormond Beach, Florida, he made his first official world record on January 28, 1904, on a standard "Hercules", as he trade-named his earlier motorcycles.

Below, Curtiss diagnoses the mud-caked two-cylinder, air-cooled power plant of one of his racing motorcycles.

*U. S. Army Dirigible No. 1, flown by her
builder, Baldwin, with Glenn Curtiss to run
the motor, successfully fulfilled all requirements in a "phenomenal" flight at Fort Myer,
Virginia, on August 12, 1908. It was by far
the most ambitious dirigible project ever
tackled in this country. Curtiss solved the
problem of a power-plant which could keep
cool for two hours of uninterrupted flying,
with power enough to drive a gas bag around
a closed circuit and carry two men, at a speed
of twenty miles per hour, by building his
first water-cooled engine. It was a four-
cylinder, aluminum-jacketed, 24-horsepower
affair.*

*Below, Curtiss weighing off for a flight in
Thomas Scott Baldwin's dirigible balloon,
"California Arrow", on June 28, 1907. He
had been building engines for dirigibles since
1904, but he had never before this taken any
personal interest in flying.*

Dr. and Mrs. Alexander Graham Bell in the garden of their country home, Beinn Breagh, near Baddeck, Nova Scotia. It was at Mrs. Bell's suggestion that the Aerial Experiment Association was formed in 1907.— Photograph copyrighted by Gilbert Grosvenor.

A facsimile of the last page of the "agree-ment to organize the Aerial Experiment Asso-ciation", one of the most fruitful of coopera-tive scientific ventures in the history of applied science.

number as Director of Experiments to be our medium of communication with the Laboratory.

We agree that the Laboratory workmen shall receive their instructions from the Superintendent of the Laboratory alone, that the Superintendent of the Laboratory shall receive his instructions from the Director of Experiments alone, and that the Director of Experiments shall receive his instructions by vote of the Association of which he is a member.

We agree that the headquarters of the "Aerial Experiment Association" shall be at Beinn Bhreagh, Near Baddeck Nova Scotia, and that, on or before the first of January, 1908, the headquarters of the Association shall be removed to some place yet to be determined within the limits of the United Stat

This agreement can only be modified by unanimous vote of the undersigned.

Witness our hands and seals at HALIFAX, Nova Scotia, this thirtieth day of September, A. D., 1907.

Notary Public

Alexander Graham Bell

G. H. Curtiss.

F. W. Baldwin

J. A. Douglas McCurdy

T. Selfridge
1st Lt. 5th F.A., USA

The Aerial Experiment Association's first experiment in Hammondsport was a bi-plane glider, which would support a man if he ran down a hill into the face of a fifteen-mile breeze.

The members of the Aerial Experiment Association and some of their fellow workers in the cause of aeronautics.

Left to right: (Standing)—Thomas Scott Baldwin, F. W. Baldwin, A. E. A. chief engineer in special charge of construction; J. Newton Williams, who was building a helicopter at the Curtiss shop; J. A. D. McCurdy, A. E. A. treasurer and chief engineer in special charge of photographic experiments; Lieut. T. Selfridge, 5th Field Artillery, U. S. Army, A. E. A. secretary.

(Seated) Alexander Graham Bell, A. E. A. chairman; G. H. Curtiss, A. E. A. executive officer and director of experiments; W. F. Bedwin, who was in charge of the Bell experimental laboratory at Baddeck.

At the top, The Red Wing, assembled on the ice of Lake Keuka, with steel runners to enhance the hope of getting into the air. The small black projectile-like object above the motor is the fuel tank.

In the middle, "Casey" Baldwin in the pilot's seat for the Red Wing's first and last flight. Photo by Harry M. Benner.

At the bottom, The Red Wing collapsed after a twenty-second flight some six or eight feet into the air. This was the first public flight in America by a heavier-than-air machine—on March 12, 1908.

J. Newton Williams and his helicopter-type of aerial machine. Curtiss, Baldwin and John McCurdy assisted in its successful "rise" up the length of a short cable, under its own power.

Below, A device to test the front elevator. Curtiss is in the driver's seat of this "wind-wagon," with Clarence Love (wearing a cap) and another mechanic standing by.

The White Wing about to take off on her first flight with Lieutenant Selfridge at the controls, and Curtiss beside him. Baldwin is standing behind the machine. Selfridge flew about 500 feet and landed without damage. Photo by Harry M. Benner.

Below, the townspeople of Hammondsport gathered on the slope bordering the A. E. A. flying field, on an unofficial holiday, May 22, 1908, the occasion of Curtiss's first flight in a heavier-than-air machine. They cheered when he rose above the tops of the grass in the White Wing. On May 27th he flew 1017 feet in 19 seconds.

The June Bug, born of the trials and errors of the Aerial Experiment Association's first two machines, which competed for the Scientific American's trophy, on July 4, 1908. The judges came to Hammondsport to see if it was possible for an aeronaut to make a scheduled flight, weather permitting. Just before sundown on that day Curtiss flew more than the required kilometer and won the first leg of the contest. This won for him Aero Club of America's No. 1 pilot's license. Photo by Harry M. Benner.

Below, An amazing picture of the startled spectators streaking behind the trophy-winning June Bug as she puffed her way to flying immortality. The plane is barely discernible just ahead of her smoke screen. Dr. Bell's daughter, Mrs. Gilbert Grosvenor (dressed in white) is being squired across the potato patch by "Casey" Baldwin.

Glenn Curtiss and John McCurdy took the wheels off the June Bug, equipped her with two floats, or pontoons, and re-christened her the Loon. On January 2, 1909, she sank without warning because one float was water-logged. For purposes of comparison with later, more amenable water-aircraft, note the slender shape and length of the pontoons on the Loon (minus her engine) on her way to the lake shore, astride an improvised cart. These floats were little more than ordinary paddling canoes, decked over with rubberized cloth.

Below, The air-cooled engine which powered the June Bug, did duty also in the Red Wing and the White Wing. In order to get the maximum power out of this engine a carburetor was fitted to each cylinder and auxiliary ports drilled to take away part of the work of the exhaust valve and prevent overheating. The engine was built from eight motorcycle cylinders which were rated at 2½ horsepower, although 2 horsepower might have been more conservative. The bore was 3¼ inches and the stroke about 3½ inches. The automatic intake valves did not contribute to high efficiency.

The little tank overhead was taken from a racing motorcycle and carried both oil and gasoline. The oil was fed into the crank case through a sight-feed oiler. The cam shaft gear was not enclosed. It was lubricated before every flight with bicycle chain graphite. All things considered, it was quite surprising that the June Bug actually flew a mile.

This ice sled was the Aerial Experiment Association's first propeller-testing device. The four-cylinder, aircooled motor was designed for use in an early dirigible balloon. The propeller was made of steel bars with a sheet-steel face, and is similar to the one used in the Red Wing. Glenn Curtiss enjoyed motor ice-boating as a sport. As it happens, he received his only disfigurement in many years of flying and racing while riding on a large motor ice sled in Baddeck, Nova Scotia.

Below, McCurdy's Silver Dart, the fourth and last of the A. E. A. machines, flown at Hammondsport in the fall of 1908. It combined the best features of the three predecessors, with some innovations including the water-cooled type engine designed for the Army dirigible, and a vertical type radiator (in front of the engine). The wings were covered with nainsook rather than expensive silk. They were "doped" with aluminum paint, which accounts for the name Silver Dart.

Glenn Curtiss still has his chin in a sling after the ice boat accident.

*La Grande Semaine d'Aviation de Cham-
pagne—the first of all the air meets, was held
August 22 to 29, 1909, on Bethany Plain, near
Rheims, France. It was the sporting event of
the decade, with many thousands of dollars
posted in prizes. All manner of aircraft was
entered and the various types afford an interesting comparison of current design tenden-
cies.*

*At the top, Curtiss flying the Curtiss bi-
plane built for the meet in his motorcycle
factory. This, his second machine, had a 50-
horsepower, water-cooled engine.*

*At the right, Louis Paulhan, of France,
rounding a pylon in his box-kite Voisin plane.
Paulhan had learned to fly two months before
the meet and already had captured an important record.*

*To the left, middle, Lefebre, another
Frenchman, flying a graceful Wright biplane.
Note runners as compared to wheels of other
planes. The Wright brothers, who had made
many record flights abroad, were not themselves represented at the meet because they
felt that the rules placed their planes at a disadvantage.*

*Bottom, left, Hubert Latham, Frenchman,
flying the Antoinette high-wing monoplane.
Note the beauty of its long, slender lines.*

The three leading contenders for the Gordon Bennett Cup race at the Rheims meet

At the top, Louis Bleriot, the idol of all Europe at the moment, because of his recent English Channel crossing. His compact little high-wing Bleriot monoplane, with its 8-cylinder, 80 horsepower engine was reputed the fastest thing aflight.

In the middle, Curtiss is standing in front of his biplane, the Golden Flyer. Curtiss beat Bleriot's time by a few seconds and captured the cup for the United States.

Below, Hubert Latham in the cozy seat of his Antoinette monoplane. He made third best time around the 20-kilometer course in the Bennett race, averaging about 40 miles an hour as compared to 46 by the American winner.

Three French aeronauts at the Rheims meet:

Above, Alfred Leblanc prepares to depart in his Bleriot monoplane, while a camera enthusiast rushes up to take his picture.

In the middle, De Rue, approaches his Voisin biplane in the helmet and leather boots over street clothes, which was covential flying garb of the day. The aviator in the black hat and boots (showing the white armband of contestants at the meet) is Santos-Dumont.

Below, Henri Farman (in leather boots and black hat) celebrated flyer and designer, prepares to take off in his Farman biplane. The slim black tank slung between the wings gives some idea of the limited gas capacity of aircraft, vintage 1909.

The Damoiselle of Santos-Dumont, leading French pioneer aeronaut and designer, has the beauty of a dragon fly.

Below, the side-lines at the initial "air-classic of the century." Ticket holders have swarmed out of the grandstands to watch the Comte de Lampert take off in his white Biplan Wright, by .means of the catapult launching tower. Peasants have filtered in also to have a look at the aerial festivities. The hatless, countrywomen, with their topknots and aprons, are in striking contrast to the lady-like fashion-plate of 1909, with her escort. Photograph by M. Rol et Cie.

Because the American aviator allowed him to sit on a narrow board wired to the top of the lower wing during a flight, at Brescia, Italy, on September 12, 1909, Gabriele d'Annunzio, Italy's poet and war flyer discovered exactly "what a creeping, crawling business life on earth was." The board on which d'Annunzio had his first trip aloft was later auctioned off for profit splinter by splinter

This photograph of the poet was inscribed, in May 1930:

    "To the very great Curtiss his first passenger and his admirer forever

                  Gabriele d'Annunzio"

dee.
192

An très grand Curtiss
son premier « passenger ».
et son admirateur pour toujou
Gabriele d'Annunzi

In the Albany Flyer, Curtiss, on Sunday, May 29, 1910, flew down the river and won a ten thousand dollar prize for the first flight from Albany to New York. This "long-distance," one-stop flight of 150 miles was made at an average speed of 52.63 miles an hour in 2 hours and 51 minutes flying time. The photograph at the top was taken at Albany before the flight. Left to right: G. H. Curtiss, Mrs. Curtiss, Augustus Post, and a proud young local flying fan.

Below, the Gill farm, near Poughkeepsie, where Curtiss stopped to refuel. A crowd gathered quickly. While the aeroplane was being prepared for the second leg of the flight, the New York Central train waited on the nearby tracks, ready to resume the race down the Hudson. The flyer got to New York first and won the rail-air race, much to the astonishment of the locomotive engineer. The train's average speed was 49.6 miles per hour or nearly 3 miles less than that of The Hudson Flyer.

A facsimile of the receipt which Curtiss handed to J. Angus Shaw, treasurer of The World.

In the excitement of his arrival and reception, Curtiss forgot for nearly two hours to deliver a letter to Mayor Gaynor of New York from the Mayor of Albany. New York's mayor presided at the banquet, at the Hotel Astor, in honor of the flyer. The photograph is of Curtiss and Mayor Gaynor.

The World

Pulitzer Building. Park Row, N. Y.
CASHIER'S DEPT

Received of The New York World
Ten Thousand $10,000.00 dollars
prize for Aeroplane flight from
Albany to New York City

May 29 - 1910

G. H. Curtiss.

An appropriately melodramatic picture of the prize-winning flight was made up and distributed to its readers by the New York World. On the whole a general gala effect is preserved for posterity's benefit. Even the skyline, in which the 41-story Singer Building still looms over down-town Manhattan, dates the lithograph.

The Albany flight having aroused wide-spread interest, many requests poured in for air shows. The Curtiss exhibition team was organized. This picture of three members of the flying troupe, taken in Cleveland, shows Curtiss wearing, for the only time in any photograph, the traditional aviator's helmet. Left to right: Eugene B. Ely, J. C. ("Bud") Mars, and Curtiss.

Aviator Ely in 1910 and 1911 made the first ship-to-shore and shore-to-ship flights, marking the inception of the airplane carrier.

On December 9, 1910, Glenn Curtiss sent letters to the United States War and Navy Departments offering to instruct officers detailed in the science of aviation. The first to be so detailed were Lieut. Theodore G. Ellyson, from the Navy, and Lieut. Paul W. Beck, from the Army; others followed. At North Island, near San Diego, where he opened a winter aviation camp, and then at Hammondsport, N. Y., Curtiss taught them to fly and worked with them on experiments to develop flight equipment.

Left to right: Lieut. J. W. McClaskey, of the Marine Corps; Lieut. Paul W. Beck, of the Army; Lieut. John H. Towers, of the Navy; Lieut. T. G. Ellyson. Curtiss is seated in the training plane, or "grass-cutter."

Beginning with 1910, a new crop of pilots was graduated each spring and fall from the Curtiss flying schools at Hammondsport, San Diego and Miami. Many of the alumni stayed on as instructors or to do experimental work. Others were sent over the world as aircraft demonstrators. This is a representative group at Hammondsport in the spring of 1913.

January 26, 1911, marked the birth of Naval Aviation, when Curtiss made the world's first flight in a seaworthy aircraft at San Diego, California. He had already demonstrated to the skeptical Naval officials that shore-to-ship and ship-to-shore flights were practicable. On February 17, 1911, he went a step further by making a flight off the water, landing alongside a battleship and being hoisted aboard, hydro-aeroplane and all.

The photograph shows the flyer with one leg slipped through the big hook of the hoisting crane just above his machine. Note the single pontoon of this early hydro-aeroplane (or seaplane in modern usage).

By adding a third wing surface (slightly smaller) Glenn Curtiss in 1911 increased the carrying capacity of his standard biplane by two hundred pounds, thereby making it possible to fly three passengers at once. He wanted to test the effect of building-up instead of widening-out. He also built the first hydro-triplane at this time, which had three wing surfaces of equal size (below). Left to right: Curtiss, Lieut. T. G. Ellyson and Lieut. Paul W. Beck.

An attempt to prove the feasibility of launching a hydro-aeroplane from a surface other than the water, such as, for example, a ship at sea. On September 7, 1911 with Lieut. Ellyson at the controls a new "hydro" for the Navy was successfully launched from a wire cable. In the photograph the device is being tested out without a pilot aboard.

Less than a month after the launching of the first hydro-aeroplane, the first amphibian took off from the water, flew through the air and came down on land at San Diego. Three days later, February 27, 1911, Curtiss made the first flight from the water with a passenger (Lieut. Ellyson) in this amphibian. It had a single pontoon, with a front elevator attached to the pontoon. The landing wheels are retracted against the wing in the photograph. Note the wing pontoons, necessary in a single-float aircraft to keep it from tipping.

In January 1912, Curtiss evolved the flying boat, the first of a long line of over-water boats, small and large, open or closed. Lieut. Ellyson is at the controls of this early type flying boat, which has a front elevator attached to the hull.

Below a late 1913 hydro-aeroplane, a standard school "hydro"—with an OX motor, on which hundreds of fledglings earned their water-wings. Left to right: Francis ("Doc") Wildman, chief instructor in the Curtiss schools, and Lincoln Beachey, wearing "bibs" or life preservers around their necks. Curtiss is standing on the runway.

Lincoln Beachey, than whom no greater pilot ever lived, according to Glenn Curtiss and virtually everybody who ever saw him, first piloted dirigibles for Thomas Scott Baldwin. In 1910 Curtiss taught him to fly at San Diego, and Beachey frequently visited Hammondsport.

In 1913 he persuaded Curtiss to build him a plane especially designed for stunting. It was a small tractor with one-piece wings and double-covered surfaces. Its large ailerons made it very maneuverable. Beachey test-hopped it before the fusilage was covered, as he always liked flying out in the open.

Lawrence B. ("Gyro") Sperry was one of many promising students of the Curtiss school at Hammondsport, where he qualified as a hydro-aeroplane pilot on October 29, 1913. With plans for the Rodman Wanamaker trans-Atlantic boat under way, he worked together with Elmer Sperry and Curtiss, on two important projects: automatic stability for aeroplanes in flight and air navigation instruments for distance flights. In June 1914 he won the first prize of 50,000 francs in the Safety Airplane Contest near Paris with a dramatic demonstration of a gyroscopic stabilizer for aeroplanes. The photograph shows Lawrence Sperry in a two-place standard Curtiss biplane, with the dual controls first developed in May 1911.

The first JN, or "Jenny" training plane was tried out on a pontoon before wheels, in July 1914. Curtiss built this tractor plane on order for the United States Army. It had the OX type motor developed in 1913. Most of the 9,000 training machines on which nearly 5,000 American aviators were trained in the World War, were Jennies (JN-4's and N-9 seaplanes).

Henry Ford visited the Curtiss plant at Hammondsport in 1912 and looked over a late 1912 type boat, which was giving rise to the new sport of aerial yachting. Many sportsmen were evolving into sportsmen-pilots in 1912 and 1913, and Lake Keuka was the scene of much flying activity, aside from the routine instruction school flights.

The boat in the picture below was painted red, and was familiarly known by the students as the "Old Red Boat." Curtiss is showing the control system to Henry Ford.

As soon as the news leaked out that Rodman Wanamaker had ordered a big boat to fly the Atlantic in an effort to win the London Daily Mail prize of $50,000, reporters and photographers flocked to Hammondsport. Every effort was made to insure a safe ocean crossing by the America, first twin-engined, enclosed cabin flying boat, including the experimental addition of a third 100-horsepower engine.

The America was christened on June 22, 1914, thoroughly flight-tested and many changes and improvements made on her throughout the summer. The pilot and co-pilot were anxious to be off, as French and Italian competition for the Daily Mail prize was looming. A set of spare parts and refueling supplies awaited them in the Azores. Everything was in readiness for the first trans-Atlantic take-off when war was declared, and the America sailed for England on the deck of an ocean liner for military duty.

The photograph below shows the America just before the christening ceremonies, with Glenn Curtiss, at the extreme left, talking to visitors.

The Langley areodrome of 1903 was taken to Hammondsport in the summer of 1914, re-conditioned and tests made to determine its ability to fly, both in its original form and with certain modifications. Curtiss wanted to obtain data for the design of a large tandem plane as well as to establish the essential "rightness" of Samuel Pierpont Langley's principle of two planes set at a dihedral angle to achieve stability in the air.

The photograph shows pilot William Elwood ("Gink") Doherty returning from a twenty-mile flight in the Langley plane powered with a Curtiss motor.

Supervising the Langley trials were Dr. Albert F. Zahm, for the Smithsonian Institution, and Charles M. Manly, chief assistant engineer to Professor Langley. The photograph below shows the Langley with the original engine, designed by Manly. He is seated at the controls, with Curtiss and Dr. Zahm in the foreground.

The anniversary of the trophy-winning June Bug flight was celebrated on July 4, 1928, at Hammondsport. Curtiss insisted on photographs of the old guard—all associated with him in aircraft production—as they faced the age of fifty. Left to right: Lyman J. Seely, Henry Kleckler, Glenn Curtiss, Harry C. Genung, Kenneth B. MacDonald, W. L. Gilmore.

Twenty years afterward, Glenn Curtiss retraced his solo flight down the Hudson of May 29, 1910, at the controls of a giant twin-motored transport plane. The anniversary flight, with a load of eighteen passengers and 2 pilots, was made in nearly half his original time at a speed of 110, instead of 54 miles per hour. The photograph below shows him waving from the cockpit of the huge Curtiss Condor biplane.

This photograph, taken at the age of fifty, is the one Glenn Curtiss liked best of himself, probably because it made him look like a "serious business man."

Literature and History of Aviation

AN ARNO PRESS COLLECTION

Arnold, H[enry] H.
Global Mission. 1949.

Bordeaux, Henry.
Georges Guynemer: Knight of the Air. Translated by Louise Morgan
  Sill. 1918.

Boyington, "Pappy" (Col. Gregory Boyington).
Baa Baa Black Sheep. 1958.

Buckley, Harold.
Squadron 95. 1933.

Caidin, Martin.
Golden Wings. 1960.

"Contact" (Capt. Alan Bott).
Cavalry of the Clouds. 1917.

Crossfield, A. Scott and Clay Blair, Jr.
Always Another Dawn. 1960.

Fokker, Anthony H. G. and Bruce Gould.
Flying Dutchman: The Life of Anthony Fokker. 1931.

Gibson, Guy.
Enemy Coast Ahead. 1946.

Goldberg, Alfred, editor.
A History of the United States Air Force 1907-1957. 1957.

Gurney, Gene.
Five Down and Glory. Edited by Mark P. Friedlander, Jr. 1958.

Hall, Norman S.
The Balloon Buster: Frank Luke of Arizona. 1928.

Josephson, Matthew.
Empire of the Air: Juan Trippe and the Struggle for World Airways.
  1944.

Kelly, Charles J., Jr.
The Sky's the Limit: The History of the Airlines. 1963.
  New Introduction by Charles J. Kelly, Jr.

Kelly, Fred C., editor.
Miracle at Kitty Hawk. 1951.

La Farge, Oliver.
The Eagle in the Egg. 1949.

Levine, Isaac Don.
Mitchell: Pioneer of Air Power. 1943.

Lougheed, Victor.
Vehicles of the Air. 1909.

McFarland, Marvin W., editor.
The Papers of Wilbur and Orville Wright. 2 volumes. 1953.

McKee, Alexander.
Strike From the Sky: The Story of the Battle of Britain. 1960.

Macmillan, Norman.
Into the Blue. 1969.

Magoun, F. Alexander and Eric Hodgins.
A History of Aircraft. 1931.

Parsons, Edwin C.
I Flew with the Lafayette Escadrille. 1963.

Penrose, Harald.
No Echo in the Sky. 1958.

Reynolds, Quentin.
The Amazing Mr. Doolittle. 1953.

Saunders, Hilary St. George.
Per Ardua: The Rise of British Air Power 1911-1939. 1945.

Stilwell, Hart and Slats Rodgers.
Old Soggy No. 1. 1954.

Studer, Clara.
Sky Storming Yankee: The Life of Glenn Curtiss. 1937.

Turnbull, Archibald D. and Clifford L. Lord.
History of United States Naval Aviation. 1949.

Turner, C. C.
The Old Flying Days. 1927.

Von Richthofen, Manfred F.
The Red Air Fighter. 1918.

Werner, Johannes.
Knight of Germany: Oswald Boelcke, German Ace. Translated by
    Claud W. Sykes. 1933.

Wise, John.
Through the Air. 1873.

Wolff, Leon.
Low Level Mission. 1957.

Yakovlev, Alexander.
Notes of an Aircraft Designer. Translated by Albert Zdornykh. n.d.